# Pragmatic Development

Essays in Developmental Science
*Series Editor: Jerome Kagan, Harvard University*

Within the field of human development, scholars are exploring diverse and exciting issues ranging from emotional and cognitive processes in infancy to the belief systems of adolescents. This series will serve to showcase those provocative works that examine core issues in human development. Themes to be explored include the role of culture in development, what animal research can and cannot tell us about the child, conduct disorders and delinquency, language and conceptual development, gender roles, and genetic influences on both intellectual and emotional processes.

*Pragmatic Development,* Anat Ninio and Catherine E. Snow

Forthcoming in the Series

*The Development of Aggression from Infancy to Adulthood,* L. Rowell Huesman and Leonard D. Eron

*The Kaleidoscope of Gender,* Nora Newcombe

# Pragmatic Development

## Anat Ninio
### *The Hebrew University of Jerusalem*

### and

## Catherine E. Snow
### *Harvard Graduate School of Education*

WestviewPress

*A Division of* HarperCollins*Publishers*

*Essays in Developmental Science*

Tables 4.1 and 4.2 reprinted by permission from *First Language*.

Published in 1996 in the United States of America by Westview Press, Inc., 5500 Central Avenue, Boulder, Colorado 80301-2877, and in the United Kingdom by Westview Press, 12 Hid's Copse Road, Cumnor Hill, Oxford OX2 9JJ

A CIP catalog record for this book is available from the Library of Congress.
ISBN 0-8133-2470-X.  ISBN 0-8133-2471-8 (pbk.).

The paper used in this publication meets the requirements of the American National Standard for Permanence of Paper for Printed Library Materials Z39.48-1984.

10   9   8   7   6   5   4   3   2   1

Dedicated to our children
Matan, Shira, Nathaniel

# Contents

*List of Tables and Figures* . . . . . . . . . . . . . . . . . . . . . . xi

*Acknowledgments* . . . . . . . . . . . . . . . . . . . . . . . . . . . xiii

1. **Introduction: What Is Pragmatics?** . . . . . . . . . . . . . . . . . 1

    1.1 Why Study the Development of Pragmatics? 1

    1.2 Defining the Domain of Pragmatic
        Development, 3

    1.3 The Limits of Pragmatics? 9

    1.4 What Does Pragmatic Development Include? 10

    1.5 The Theoretical Framework and Scope
        of This Book, 12

2. **The Communicative Uses of Speech** . . . . . . . . . . . . . . . . . 15

    2.1 What Is a Meaningful Verbal-Communicative
        Act? 16

    2.2 Identifying Types of Communicative Uses of
        Speech, 18

    2.3 A Proposal for the Classification of Verbal-Social
        Meanings, 21

    2.4 The Ninio and Wheeler Taxonomy and Coding
        System for Communicative Acts, 31

    2.5 Other Coding Systems Derived from the Ninio
        and Wheeler Taxonomy: FCA, INCA-A,
        PICA-100, 39

    2.6 Central Questions About the Development of the
        Communicative Uses of Speech, 43

3. **Prelinguistic Communication and the Transition to Speech** . . . . 45

    3.1 Prelinguistic Development, 45

    3.2 The Transition to Speech, 48

4. **The First Stage of Speech Use** . . . . . . . . . . . . . . . . . . . . 59

    4.1 The Characteristics of Early Single-Word
        Utterances, 59

    4.2 The Pragmatics of Early Speech, 67

    4.3 Developmental Trends in the Expression of
        Communicative Intents, 72

4.4 Learning to Express Communicative Intents in
     the Single-Word Stage, 79

5. The Acquisition of a Verbal-Communicative Repertoire . . . . . 81

   5.1 The Size of Children's Verbal-Communicative
        Repertoire in the First Two Years, 83

   5.2 General Trends in the Order of Acquisition of
        Communicative Acts, 84

   5.3 Developments in the Elicited Verbal Behavior
        System, 88

   5.4 Developments in the Marking System, 90

   5.5 Developments in the Discussion System, 93

   5.6 Developments in the Action-Negotiation
        System, 96

   5.7 Summary: Order of Acquisition of
        Communicative Acts, 103

6. Participation in Verbal Interaction . . . . . . . . . . . . . . . 107

   6.1 The Ninio Longitudinal Observational Study, 107

   6.2 The Harvard Longitudinal
        Observational Study, 127

   6.3 Refining Verbal Communication, 135

7. Children as Conversationalists . . . . . . . . . . . . . . . . 143

   7.1 Overview of the Problem, 143

   7.2 Turn-taking as the Basis of Conversation, 147

   7.3 Topic Selection and Topic Maintenance, 152

   7.4 Repair, 162

8. The Pragmatics of Connected Discourse . . . . . . . . . . . 171

   8.1 Overview, 171

   8.2 Assessing the Listener's State of Mind, 173

   8.3 Narratives, 175

   8.4 Explanations, 187

   8.5 Definitions, 189

   8.6 Summary, 191

References . . . . . . . . . . . . . . . . . . . . . . . . . . . 193
About the Book and Authors . . . . . . . . . . . . . . . . . . 215
Index . . . . . . . . . . . . . . . . . . . . . . . . . . . . . . 217

# Tables and Figures

## Tables

2.1 Major categories of communicative function identified in various coding systems . . . . . . . . . . . . . . . . . . . . . . 20

2.2 Types of verbal interchanges according to interactive function . . . . . . . . . . . . . . . . . . . . . . . . . . . . 32

2.3 Speech act codes, categories, and definitions, by major pragmatic force . . . . . . . . . . . . . . . . . . . . . . . . . . 37

2.4 Interchange categories of the abridged INCA-A coding system . . . . . . . . . . . . . . . . . . . . . . . . . . . . . 41

4.1 Examples of communicative intents verbally expressed by 10- to 12-month-old children . . . . . . . . . . . . . . . . . 65

4.2 Distribution of children's utterances according to type of speech use, by number of children and tokens produced . . . . 66

4.3 First 10 steps in the acquisition of communicative intents according to the Parental Inteview Questionnaire . . . . . . . . 71

4.4 Examples of constant-type mapping rules . . . . . . . . . . . . 75

4.5 Examples of variable-type mapping rules . . . . . . . . . . . . . 77

5.1 Order of acquisition of the first communicative intents between 8 and 24 months, according to the Parental Interview Questionnaire . . . . . . . . . . . . . . . . . . . . . 86

6.1 Number of different talk interchanges participated in by children and by mothers in a 30-minute interactive session, by children's age . . . . . . . . . . . . . . . . . . . . . 109

6.2 Number of different speech acts used by children and by mothers in a 30-minute interactive session, by children's age . . . . . . . . . . . . . . . . . . . . . . . . . . 111

6.3 Distribution of utterances emitted by children in a 30-minute interactive session, by type of major speech use and by children's age . . . . . . . . . . . . . . . . . . . . . 113

6.4 Basic indicators of communicative performance for mothers and children . . . . . . . . . . . . . . . . . . . . . . 130

6.5 Mean percentage of interpretable maternal and child communicative acts in each of the most frequently occurring interchanges . . . . . . . . . . . . . . . . . . . . . 133

6.6 Contribution of nonverbal information to interpretability
    of children's communicative attempts . . . . . . . . . . . . . 138


7.1 Repair utterances by children and parents . . . . . . . . . . . . 164


**Figures**

2.1 A schematic model of states and events of face-to-face
    interaction . . . . . . . . . . . . . . . . . . . . . . . . . . . . 24

2.2 A model of states and events of face-to-face interaction
    and types of talk interchanges relating to them . . . . . . . . 30

5.1 Distribution of number of different communicative acts as
    a function of age . . . . . . . . . . . . . . . . . . . . . . . . . 85

6.1 Mean number of different types of verbal interchanges in
    which children took part in a 30-minute interaction,
    by age . . . . . . . . . . . . . . . . . . . . . . . . . . . . . . 109

6.2 Mean number of different speech acts produced by
    children in a 30-minute interaction, by age . . . . . . . . . . . 111

6.3 Relative frequency of utterances produced by mothers and
    children, by type of major speech use and by age

    a: Performative or game verbalizations . . . . . . . . . . . . . 115

    b: Discussions of present topics . . . . . . . . . . . . . . . . 116

    c: Action negotiations . . . . . . . . . . . . . . . . . . . . . 117

    d: Self-directed action directives . . . . . . . . . . . . . . . 118

    e: Attention negotiations . . . . . . . . . . . . . . . . . . . 119

    f: Polite and other markings of events . . . . . . . . . . . . 120

    g: Clarification of communication . . . . . . . . . . . . . . . 121

    h: Discussions on nonpresent topics . . . . . . . . . . . . . . 122

6.4 Distribution of four types of action-negotiation
    interchanges in maternal and child speech, by age

    a: Initiate a new activity . . . . . . . . . . . . . . . . . . . 123

    b: Regulate hearer's acts . . . . . . . . . . . . . . . . . . . 124

    c: Attempt to end activity . . . . . . . . . . . . . . . . . . . 125

    d: Propose addition of a recursive act . . . . . . . . . . . . . 126

# Acknowledgments

Thanks are due to the foundations that supported our work. The preparation of the communicative coding system was supported by Grant No. 2467/81 from the United States–Israel Binational Science Foundation (BSF), Jerusalem, Israel, to Anat Ninio and Carol Eckerman. The research reported in this book was supported by Grant No. 84-00267/1 from the BSF, to Anat Ninio and Catherine Snow; by grants from the Israeli Academy of Sciences and the Israel Foundations Trustees (Ford Foundation) for research on the development of verbal expression of communicative intents, to Anat Ninio; by the National Institutes of Health for support of research on communicative intents through HD 22338, to Catherine Snow; by the Ford Foundation and the Spencer Foundation for support of the Home School Study of Language and Literacy Development, to Catherine Snow.

We want to thank Yoram Ben-Yehuda, Ruth Berman, Shoshana Blum-Kulka, David Dickinson, Ahuva Fuchs, Harel Goren, Vibeke Grøver Aukrust, Jane Herman, Alison Imbens-Bailey, Barbara Pan, Pamela Rollins, Benny Shanon, Patton Tabors, Polly Wheeler, Kendra Winner, and Lilach Yishay for being stimulating collaborators and conversational partners and for insightful comments on the manuscript of this book. Thanks are due to Simon Dik, who stimulated an interest in linguistic pragmatics that persists in his students and colleagues, transcending his too-early death. We wish to thank Jose Luis Linaza-Iglesias and the members of the Department of Developmental and Educational Psychology, Universidad Autónoma de Madrid, for their hospitality and companionship and the Ministry of Science and Education of the Spanish government for its sabbatical support to Catherine Snow during preparation of the manuscript.

*Anat Ninio*
*Catherine E. Snow*

# 1

# Introduction:
# What Is Pragmatics?

## 1.1 Why study the development of pragmatics?

Consider the following four scenarios, all real incidents:

*Example 1.1.*     Two faculty members whom we'll call Amy and Ben had worked in the same department for several years and had been co-teaching a course since September. In April students in the course gave presentations about their own research in two parallel sessions organized around research themes. Amy and Ben had agreed that one of them would attend each of the sessions. Amy arrived just as the sessions were scheduled to start and encountered Ben in the hall. Conscious of the time, Amy tried to figure out which room she should enter.

| | |
|---|---|
| Amy (hurriedly): | Are you narrative, or are you emotional development? |
| Ben (slowly): | Well, as you know I've done work on emotional development, in fact I just published a paper on emotional development, and I've done work on narrative development as well, in fact one of the students presenting on narrative development is my advisee and has been working with me on the research she is presenting. |
| Amy (gritting her teeth): | So which session do you want to go to? |

*Example 1.2.*    At a meeting to plan a sales campaign, a middle-aged member of the sales staff we'll call Cal is seated next to a recently hired colleague we'll call Dee; Cal and Dee are friendly in their professional context but have no personal social relationship. About two hours into the meeting, during a discussion of new market development, Dee leans over and whispers to Cal:

Dee:        Your left sock is inside out.

*Example 1.3.*    Several convention goers board a courtesy bus scheduled to leave at 7:45 A.M. for the convention center. The bus driver, behind the wheel, is reading a newspaper. Passengers, mostly strangers to one another, are making desultory conversation about the weather, the early hour, the convention, and so on. At 7:52 a middle-aged male passenger seated close to the driver glances at his watch, then says:

Passenger:    What time do we get to the convention center?
Driver:        When we pull up to the front door.

The general conversation stops. After a noticeable pause, the questioner says:

Passenger:    Well, I wouldn't want to get there any sooner.

The bus driver responds, in a noticeably friendlier tone:

Driver:        There's so little traffic at this time of day, I'll be too early at the next stop if I leave here on schedule.

*Example 1.4.*    An intensive introductory Spanish class is being taught during the summer session by José, a Puerto Rican doctoral student in Spanish literature. About half an hour into the class one morning, Philip, a college senior taking the course for extra credit, beckons José and whispers something to him. José turns his back to the class and unmistakably (even from the back) zips his fly. He then proceeds with the drill.

The first two scenarios reveal pragmatic failures. In the first case, Amy was evidently insufficiently explicit in seeking information about which session Ben wanted to attend, whereas Ben was somewhat incompetent at judging what kind of information Amy might be seeking. Their minor communicative breakdown was eventually repaired, but not without some potentially negative effect on their relationship—Amy might have exited the interaction thinking Ben was egotistical, and Ben may have been thinking Amy was obtuse, unpleasant consequences for close colleagues.

The second violation involved less a potential for misunderstanding the speaker's intent than a failure to have understanding of her reasons for speaking. Why would someone mention an inside-out sock in a situation where it cannot be remedied? Why would Dee assume that Cal cared to remedy this relatively minor sartorial deviation? Bringing up a personal failing that is not remediable is clearly rude (*You're bald,* or *That's a nasty scar on your cheek*). On the other hand, as example 1.4 shows, mentioning something that can be fixed might be considered a favor, at least among friends (*You have spinach on your teeth,* or *Can I take this price tag off for you?*). Where does mentioning an inside-out sock at a business meeting fit on this continuum? Is it rude or an invitation to greater intimacy?

The third and fourth examples represent pragmatic successes. After the passenger in 1.3 asked a question that was interpreted as a challenge, the driver created a situation of frank conflict. The passenger would have lost face by accepting the driver's refusal to provide the requested information and might have created an incident by demanding an answer. Instead, he hit upon a response that established an affiliative relationship with the driver, thus providing the driver with a basis for reinterpreting the original question as a simple request for information rather than a complaint. The passenger was clearly a skilled pragmatician, someone we would all like to have around during awkward social situations.

Philip in 1.4 was less adept than the passenger but nonetheless handled a classically difficult situation with some delicacy, managing to convey information about José's state of undress while maintaining at least an illusion of privacy. Although everyone in the class knew what Philip had said, the fact that he whispered it and that José turned his back to zip up created a social fiction that the embarrassing event had never occurred.

## 1.2 Defining the domain of pragmatic development

Our ultimate goal is to understand how children develop abilities of the types displayed by the bus passenger and by Philip and to consider why violations such as those displayed by Amy, Ben, and Dee are not infrequent. The examples illustrate just a few of the phenomena that comprise pragmatics. Other violations include interrupting a speaker, telling a joke or an anecdote twice to the same person, dominating a conversation, using direct demand forms in social relationships where polite requests are expected and vice versa, failing to answer questions posed by one's interlocutor, using a first name or intimate address form with an elder or a superior, failing to greet acquaintances, and so on. Since the potential for pragmatic violations is vast, coming to understand how it is that most adults end up abiding by most pragmatic rules most of the time is a considerable challenge.

Obviously, development does not consist only of learning to avoid violations. Before children can learn in which social situation it is appropriate to emit a direct demand and in which a polite request, they have to understand what demands and requests are and learn the verbal forms for their expression. A three-month-old can neither order people around nor ask them nicely for a favor. Similarly, she fails to answer questions not out of impoliteness but because she has not yet learned that questions and answers exist in the social world. Thus, even before the sophisticated abilities involved in the avoidance of pragmatic violations are considered, we need to understand the acquisition of the fundamental store of knowledge necessary for the social uses of language. Children need to learn how to formulate their social moves through language in a form interpretable by their interlocutors and to interpret correctly the interpersonal significance of others' verbal overtures. The acquisition of these skills is the topic of this volume.

What is the extent of the pragmatic rules children must learn? Pragmatics is a branch of linguistics concerned with speech use, and studies of pragmatic development are concerned with how children acquire the knowledge necessary for the appropriate, effective, rule-governed employment of speech in interpersonal situations. Like developmental psychology in general, studies of pragmatic development address questions of the following sort: What is the age of onset of particular skills? By what processes are these skills acquired by the child? What factors influence the speed and order of acquisition of these skills? What sorts of individual differences emerge? Questions just like these are also asked about the acquisition of both grammar and the lexicon. What distinguishes pragmatics is the considerable disagreement about exactly what knowledge and skills constitute the domain of pragmatic development.

Those who study pragmatics struggle to define their domain of inquiry so it does not become coextensive with linguistics on the one hand and so it remains distinct from the rules that govern all of social interaction on the other. Traditionally, linguistics is parsed as having three domains of analysis: grammar, semantics, and pragmatics. These are distinguished by the criteria for correctness or adequacy used to assess performance. Grammatical rules prescribe formal correctness, and violation of these rules produces ungrammatical sentences that might, however, be perfectly adequate in the semantic and pragmatic domains, for example, *The door are open. Could you please to close it?* Semantics is the system that prescribes meaningfulness and provides rules that enable sentences to be judged as uninterpretable (*The most eligible bachelor of Peoria just got married for the fourth time*), false (*Two plus two makes seven*), or meaningless (*Hordes of principles contemplate curtain rods*) although perhaps grammatical. Pragmatic rules, on the other hand, define appropriate and effective language use—using language in such a way that one's own communicative goals are achieved without giving offense or causing misunderstanding. Thus, grammatical, meaningful, true sentences (e.g., *Your left sock is inside out*) might well violate pragmatic rules of appropriateness.

We have defined developmental pragmatics, then, as the acquisition of "knowledge necessary for the appropriate, effective, rule-governed employment of speech in interpersonal situations." This apparently simple definition soon leads us, though, into considerable complexity. Clearly, children have to learn how to use language in order to make statements, to ask questions, to request, to greet, to refuse, and so on; these are the so-called *illocutionary* speech acts (Austin, 1962; Searle, 1969). These are manifest communicative acts for which a speaker expresses a willingness to be held accountable that are furthermore characterized by the presence, at least some of the time, of overt linguistic markings, such as the interrogative grammatical mood for questions. Even in cases when such explicit linguistic markers of intents are absent, for example, in indirect requests, the linguistic community shares certain conventions for the expression of communicative intents in utterances. Without such shared guidelines, we would be unable to interpret correctly what type of illocutionary act speakers intend their interlocutors to hear them making. Illocutionary acts thus qualify as a clear instance of linguistically signaled uses of speech that are appropriate and effective only when produced in accordance with certain rules. Speech acts, therefore, are centrally within our domain of inquiry.

Where, though, should we draw the limits of linguistic pragmatics? When the British heroine of the movie *L.A. Stories,* on first arriving in Los Angeles, makes a mildly dirty joke in front of a group of locals in a restaurant, she shocks everyone speechless. English is her native language, and she has no problem being understood at the level of lexicon, grammar, or illocutionary intent. Nevertheless, she has committed a violation of the rules that govern speech use in her host community. Although in Britain well-bred women can tell jokes using four-letter words in polite company, in certain Los Angeles circles one cannot. This generalization, which most people would relegate without argument to the domain of pragmatics, is a cultural norm defining correct behavior in London versus Los Angeles, equivalent to other cross-cultural differences like *Use a knife and a fork throughout the meal* in London versus *Cut your meat into small pieces at first, then transfer your fork to your right hand and use only that to actually consume the meal* in Los Angeles.

Rules about using both four-letter words and forks might be found in books of etiquette that prescribe social niceties; we lack guidelines about how politeness rules for speech should be distinguished from politeness rules for the use of cutlery, precedence rules for entering and leaving rooms, rules for sitting down and getting up, rules for shaking hands, for how to dress, for offering and accepting food, and so on. Politeness rules for speech form an integrated system with the societal regulation of interpersonal behavior in general. To describe linguistic politeness rules and to study how children are socialized into using them, we need to consider the totality of a culture. An analogy is the linguist's attempt to chart the semantics of the kinship terminology within a newly discovered language; describing kinship terms and the rules for their use requires an understanding of social relations, rules for marriage and inheritance, customs regarding who is responsible for rearing, naming, educating, and indulging children, rules concerning who can live together, who can eat together, and so on. All of this knowledge is prerequisite to defining terms like *aunt* or *cousin* (see Goldfield & Snow, 1992). Consider, for example, the use of the terms *Auntie* and *Uncle* for older family friends in American English—a 'meaning' for aunt and uncle that can only be understood by considering the nature of social relations between the older and the younger generations, within and outside families. The study of kinship terms, at its core a linguistic issue, has been a cornerstone of modern anthropological analyses of entire societies (Goodenough, 1951; Wallace & Atkins, 1960); similarly, linguistic pragmatics inherently involves the study of culture and society.

Are we saying, then, that a developmental pragmaticist who is interested in the acquisition of the polite uses of speech must become an anthropologist? Some researchers in this domain *are* in fact anthropologists, interested in the socialization of culturally varying behavior. Others—psychologists or linguists by training—acquire the required expertise in cultural analysis. Most studies of how children are taught to speak in pragmatically appropriate ways include background information on the social structure and familial arrangements of the society under study, and many provide information about social and personality development, not just about issuing directives, selecting forms of address, and other such linguistic politeness rules.

We have come a long way from what we originally defined as a psychological-developmental study of one of the branches of linguistic knowledge. It is impossible to study or to understand certain kinds of language behavior without straying into the study of societies and cultures. It is, furthermore, very difficult to draw the lines among those culturally determined phenomena that have to do with language proper, those that are incidentally carried out by speaking, and those that merge linguistic and cultural rules. For example, the rules for "polite" speech forms in Japanese are described in grammar books, but employing them correctly requires an understanding of social categories like gender, age, and class.

The distinction between linguistic pragmatics and culture is not the only fuzzy boundary to be dealt with. Pragmatics has an interface as well with skill at producing great literature, sermons, and political speeches. For example, was Martin Luther King's success in moving people's hearts and minds through his public speaking attributable to his exceptionally good grasp of the rules of rhetoric, pragmatic rules that can be described formally? Or was King's success attributable to the depth of his understanding of and empathy for his listeners? In other words, is being an effective—as opposed to an errorless—communicator part of an individual's *linguistic* abilities in any sense?

To take another, more mundane example: Ken has a chronically noisy neighbor who ignores all entreaties to be quieter. At 2:00 A.M. the neighbor has his TV blaring. Ken, yet again, knocks on the door and says, *Your TV is very loud.* The neighbor responds characteristically, *So what?* and slams the door in Ken's face. This was an ineffective request.

An hour later Ray, Ken's cousin who is visiting from out of town, has had enough of the noise. He knocks on the neighbor's door, but instead of repeating Ken's indirect appeals assumes a furious expression and says, *If you don't turn your TV down immediately, I'll call the police*. The neighbor complies. This was an effective request.

Why did Ken not use this effective strategy? We could say that he is not assertive enough, that he has a shy and mild personality. We could even call him a coward, someone who lets himself be bullied because he is unable to stand up for his rights. In other words, we might be inclined to seek an explanation for his failure in terms of his character and his understanding of human affairs rather than in terms of some deficit in his knowledge of language per se.

Another story. Peter and Susan are watching a police drama on TV. Just as the hero is about to be pushed into the path of an oncoming train, Peter turns to Susan and says, *Maybe we should go to Florida for our vacation instead of Oregon, what do you think?* Susan says *Shh!* This is clearly an ineffective suggestion. But would anyone who saw Peter's utterance written down on the page without the accompanying story be able to say there was anything wrong with it as a potential suggestion? Peter may not have very good timing, but he certainly knows how to formulate a standard suggestion.

The issues of what makes someone a convincing public speaker, an effectively assertive neighbor, or a sensitive spouse are interesting and important ones. But are the skills necessary for effective speech use—for getting oneself heard, for convincing an audience, for getting one's way, for intentionally impressing, pleasing, annoying, or amusing others—actually language skills? Perhaps language skills only include knowing how to put a sentence together so it sounds like a suggestion and not the ability to avoid blurting out the suggestion at an inappropriate moment. Or perhaps this distinction is artificial, and everything to do with the use of speech in interpersonal situations—the timing, the intonation, the precise choice of words, the selected degree of forcefulness—is a choice based on a person's pragmatic know-how. We simply don't know where to draw the line between linguistic pragmatics and social effectiveness.

The problem of drawing the boundary between formal language structure and social language use is ubiquitous in linguistic analysis. How does one interpret a sentence like *The city will fall tomorrow* unless one knows a great deal about the conditions of its use: the date on which it was produced, the qualifications of the speaker to make such a pronouncement, and the identity of the audience? Is it a threat or a prediction, a statement about a state of affairs or a request for aid? Whereas formal linguists might decline to describe the illocutionary force of the utterance as an issue outside grammar or semantics, they do have to deal with interpreting words like *tomorrow* (and an additional very long list of deictic and indexical lexical items), whose meanings depend crucially on conditions of use.

Indeed, it is far from clear that we can distinguish between language in the abstract and its use. An influential school of thought chiefly associated with Wittgenstein (1953), which has considerable following among other philosophers and linguists (e.g., Allwood, 1981; Alston, 1964; Fillmore, 1971; Gibbs, 1984; Grice, 1957; Strawson, 1970), argues that all linguistics is nothing but a question of speech use, of pragmatics. In this view, the formal aspects of language—lexicon, grammar—are no more than tools for the production of intelligible speech acts. Focusing on a limited aspect of language, such as morphology, might mislead one into thinking it is an autonomous system, a separate field of inquiry. But a broader, deeper look prevents one from elevating the means to the status of end. Although working out the details of such a holistic, use-conditional language system is extremely difficult, formal grammars built on pragmatic principles have been suggested by several linguists (e.g., Dik, 1978; Halliday, 1985; Van Valin, 1993). If these so-called Functional Grammars are successful, all boundaries between pragmatics and other aspects of language may be obliterated.

The difficulty of limiting the proper concerns of pragmatics is perhaps best illustrated in the context of a fundamental question: What is a meaningful sentence? What is it that turns a vocalization into a means of conveying thought from person to person? This is an extremely complex question that might be illuminated with a negative example. Baier (1967) gave the following example for the entry "Nonsense" in *The Encyclopedia of Philosophy:* a person uttering the sentence *The water is now boiling* in the middle of a marriage ceremony. Even though the sentence itself is a perfectly ordinary declarative sentence and everybody hearing it understands the words, nobody can understand why it was said. The use the speaker had in mind for that sentence in those circumstances, for that audience, is incomprehensible. It is impossible to attribute any kind of point to this utterance, so in spite of its impeccable grammar and vocabulary it is meaningless. One needs, however, to know all sorts of things about marriage ceremonies to understand why the speaker should not have produced this utterance unless he wanted to be hospitalized as insane. Goffman (1983), in a posthumous article "Felicity's Condition," pointed out that violating the rules and conventions that tie sentences to their contexts is at best socially inappropriate and ultimately makes for an intolerable breach of normality, a violation society cannot condone. Our question is whether the knowledge required to produce meaningful utterances in the wedding context (knowledge about society's arrangements for the public ratification of personal relations, about religion and sanctity, about ritual and its functions) is properly included under knowledge of **language.** The concept of meaningfulness appeals to a very large and a priori unspecifiable store of information about the contexts in which talk takes place; apparently, people must master, remember, and constantly monitor an encyclopedic store of facts in order to produce meaningful utterances and interpret others' speech as intelligible.

This problem does not emerge only when speakers produce full sentences. Even interpreting a single word in most uses requires an encyclopedic rather than a dictionary-based level of knowledge about the word's meaning. A familiar example of this phenomenon, from Schank and Abelson (1977), is the impossibility of understanding uses like 'the menu' or 'the check' in a story about going to a restaurant unless one's knowledge of the meaning of the word *restaurant* includes considerable contextual information about the restaurant script. Only with considerable knowledge of the world, society, and human psychology can we interpret others' utterances or produce interpretable utterances ourselves.

Is there no limit to how much of human affairs we should include under pragmatics? Assertiveness and sensitivity, justice and charisma, religion and culture—is there anything human that is not a proper part of the study of language use? Apparently not. Speech is an immensely important, central element of human life, interwoven with practically every strand of our existence. This is what makes the study of children's gradual mastery of speech uses such a varied and intriguing subject.

## 1.3 The limits of pragmatics?

Not everybody would agree, though, that all aspects of social effectiveness, politeness, interpersonal sensitivity, and cultural understanding should be incorporated under the label of pragmatics. The term *pragmatics* denotes a branch of linguistics rather than the study of communication, social interaction, or the behavioral organization of talk (for a review, see Kendon, 1979). Pragmatics is the branch of linguistics concerned with language use, to be distinguished from syntax and semantics, which deal, respectively, with the form and meaning of sentences. The difference is best illustrated by the criteria used in evaluating a speaker's performance in the three domains. As discussed earlier, the pragmatic success of an utterance depends not on grammaticality (the syntactic criterion) or interpretability (the semantic criterion) but on the appropriateness or *felicity* of an utterance on the occasion it is produced (Austin, 1962; Lyons, 1977). The trichotomy of syntax, semantics, and pragmatics originated with Morris (1938), who defined syntax as the study of the formal relations of signs to one another, semantics as the study of the relations of signs to the objects they denote, and pragmatics as the study of the relation between signs and their interpreters—the speaker and addressee(s). With minor modifications, the very same distinctions underlie present-day mainstream linguistics; except for the group of linguists mentioned earlier who advocate Functional Grammars, the rest of the field makes a clear differentiation between the formal rules governing the construction of correct sentences and the ways in which those sentences are used.

Most linguists see language as an autonomous system of fixed symbols and abstract rules for their lawful combination, defined independently of their possible contexts of use. The uses people make of well-formed and meaningful sentences are not seen as the concern of linguists any more than weapons dealers take responsibility for murders committed with guns they have sold.

Speech use is, however, incorporated into formal linguistic theory in certain cases, for example, when conditions of use have a direct effect on the structure or meaning of sentences. For instance, linguistic expressions that point to contextual information rather than symbolize context-independent, abstract concepts exist in every language. These expressions are the *deictic,* or *indexical,* elements of language: pronouns, locatives such as *here* or *there,* temporal terms such as *today* or *tomorrow,* verbs like *come, go, bring,* and the like. Because these expressions receive different interpretations in different contexts of use, the meaning of a sentence containing them is not absolute but is relative to their situated use. Since these deictic terms are bona fide lexical items, it is impossible to exclude the rules governing their use from linguistics proper. On the other hand, they are not easily incorporated in linguistic theories developed to deal with context-independent linguistic entities. It was therefore proposed (cf. Bar-Hillel, 1954; Kalish, 1967; Montague, 1968) that linguistic theory proper be complemented by a separate pragmatic component dealing with indexical or deictic expressions.

The pragmatic component was later extended to include several heterogeneous phenomena that exhibit a direct effect of speech use on the form and interpretation of sentences. These phenomena include the control of presuppositions and implicature (Keenan, 1971; Kempson, 1975); speech acts that involve such purely grammatical features as mood, performative sentence structure, a propositional core, and so on (cf. Lyons, 1981; Searle, 1975); certain aspects of discourse structure, such as rules governing definite reference and anaphora; and rules of politeness, such as the use of honorifics (but see Levinson, 1983). These phenomena have little in common except for the feature that it is impossible to formulate the rules governing them in a use-independent way. In consequence, many experts on pragmatics have lost hope of characterizing the domain coherently with a single definition and provide instead lists enumerating the various phenomena of inquiry (cf. Stalnaker, 1972).

## 1.4 What does pragmatic development include?

Given the range of definitions of "pragmatics" currently in use, it is not surprising that pragmatic development is a heterogeneous field. Researchers using the label *developmental pragmatics* or *pragmatic development* for their own work study a wide range of disparate subjects whose communality is that they have some connection with both language and social interaction. Many aspects of children's language development have been treated in studies that present themselves as focusing on pragmatics—more than we can deal with effectively in this volume. We present here a list of topics most frequently studied under the rubric *pragmatic development,* together with examples of studies done on each topic. This list is designed to help the reader place our own work, presented in the following chapters, in the context of others' contributions to our understanding of children's uses of language. The present volume focuses on the first three topics in this list.

1. The acquisition of communicative intents and the development of their linguistic expression, including the conduct of communication prior to the emergence of speech—that is, by vocalizations and gestures (e.g., Bates, 1976; Bates, Camaioni, & Volterra, 1975; Bruner, 1983; Carpenter, Mastergeorge, & Coggins, 1983; Carter, 1979; Dale, 1980; Dore, 1975, 1978; Garvey, 1975; Greenfield & Smith, 1976; Halliday, 1975; Lock, 1980; Nelson, 1985; Ninio, 1992; Wells, 1985)

2. The development of conversational skills and the acquisition of rules that govern turn-taking, interruptions, back channeling, signaling topic relevance or topic switch, and so on (e.g., Bruner, 1983; Dorval & Eckerman, 1984; Forrester, 1992; Kaye & Charney, 1980; Lieven, 1978b; Snow, 1977a, 1979)

3. The development of control over the linguistic devices used to organize discourse in ways that are cohesive and genre-specific (e.g., Bates, 1976; de Villiers & Tager-Flusberg, 1975; DeHart & Maratsos, 1984; Greenfield & Smith, 1976; Hicks, 1990; Maratsos, 1973)

4. Pragmatic learning processes that operate in children's entry into language, such as the acquisition of novel linguistic forms by pairing them with their inferred communicative function rather than with their semantic meaning (e.g., Antinucci & Parisi, 1975; Bates, 1976; Bruner, 1983; Halliday, 1975; Nelson, 1978; Ninio, 1992; Ninio & Snow, 1988; Ninio & Wheeler, 1984a, b)

5. The acquisition of rules of politeness and other culturally determined rules for using speech (e.g., the work reported in Ochs & Schieffelin, 1979; see also Ochs, 1988; Schieffelin, 1990; Schieffelin & Ochs, 1986)

6. The operation of pragmatic factors in the acquisition of deictic forms, such as pronouns and deictic locatives (e.g., Charney, 1980; Clark, 1978a; Dale & Crain-Thoreson, 1993; Loveland, 1984; Oshima-Takane, 1988)

7. Pragmatic factors influencing language acquisition, such as the interactive context of language use in early childhood (Bruner, 1983; Cazden, 1970; Chapman, 1981; Fletcher & MacWhinney, 1995; Lieven, 1978a; Snow, 1977a, 1979, 1983b, 1995); the role of maternal input and scaffolding behavior in the acquisition of linguistic forms (e.g., Mervis & Mervis, 1988; Moerk, 1976; Nelson et al., 1984; Newport, 1977; Ninio, 1985; Ninio & Bruner, 1978; Ochs & Schieffelin, 1984; Sachs, Brown, & Salerno, 1976; Snow, 1972, 1977b; Tomasello & Todd, 1983); and, more marginally, pragmatically based explanations for otherwise puzzling acquisition biases (e.g., Benedict, 1979; Stephany, 1986; Wales, 1986)

## 1.5 The theoretical framework and scope of this book

In this book we adopt a relatively liberal definition of the domain of developmental pragmatics. We shall be concerned not merely with children's acquisition of those aspects of speech use that have obvious formal correlates but also with their growing mastery of a variety of skills necessary for the appropriate and effective employment of speech in interpersonal situations.

The overall theoretical framework of this book is an empiricist, interactionalist, context-oriented model of behavior and development, nowadays often referred to as Cultural Psychology (Shweder, 1990). Cultural Psychology rests on the philosophical foundations of the so-called constructivist conception of meaning; namely, on the notion that meaning is an interpersonal construct. This approach was developed independently but more or less simultaneously by both sociologists and philosophers of language. Sociologists have pointed out that social reality is a subjective entity, coconstructed by its participants (Bateson, 1955; Berger & Luckman, 1967; Cicourel, 1970; Goffman, 1974; Harré, 1979). Philosophers of language offered an analysis suggesting that the very concept of linguistic meaningfulness must be derived from a set of interpersonal communicative goals the speaker of an utterance intends the addressee to recognize (Grice, 1957; Strawson, 1970).

The legacy of these thinkers to psychology has been the axiom that meaningful participation in the social life of a group, as well as meaningful use of language, involves an interpersonal, intersubjective, collaborative process of creating shared meaning. This has caused a reconceptualization of accepted models and research paradigms in various fields of psychology (Barker, 1968; Mischel, 1968; Tajfel, 1972). Developmental psychologists were influenced by the implication that no child, however young, should be seen as the passive recipient of input from the environment; rather, the child should be viewed as a participant in collaborative interpersonal encounters in which the meaningfulness of behavior is coconstructed by the participants (Bruner, 1983).

Taking this approach, we view children's growing mastery of the interpersonal uses of speech as a focal component of the process of *enculturation* that human beings undergo from birth through adulthood. Fundamentally, we consider the development of pragmatic skills a process of *social* development— the accumulation of knowledge necessary for the successful conduct of interpersonal affairs through the medium of language.

Obviously, this definition overlaps only partially with the linguistic definition of pragmatics. In fact, as we pointed out in Section 1.2, all of the formal aspects of language can be viewed as component skills necessary for pragmatic success. In so-called functionalist linguistic theories, this is precisely the view advanced concerning the primacy of pragmatics over semantics and syntax. We shall not, however, expand the definition of developmental pragmatics used in this book to cover all of language acquisition. The topics we cover fall generally within the phenomena most linguists would regard as belonging to pragmatics.

We shall not review research and theories on the development of semantic and grammatical competencies unless they have a close connection to pragmatic development. Further, we shall not present developmental work based on a radical functionalist orientation, such as work by Bates and MacWhinney (1982) or Van Valin (1991), in which no principled distinction is made between pragmatics and the rest of language. We start by acknowledging the value of distinguishing among syntax, semantics, and pragmatics, although we push the boundary between pragmatic and social skills farther away from language proper than most linguists would.

We depart from the linguist's delimitation of pragmatics by including in our conceptualization of pragmatic skills various types of social skills and knowledge not, strictly speaking, linguistic in nature but crucial for pragmatic achievements. These include social-cognitive concepts defining types of social situations; procedural skills, such as turn-taking, necessary for the conduct of conversations; cultural knowledge underlying social appropriateness criteria; and the individual social skills necessary for appropriate and efficient employment of speech in various situations. In other words, we see developmental pragmatics as a field of study situated in between the disciplines of language development and social development, with blurred boundaries at both extremes.

The topics we deal with in this book represent, then, a somewhat idiosyncratic parsing of the field of developmental psychology, but one we feel brings together under the rubric *developmental pragmatics* inextricably interrelated phenomena that have traditionally been treated separately. We organize our discussion under three topics, which represent, in our view, the major achievements of language learners within the domain of pragmatics:

1. The development of the rules governing the communicative uses of speech
2. The development of conversational skills
3. The development of the ability to produce extended discourse and genre-specific forms

The focus on these three topics excludes several issues others would include under pragmatic development (see list in Section 1.4).

The topics we focus on are central to issues of appropriateness in language. They are also topics on which we have both done research, alone and together. Although we attempt to situate the most important studies done by our colleagues in each of these fields and to acknowledge our own intellectual antecedents, we draw most heavily on our own work. We have been working concurrently in fields that are traditionally fairly separate, namely, speech acts, conversation, and extended discourse. Thus we have been struggling explicitly both to locate and to transcend the boundaries among these domains of knowledge within pragmatics. Our goal, then, is not to offer a complete review of work that has been done in the field of pragmatic development. Rather, we try to present a map of the terrain and its surrounding territories on which we hope the reader can identify the major landmarks and perhaps as well note the large uncharted tracts.

A coherent picture of pragmatic development must go beyond describing development in the three identified domains, though. It must make explicit the relations among the emergence of speech acts, conversational skill, and extended discourse, rather than treating them as separate topics. These three accomplishments are related in a number of ways, the most important of which is that each provides the context for the development of the other two. Thus, for example, conversation-like interactions provide an opportunity for children to acquire their first conventional speech acts, but the continued development of conversational skills requires that children acquire more sophisticated speech acts, like asking and responding to questions. Children's autonomous extended discourse skills emerge from the collaborative production of extended discourse in conversational exchanges, which in turn depend on the ability of the child to engage in the speech acts associated with discussions. These three developments are intertwined and mutually dependent, although they are also concurrent and autonomous. They reflect, respectively, children's growing abilities to relate their own utterances to interpersonal activities, to utterances produced by the interlocutor, and to the interlocutor's state of mind—three increasingly challenging contexts for the production of appropriate and effective speech.

# 2

# The Communicative
# Uses of Speech

Children's developing mastery of the uses of speech for communicative purposes is the topic of this and Chapters 3–6. Our first task is to provide definitions and a basis for categorizing communicative acts.

It is commonly recognized, in light of theoretical work by philosophers such as Austin (1962), Grice (1957), Searle (1969, 1976), and Vendler (1972), that the interpersonal use of speech involves types of knowledge that go beyond the rules of syntax and semantics. Speech is used to perform social acts, for example, to greet, to request, to regulate an activity with a companion, or to draw another's attention to something. A major developmental task in the domain of pragmatics is learning to use speech for the performance of such social-communicative acts.

These acts consist of the intentional and overt communication of some content to another person. From a developmental point of view, two questions are of interest: First, what type of communicative intents can children express at various ages, and second, by what linguistic means can they express these intents at various points in the course of development?

The two questions are often confounded in discussions of pragmatic development. Developmental trends in types of speech acts produced by children are seen as reflecting their growing linguistic ability rather than their increasing mastery of the contents being communicated. In particular, the role of social-conceptual development tends to be overlooked. It is easy to see that the verbal expression of communicative intents undergoes development throughout the early years, but it is less self-evident that there should be an age-related development in the kinds of communicative intents children can control. However, as argued in Chapter 1, the production of verbal-communicative acts requires not only adequate verbal skills but also the mastery of a host of social-cognitive capacities. We argue that the generation of verbally expressed communicative acts is a componential skill involving several different types of competencies. These include:

1.  Intentionality, or having the will to affect the addressee by some purposeful behavior
2.  Control of communicative intentionality, that is, the formulation of intents concerned with achieving an understanding of a message by an addressee
3.  Control of a range of different types of communicative intents, encompassing different types of social-cognitive and linguistic concepts
4.  The ability to express intents conventionally, effectively, and politely

Each of these skills needs to be fully mastered to arrive at the complete adult control of verbal-communicative behavior. Some, such as intentionality, are prerequisite to even the most rudimentary communicative acts. In the case of other component skills, such as social-cognitive concepts of various types, it is not necessary that children possess their full range to begin emitting intentional verbal communications. However, since such component systems develop only gradually over the first years of life and may even continue to develop in mid- and late childhood, they may cause age-related limitations in the range of communicative intents mastered.

Moreover, children's ability to understand the social-cognitive concept underlying some type of communicative act is not independent of the mastery of the verbal forms by which that act is typically expressed in their environment (see Section 4.1). The limitations of children's linguistic knowledge at any given stage in development thus put additional constraints on the kinds of speech uses they can understand and come to produce on their own.

## 2.1 What is a meaningful verbal-communicative act?

In investigating the development of the speech-act system in children, the first problem is to decide what child behaviors to consider instances of meaningful, intentional communication, and the second is to decide which intentional communications are linguistic, that is, conventional. These questions could be interpreted as an attempt to define the domain of linguistic pragmatics, but rather than enter into high theory we focus on these questions as methodological issues in developmental research: How do we recognize the emergence of verbal communicative acts in young children, and how do we distinguish meaningful from other communicative verbalizations? Although these questions might seem quite basic and agreement on the answers prerequisite to starting work on the development of pragmatics, in fact many different answers have been given (see Section 4.1).

The definition adopted here draws on theoretical literature in anthropology (Bateson, 1955; Hymes, 1972), sociology (Goffman, 1974; Gumperz, 1971), and the philosophy of language (cf. Austin, 1962; Halliday, 1975; Searle, 1969). We impose two criteria in order to consider an utterance an instance of meaningful language use, one formal and one functional.

First, the expression used (or at least the phonetic target) is verbal and not merely vocal: It consists of conventional or semiconventional forms accepted in the speaker's speech community. This criterion distinguishes between language and nonlinguistic vocal productions. Words and sentences—that is, forms that are conventionally and arbitrarily restricted in phonetics—are included, as are semiconventional exclamations, onomatopoeia, nicknames, and so forth. In other words, meaningful speech involves the use of a conventional and arbitrary vocal *code*. Of course, we recognize the difficulty of applying this criterion in practice, given the gradual transition between preverbal babbling and early conventional words on all phonetic and phonological analyses; nonetheless, the criterion of a linguistic code is one we maintain in principle.

Second, the utterance is amenable to interpretation by its addressee as an intentional social or communicative act. Communication is by definition an interpersonally construed social phenomenon. It does not consist of the mere emission of informative signals a listener can interpret; for instance, if one's interlocutor suddenly pales and starts to buckle at the knees, he is certainly emitting an informative signal about his current state of health but one that would not be strictly interpreted as the production of a communicative act on his part.

Rather, communication in the strict sense consists of the planful emission of signals intended to be interpreted by the recipient, produced on the assumption that the addressee shares a conventional system of codes for conveying messages and an understanding that intentional communication is taking place. This is basically the criterion the philosophers (mainly Grice, 1957, and Strawson, 1970) developed as defining meaningful language use in general. The very foundation of communication is an understanding among participants that communication is taking place; this understanding generates what philosophers call a "nonnatural" or "linguistic" meaning for vocalizations produced in social settings. Communication is what the speaker and the addressee agree on as communication; it is an interpersonal, not a private, event.

These two criteria, relating to the form and the function of verbal-communicative acts, are similar in that they emphasize the conventional or nonnatural characteristics of meaningful speech uses. The use of speech for communication is a social or culturally determined behavior, qualitatively different from spontaneous, unintended, and naturally informative transmission of signals between two living organisms of whatever kind, including two human beings. Verbal communication belongs to the domain of culturally *constructed* behaviors, those whose meaning inheres in interpretation. *Do you have a match?* is a social, communicative act whose meaning depends on the story the speaker tells herself (a straightforward desire for a cigarette? a friendly social initiative? a flirtatious move?). It is successful as a communicative act if the story constructed by the addressee converges with that of the speaker. Participation in such shared construction of reality by a developing child is thus an important landmark in the process of becoming a member of human society.

## 2.2 Identifying types of communicative uses of speech

Having defined what counts as a communicative use of speech, we need to identity and distinguish among types of communicative uses of speech. To study the development of control over speech acts, we need a vocabulary for talking about different types of communicative acts. For such basic questions as what kinds of acts children produce at any developmental point or in what order they appear in children's speech, we must make principled distinctions among different speech uses. In other words, we need some criteria for determining whether two different utterances represent the same kind of communicative act.

Since the mid-1970s, although considerable research effort has been devoted to pragmatic analyses of child speech, no generally agreed-upon method of analysis (comparable, for example, to vocabulary testing) or metric of development (comparable, for example, to Mean Length of Utterance [MLU] for grammatical development) has emerged. There are no "natural" criteria for discriminating among distinct types of communicative acts. The variety of category systems used in research on pragmatic development clearly demonstrates that intuitions about how to categorize and distinguish communicative acts differ fundamentally. There is also no agreed-upon theory of communicative uses of speech from which similar category systems could have been derived by different research groups; different researchers (for example, Dore, 1974, and Halliday, 1975) operate with fairly dissimilar conceptions of speech uses. Since different researchers have used mutually incompatible typologies of communicative acts, comparing and synthesizing their various findings is nearly impossible.

Furthermore, because language transcription and pragmatic analysis are time-consuming, most of the studies have used rather small samples, leaving some doubt as to the generalizability of the findings. Yet another problem of generalizability is that some of the most widely used coding systems (e.g., Bates, 1976; Bates et al., 1979; Dore, 1974; Halliday, 1975; McShane, 1980) were designed for very young children, with categories specific for this population. Data from studies using these coding systems are difficult to compare with studies on older children's more complex communicative systems.

In addition, studies using the most detailed and theoretically founded coding systems have typically concerned themselves with a subset of formal structures (e.g., Keenan, 1977, looked only at repetitions), of communicative categories (e.g., Garvey, 1975, looked only at requests for action; Garvey, 1977, only at clarification requests; Corsaro, 1979, Ervin-Tripp & Gordon, 1986, and Menn & Haselkorn, 1977, only at requests), or of situations (Moerk, 1975, looked only at teaching interactions; Ninio, 1980, 1983b, and Ninio & Bruner, 1978, only at book-reading routines). The findings from these studies obviously cannot be taken to indicate children's overall pragmatic abilities.

The more comprehensive systems that have been developed for coding the speech acts of older as well as younger children are totally inconsistent with one another. A comparison of three of the most widely used systems, by Dore (1978), Tough (1977), and McShane (1980) (see Table 2.1) shows that they emphasize very different aspects of the production of communicative acts. Tough's system makes distinctions at a cognitive level, Dore's reflects something close to illocutionary force at the utterance level, and McShane's concentrates on the kind of activity children are engaged in. This difference of conception and emphasis creates incompatible typologies of communicative speech uses.

What accounts for this lack of consensus on types of communicative acts? The basic problem appears to be the absence of a firm theoretical basis for deriving a systematic category system. As a consequence, many of the coding systems for pragmatic meanings are internally incoherent, confusing functional with semantic levels of analysis (e.g., Greenfield & Smith, 1976) or functional with formal bases for categorization (Dore, 1978). Some systems include coding categories that do not designate illocutionary or communicative acts at all. For instance, Wells (1985) has a category **Wanting** (in addition to an illocutionary act–type category called **Direct Request**); Astington (1988) codes acts like **Deceive** or **Persuade**, neither of which refers to a speaker's illocutionary act but rather to the *perlocutionary goals* the speaker wants to achieve (see Ninio & Snow, 1988, for further discussion).

Moreover, in the absence of a clear theory on which to base decisions about how many speech acts to distinguish, the level of detail adopted by a particular investigator may reflect personal preference rather than any particular theoretical stance. Coding systems are often developed empirically and thus are greatly affected by the nature of the interactive situation in which the data are collected, yielding much otherwise unmotivated variability in the number of communicative acts differentiated. Many systems are fairly simple, distinguishing only a small number of communicative categories, presumably to ease coding and to raise reliability. Folger and Chapman (1978), for example, have 12 categories of communicative intent for mother as well as child, whereas Dore (1978) distinguishes 38. Although the practical advantage of limiting the number of coding categories is clear, such abbreviated systems cannot reflect the rich communicative capacities of even very young children.

TABLE 2.1   Major Categories of Communicative Function Identified in Various Coding Systems

Dore (1978) (38 total distinctions; first 4 identified as most important)
| | |
|---|---|
| Requestives: | solicit information or actions |
| Assertives: | report facts, state rules, convey attitudes, and so on |
| Responsives: | supply solicited information or acknowledge remarks |
| Regulatives: | control personal contact and conversational flow |
| Expressives: | nonpropositionally convey attitudes or repeat others |
| Performatives: | accomplish and establish acts/facts by being said |

Tough (1977) (37 total distinctions)
| | |
|---|---|
| Directives: | self-directing, other directing |
| Interpretive: | reporting on present and past experiences, reasoning |
| Projective: | predicting, empathetic, imagining |
| Relational: | self-maintaining, interactional |

McShane (1980) (16 distinctions)
| | |
|---|---|
| Regulation: | attention directives, requests, vocatives |
| Statement: | naming, description, information |
| Exchange: | giving, receiving |
| Personal: | doing, determination, refusal, protest |
| Conversation: | imitation, answer, follow-on, question |

*Source:* A. Ninio, C. E. Snow, B. A. Pan, and P. R. Rollins. 1994. "Classifying Communicative Acts in Children's Early Utterances." *Journal of Communication Disorders* 27: 158–187.

Many systems group speech acts into broader categories, for example, directives and statements. Although one might expect greater comparability across systems at this higher level of organization, the underlying differences in conceptualization emerge here as well (see Table 2.1). Dore's category of **requestives** has no parallel in Tough's or McShane's system, for example, and although Dore's **assertives** probably overlap with McShane's **statements**, it is unclear where such acts would fall in Tough's system.

Empirical studies on developmental pragmatics that do use category systems derived from theory typically select Searle's Speech Act Theory (1969, 1975) as their theoretical foundation. Searle's theory offers not only a taxonomy of speech acts but also a particular conceptualization of what communicative acts are: exclusively individual utterances and their categorization into subtypes. Coding systems built on this theory share a limitation inherent in any system coding only for speech acts—they cannot acknowledge any higher-level organization of talk beyond the single utterance. Talk is organized on several levels simultaneously; a principled distinction should be made among the level of the single utterance, its relationship to preceding and following utterances, and the type of discourse in which it is embedded (Goffman, 1976). As insightfully discussed by Chapman in her review (1981), coding schemes used in developmental pragmatic research typically fail to discriminate among, or successfully to integrate, three commonly recognized levels of analysis: utterance, conversational discourse, and social interaction. Whereas some coding schemes are fairly good at one level or another (e.g., Bloom, Rocissano, & Hood, 1976, at discourse; Dore, 1978, at the utterance level), many mix levels of analysis, and none covers all the levels within one coding scheme. (For further discussions of widely used coding schemes, including those designed for application to populations of children with handicaps, see also Chalkley, 1982; Chapman, 1981; Dore, 1979; Ninio & Wheeler, 1984b; Ninio et al., 1994.)

## 2.3 A proposal for the classification of verbal-social meanings

Ninio and Wheeler constructed a taxonomy, that is, a systematic typology, of communicative acts (Ninio, 1983b, 1986a; Ninio & Wheeler, 1984a, b), to study the development of speech production in young children and, more specifically, the development of the production rules young children employ to verbalize communicative intents. As discussed in the previous section, coding systems then in use for the categorization of communicative intent were not sufficiently detailed or systematic for this purpose, and most had serious theoretical and empirical shortcomings (see also Chalkley, 1982; Chapman, 1981; Dore, 1979). Moreover, the dominant theory of utterance meaning, Searle's Speech Act Theory (1969, 1975), had been repeatedly criticized as a conceptualization of actual situated utterances, for focusing on individual utterances as the unit of analysis, and for its simplistic model of the organization of talk and of social acts (cf. Dore & McDermott, 1982; Edmondson, 1981; Levinson, 1983; Ninio, 1986a; Streeck, 1980). A systematic analysis of communicative action required a basis not just in the work of Searle but also in models of discourse analysis that acknowledged the organization of talk into larger units (e.g., Dore & McDermott, 1982; Labov & Fanshel, 1977; Sacks, Schegloff, & Jefferson, 1974; Sinclair & Coulthard, 1975), as well as in theories of social action and social meaningfulness (e.g., Goffman, 1974; Rommetveit, 1974; see Sections 2.3.1, 2.3.2).

Ninio and Wheeler's goal was to develop a category system that would capture discrete, psychologically real types of communicative acts in mother-child interaction. However, this goal immediately raises a question: Does such a system of discrete categories actually exist for either children or adults? "Rules" imply some form of internal representation of fixed options or meanings the speaker has recourse to when producing or interpreting utterances. The presupposition that such fixed representations exist—for word meanings, for utterance meanings, or for any other type of social meaning in the broadest sense—has been repeatedly challenged ever since Wittgenstein (1953) by both ethnomethodologists (Cicourel, 1970; Garfinkel, 1967) and linguists and psycholinguists (Gibbs, 1984; Shanon, 1994). Social or verbal meanings are said by many to be created ad hoc in each unique set of circumstances, to be essentially momentary and unique. In consequence, some branches of sociology have abandoned attempts at formalization of types of speech uses. Instead, they concentrate their efforts on understanding how addressees recreate the intended meaning at a particular moment of verbal interaction without attempting to classify the type of meaning according to a preexisting typology. They view utterance meanings as forming an infinite and indivisible continuum rather than as a set of clearly discriminable subtypes.

In this intellectual climate, setting a goal of formalizing pragmatics may appear anachronistic. Nevertheless, there is some basis for believing that utterance meanings do constitute discrete categories rather than a field or space of options flowing into each other. We will argue that a finite system of distinct and separate types of social-linguistic concepts underlies utterance meanings and in turn precludes the generation of an infinite variety of utterances.

### 2.3.1 The principles underlying the construction of the Ninio and Wheeler taxonomy of communicative acts

The taxonomy of verbal-communicative acts proposed by Ninio and Wheeler (1984b) represents an attempt to classify speech acts based on how an utterance relates to its context. The basic insight on which the taxonomy is built is that speech is a type of social behavior, and as such, utterances are social acts that are meaningful as moves in the currently operative social situation (cf. Goffman, 1976; Wittgenstein, 1953).

According to the "constructivist" account of social behavior, the meaning-fulness of any kind of action is derived from its being systematically related to some agreed-upon definition of what is going on between the participants in a social scene (Bateson, 1955; Goffman, 1974; Gumperz, 1971; Hymes, 1972; Scheflen, 1974). In Scheflen's words, "Meaning applies . . . to a relation between behavior and context" (p. 179). The same is true of language; utterance meaning is a type of social meaning (Halliday, 1975). Thus talk, as a kind of social action, also derives its meaningfulness from having a systematic relationship with the interactive context. To understand what has been said is first to understand what is happening in face-to-face interaction *through* uttering the utterance.

Talk both defines and is defined by the currently operative social reality. When what is said cannot be assimilated into the current definition of social reality, it is meaningless. Recall the example in Section 1.2: When somebody says *The water is now boiling* in the middle of a marriage ceremony, the result is nonsense (Baier, 1967). Thus, to make principled distinctions among types of utterances, one should look for differences in the ways speech contributes to the definition of the situation and in the ways it is interpreted in light of that definition.

In identifying the dimensions along which communicative acts differ, the question then becomes how an utterance relates to, or is interpreted in terms of, the currently defined social reality. This question can be decomposed into two: First, *what* is the state or event or entity of social reality that the current speech act relates to, and second, *how* does the speech act relate to, define, or constitute that state or event of social reality? It appears that there is a finite number of different states and events in terms of which people construe face-to-face interaction, as well as a finite number of distinct ways in which speech operates on the immediate social reality. These two dimensions are taken jointly as defining the *social* meaning of utterances formalized by the taxonomy. Distinct types or categories of utterance meaning exist precisely because the conceptual systems underlying utterance meaning—social-cognitive concepts, such as interactive states or actions, and linguistic-communicative concepts, such as kinds of meaning operations on contextual arguments—are themselves finite systems of discrete categories rather than infinite and indivisible continua.

### 2.3.2 A model of face-to-face interaction

To answer the question of how talk relates to immediate social reality, we need a model or theory of face-to-face interaction. Such a model must identify the system of social-cognitive concepts of different types of states and events that are used by participants in interaction in defining the current situation. The formulation of such a model in the Ninio and Wheeler project relied on two different sources. The first was mothers' descriptions of videotaped interaction sessions in which they had participated, which were content analyzed (Ninio & Wheeler, 1984a). The second was the theoretical writings of sociologists such as Goffman (1953, 1964, 1974) on the nature of face-to-face interaction.

From both sources the following emerged. Participants defined or "framed" the current social reality on several levels simultaneously. These can be viewed as hierarchically embedded definitions going from the most general to the most specific. Figure 2.1 presents a schematic model of the different states and events of face-to-face interaction.

The key element in this taxonomy of interactive states is the *degree* of communality or intersubjectivity achieved. Intersubjectivity is a state in which two or more persons share a feeling of "togetherness," of being united in their concerns and actions. But intersubjectivity is not an all-or-nothing affair, nor is it a constant state achieved by two individuals vis-à-vis each other, like a long-term relationship. Rather, intersubjectivity can be thought of as the momentary achievement of some position between separateness and unity that requires interpersonal "work" to establish and sustain.

The model starts—from the outside in, as it were—with the most general distinction among face-to-face interactive states, the distinction between co-presence and separation. Being within each other's range of vision or hearing is apparently the crucial factor for even a minimal feeling of togetherness in humans. Even if nothing is happening, co-presence offers the possibility of

FIGURE 2.1    A Schematic Model of States and Events of Face-to-Face Interaction

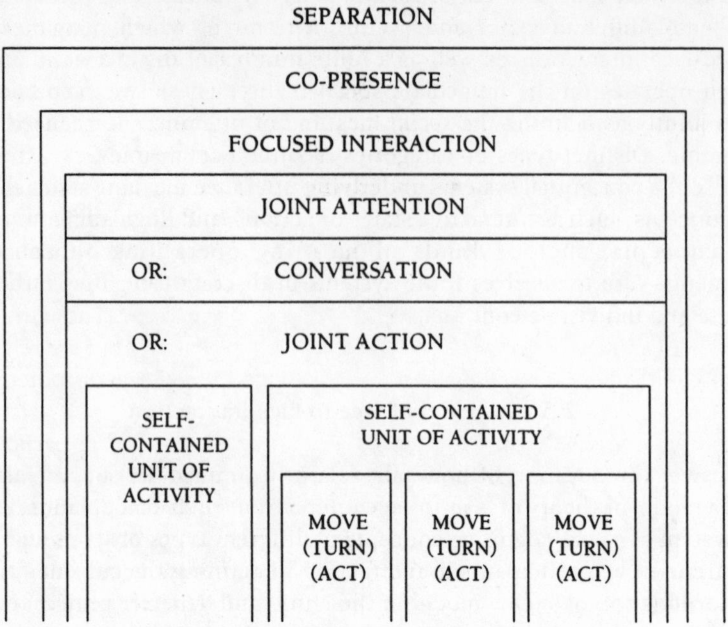

SEPARATION

CO-PRESENCE

FOCUSED INTERACTION

JOINT ATTENTION

OR:    CONVERSATION

OR:    JOINT ACTION

| SELF-CONTAINED UNIT OF ACTIVITY | SELF-CONTAINED UNIT OF ACTIVITY | | |
|---|---|---|---|
| | MOVE (TURN) (ACT) | MOVE (TURN) (ACT) | MOVE (TURN) (ACT) |

*Source:* A. Ninio. May 1983. "A Pragmatic Approach to Early Language Acquisition." Paper presented to the Study Group on Crosscultural and Crosslinguistic Aspects of Native Language Acquisition. Institute For Advanced Studies, Hebrew University, Jerusalem, Israel.

mutual visual monitoring and a potential for focused interaction (see Goffman, 1964, p.63).

Focused interaction occurs when the participants are attending to the same perceptual or mental focus. This might involve interacting around a joint focus of perceptual attention, carrying on a conversation about a jointly contemplated topic, or achieving intersubjectivity by carrying out a joint activity (see Goffman, 1976, pp. 308–309). In all of these cases, a higher degree of intersubjectivity is achieved than occurs if the participants merely remain in each other's presence in a state of unfocused co-presence.

Each of these types of focused interaction (or encounter) can be further articulated into smaller structural units with their own boundaries, an articulation that can continue recursively to ever more elaborate embeddings of units within units. The more deeply a unit of coaction is embedded within the shared definition of the joint action, and the more specific the definition of what the participants are doing together at that moment, the higher the level of intersubjectivity thereby achieved. For example, a novice driver may share with the driving instructor the general definition of the current situation as one of a driving lesson, but the two may not share the meaning of the specific actions to be performed at a particular moment, like simultaneously depressing the clutch and brake pedals while downshifting before stopping. To the extent that one participant does not understand in detail what is going on and the other does, there is less intersubjectivity between them than could have been achieved between equally expert drivers in the same circumstances.

In addition to being in any of these hierarchically embedded states of some focused activity, interactants may at some moment be in transition between any two given interactive states. For example, they might have just finished one activity and not yet started on another one; they may have completed some component of a joint project and be about to start on the next. These times "in between" are not, properly speaking, part of a shared activity but are relatively diffuse and formless intervals; in a classroom setting, they have the potential to develop into pandemonium.

Lastly, breakdowns of frame might occur when one of the participants discontinues the expected flow of events. Lapses of attention or of action eject the participants momentarily from a shared definition of the situation; one of them appears to be doing something different from what the other thought they were doing together. The suddenly inattentive conversational partner may be listening to some conversation overheard from the corner of the room instead of answering a question in the current conversation; the inattentive student may be remembering events of the previous evening instead of copying the formula from the blackboard; the small child may stop listening to the story the adult is telling, turn around, and start to crawl away. In all of these cases the previously shared definition of the interpersonal situation appears to have evaporated in an instant; there is no assurance that participants will persist from one minute to the next at their level of "togetherness." Intersubjectivity is an on-line achievement, not a passive *given* of human affairs.

To summarize the model presented in Figure 2.1, we list the states or events of social situations, from the general to the specific:

- Co-presence/separation/transitions between them
- Focused interaction/unfocused co-presence/transitions between them
- Types of focused interaction: joint attention/conversation/joint action
- Beginning/middle/discontinuity/end of focused interaction
- Self-contained units of focused interaction and their boundaries
- Acts/their boundaries/between-act breathing spaces
- Other elements of immediate social situation: roles, turns, moves

These states are organized in a hierarchically embedded scheme, so that the more specific are substates of the more general. According to the theory, at each particular moment participants define the current social reality ("what is going on") simultaneously on its several levels. It follows that the more general or global states, such as being in co-presence, involve simpler definitions than the more specific situations embedded deeper in the hierarchy. For instance, a single turn at a game in which one participant throws a ball to another may be "framed" by the following simultaneous definitions:

*We are in co-presence.*
*We are engaged in focused interaction.*
*We are engaged in a joint activity consisting of ball tossing/catching.*
*I am performing a turn of the game in the role of the active "pitcher."*

The complete definition of the situation can be paraphrased by the following:

*I am performing a turn of a joint activity consisting of ball tossing/catching in the role of the active "pitcher" while in focused interaction with my mother in each other's presence.*

The more elements a definition requires, the more complex it is. The same principle applies to changes of state: Global changes of interactive state, such as someone leaving, involve fewer elements in their definition than, for example, switching the participants' roles in the midst of an ongoing, agreed-on activity. Leaving could be defined by the participants as something like:

*Our mutual situation changes from co-presence to separation.*

Switching roles may require a more complex definition:

*Participant A will stop filling the role of the active "pitcher," and this role is going to be taken over by Participant B, while A and B continue to be engaged in a joint activity consisting of ball tossing/catching, remaining in focused interaction, remaining in co-presence.*

Obviously, these are rough paraphrases of the actual terms in which people define to themselves what is going on in the social scene. The crucial claim is that whatever the form these definitions take, participants' framing of the social situation will increase in complexity as the states involved become more and more specific.

### 2.3.3 The relation of talk to current social reality

Given this system of participant-defined interactive states and events, the next question is how speech functions to establish, sustain, or modify the current definition of social reality. There are several qualitatively different modes of employing speech, each representing a different type of relationship of speech to the interactive situation.

1. Utterances may explicitly *negotiate* the occurrence and characteristics of future states and events. Negotiations consist of directives to the hearer to bring about some future state of affairs, of commitments by which the speaker undertakes to bring about some state of affairs, and of declarations some state obtains. In addition, the giving and requesting of information necessary for effective negotiation is also seen as a type of action negotiation.

2. Utterances may *mark, signal,* or *acknowledge* the occurrence of some happening, thereby turning it into a ratified, publicly acknowledged event of social reality. For example, a greeting ratifies a meeting, or an expression like *That's it!* publicly marks the completion of an action. Markings are contingent on the occurrence of the event but do not describe or indicate it, since the event is not represented verbally by the utterance.

3. Speech may be employed to establish and sustain a state of conversation in which utterances are used to discuss some topic. Discussions consist of the exchange of information (or, more precisely, of statements, claims, or propositions) on the relevant topic. The heart of discussions, in this restricted sense, is a commitment of speakers to the truth of their propositions. Propositions on the shared topic may be claimed to be true or false, queried, agreed with, disagreed with, and so forth.

4. Utterances may be used to *perform* or *enact* verbal moves of rule-bound activities, such as games. Performances of verbal moves in games and so on count as meaningful units only within the framework of those games. That is, the meaning of such utterances is describable only in reference to the relevant nonlinguistic game and its rules.

5. Utterances may *evaluate* past, ongoing, and future actions of the participants.

In addition to operating on the states and events of the immediate social situation, speakers also engage in types of talk that represent operations on previous communications or texts. These include the following:

6. Speech may *acknowledge the reception* of previous communicative messages. Acknowledgments of the reception of past communications signal that the present speaker was paying attention to the verbal or nonverbal message addressed to him or her in the previous move. The prototypical context is one in which one participant calls the other, who then responds with an acknowledgment:

Mike:   Susan!
Susan:  What?

However, back-channel–type, conversation-monitoring moves are also frequent in interaction; a participant being addressed may from time to time insert a *Yeah* into the other's monologue to signal that he or she is being attentive. Formally, such speech uses are markings, similar to greetings or action-completion signals discussed previously; they turn the speaker's state of attentiveness into a publicly acknowledged fact.

7.  Utterances may involve *metacommunication* about unsuccessful communication. Metacommunications consist of demands for clarification or confirmation of the meaning of the hearer's past communications or of various statements about them. For example:

Mike:     I got that letter yesterday.
Susan:   Which letter?

Susan's clarification request communicates to Mike that he was unsuccessful in referring to the letter he had in mind by the vague deictic expression "that letter" and that he has to be more specific to ensure that Susan knows what he is talking about. In a more extreme case of communication failure, Susan may have responded by *What?* or *Eh?*, signaling that practically nothing of Mike's utterance was received by her, because of either her failure to hear it or some serious problem with understanding it. She might also have said, *I don't hear you, or I don't know which letter you are talking about,* and so on, stating her problem rather than using a question form. In all of these cases, speech is used not merely to signal communicative failure but also to request a repair of the original communication, a complexive meaning specific to metacommunication.

8.  Lastly, utterances may be used to *edit the text* of previous talk. Text editing consists of imitations, completions, corrections, or paraphrases of previous utterances. When text editing is of someone else's utterances, the present speaker does not take responsibility for the meaning of the utterance manipulated, only for its form. For example:

Child:    This is a hippotatamus.
Mother: Hippopotamus. No, it is an elephant taking a bath in the river.

Mother's first utterance is not to be taken as a statement that the picture shows a hippopotamus nor as an agreement with the child's labeling but only as a correction of the child's pronunciation of this word.

These distinctions among major types of speech use correspond to what Searle (1969, 1976; Searle & Vanderveken, 1985) called the *illocutionary point* of utterances; namely, they differ in the kind of point the speaker makes when he or she generates one or another type of utterance. It is possible to demonstrate that utterances belonging to different categories achieve meaningfulness on a different basis (Ninio, 1986a). In the philosophical literature, it is generally accepted that an utterance is meaningful if it can be tied to a set of contractive conditions that make a crucial difference to its interpretation. Thus, statements are meaningful because of, or to the extent that, there exist identifiable conditions in which what is claimed is indeed true and others in which it is false. Without some such connection to matters external to the speech event, an utterance would remain a mere emission of sounds rather than constituting an interpretable and meaningful human act. For example, as Austin pointed out (1961, pp. 50, 70), a statement cannot refer to itself; it is meaningless to say *What I am saying now is true/false* (although, of course, this can be said about a *following* statement). This is true for all acts of speech: A request cannot request itself to be said, a declaration cannot declare itself, and so forth.

The central difference among the types of speech uses listed earlier lies precisely in the kind of "external conditions" they are connected to. Statements, which are the building blocks of conversations, are the only kind to derive their meaningfulness from possessing truth conditions; a speech act like saying *boo* in the game of peek-a-boo cannot be said to be true or false, nor can the utterances that make up action negotiations, for example, requests or refusals. Each type of speech use has its own version of "meaningfulness conditions," which is another way of saying the types differ in the way speech relates to reality.

Figure 2.2 presents the model of interactive states and events shown in Figure 2.1, with types of speech superimposed on it. The speech events marked on the model are *talk interchanges* (Goffman, 1953). Single utterances seldom function by themselves; rather, stretches of talk made up of two or more turns at speaking by the participants form a higher structural unit, functioning together to further some interactive business. In the Ninio and Wheeler system, interchanges are formally defined as stretches of talk that are unified in serving a common interactive function, namely, by relating similarly to one specific element of social reality. The operation shared by several interconnected utterances on the same contextual argument is one of the limited number of specific *modes* of employing speech that were listed previously. For example, when participants negotiate the transition from separation to co-presence, one may call out to the other, requesting that the other join him or her, and the other may answer by agreeing (or refusing) to come. The exchange as a whole relates to a future event of the participants entering co-presence, and its relationship to this future event is that of the meaning-operation of **negotiation**. Within the interchange, each of the individual utterances makes its specific contribution to the business at hand: The first utterance is a request, the second an agreement; these are specific moves carrying out negotiation. Talk thus possesses at least *two* levels of organization, the individual utterance and the talk interchange in which it is embedded and to which it contributes.

It is important to emphasize that not all talk is concerned with establishing and acting out interactive situations. Some talk is metacommunicative, that is,

FIGURE 2.2    A Model of States and Events of Face-to-Face Interaction and Types of
Talk Interchanges Relating to Them

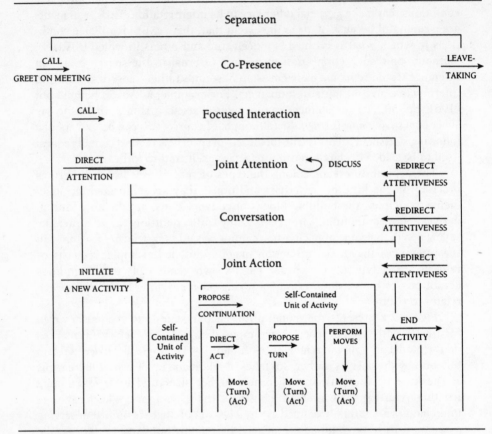

*Source:* A. Ninio. May 1983. "A Pragmatic Approach to Early Language Acquisition." Paper presented to the
Study Group on Crosscultural and Crosslinguistic Aspects of Native Language Acquisition. Institute for
Advanced Studies, Hebrew University, Jerusalem, Israel.

concerned with talk itself—for example, talk dealing with the clarification of
a failed message. Because such talk may appear in the context of any kind of
talk interchange regardless of its situational arguments, it is not displayed in
Figure 2.2.

Among the different types of speech uses, verbal moves of interactive
formats (e.g., games) possess the simplest and most immediate relationship
with their interactive context: They are completely fused with their context,
and they constitute inseparable parts of it. Descriptions or negotiations of the
context are already somehow removed from it, as the speaker talks *about* the
context rather than enacting it. Metacommunicative interchanges have the
most distant relationship to the interactive context; these are yet one stage

removed from the ongoing interactive situation, because they are *about* talk
that may be *about* the interaction itself.

## 2.4 The Ninio and Wheeler taxonomy and coding system for communicative acts

On the basis of this theoretical model of the organization of talk, a taxonomy
of verbal communicative acts was developed together with a set of coding
instructions for identifying the relevant acts in interaction (Ninio & Wheeler,
1984a, b, 1988). We present this taxonomy in some detail because it forms the
basis for many of the findings we report in subsequent chapters. The taxonomy
identifies three levels on which talk is organized: the interchange, the utterance,
and the interutterance discourse relations levels.

### 2.4.1 The interchange level of the taxonomy

The taxonomy, in its 1984 version, distinguishes 63 distinct types of talk
interchanges (plus 2 kinds of uncodable speech). These are presented in Table
2.2. In later revisions, onomatopoeic vocal games were further classified into
subtypes, raising the number of different interchanges codable to 70. The
interchange categories represent the cross-classification of talk exchanges according to mode of speech use and the kind of contextual argument talk relates
to. In other words, the Interchange categories of the taxonomy distinguish talk
exchanges not only by the kind of operation they exert on social interaction but
also by the states and events they operate on.

   **Negotiations** are distinguished according to the state or event that is being
decided on. Choices about the future of the interaction are made on various
levels, from the most general decision about whether the interactants will
remain in each other's presence to minute details of an ongoing activity, for
example, who is to perform the next move.

   **Markings** are differentiated according to the event that is acknowledged—
for example, Meeting, Returning to co-presence, Parting; Going to sleep; Hearer
about to eat or eating; Hearer having sneezed or burped; Fall of object;
Completion of action; Object transfer, and so on.

   **Evaluations** are distinguished according to whose action is being evaluated:
Hearer's or Speaker's.

   **Discussions** are distinguished according to the immediateness of their
topic: Topic is the focus of joint attention, a recent event, the nonpresent or the
nonobservable, and so on.

   **Performances** of verbal moves in games are differentiated according to
the specific game being played, for example, swinging game, peek-a-boo,
jumping game, telephone talk. In the revised version, vocal games consisting

32

TABLE 2.2   Types of Verbal Interchanges According to Interactive Function

### MANAGEMENT OF THE TRANSITION BETWEEN SEPARATION AND CO-PRESENCE

| | |
|---|---|
| CFA: Call from afar | Function: to get hearer into speaker's presence; to interact with hearer when not in co-presence with speaker |
| GMO: Greet on meeting | To mark entering into co-presence |
| MCP: Mark co-presence | To mark co-presence of speaker and hearer after a separation |

### MANAGEMENT OF THE TRANSITION BETWEEN CO-PRESENCE AND SEPARATION

| | |
|---|---|
| GPO: Greet on parting | To mark approaching separation |
| GNO: Wish good night | To mark approaching separation because of going to sleep |
| LTT: Temporary leave-taking | To negotiate an intention to leave hearer for a short while; to prepare hearer for leaving her or him; to take leave |
| −LTT: Prevent hearer from leaving | To stop or prevent hearer from leaving |

### INITIATING FOCUSED INTERACTION: ESTABLISHING MUTUAL ATTENTIVENESS AND PROXIMITY

| | |
|---|---|
| CAL: Call | To demand attentiveness from hearer; to direct hearer's attention to speaker; to get hearer to approach speaker to make interaction possible |
| SAT: Show attentiveness | To demonstrate that speaker is paying attention to hearer |

### REESTABLISHING FOCUSED INTERACTION AFTER A BREAK

| | |
|---|---|
| ICS: Initiate: "come and start" | To redirect hearer's attention to the performance of a new activity after it had been agreed that activity will be performed but hearer has become inattentive |
| RCN: Renew: propose continuation of activity after a break | To redirect hearer's attention to the performance of an ongoing activity after a break in the activity, for example, because of hearer's inattentiveness |

### WITHDRAWING FROM INTERACTION

| | |
|---|---|
| WFI: Withdraw from interaction | To inform hearer that speaker is about to withdraw from interaction, although he or she will remain in hearer's presence |

### MANAGEMENT OF JOINT ATTENTION

| | |
|---|---|
| DHA: Direct addressee's attention | To achieve joint focus of attention by directing hearer's attention to objects, persons, and events in the environment |

### HOLDING CONVERSATIONS ON PRESENT TOPICS

| | |
|---|---|
| DJF: Discuss joint focus of attention | To hold a conversation on something observable in the environment that both participants attend to, for example, objects, persons, ongoing actions of hearer and speaker, ongoing events |
| DRE: Discuss a recent event | To hold a conversation on immediately past actions and events |
| DHS: Discuss addressee's inner state and feelings | To hold a conversation on hearer's nonobservable thoughts and feelings |

(continues)

TABLE 2.2   (continued)

| | |
|---|---|
| DSS: Discuss speaker's inner state and feelings | To hold a conversation on speaker's nonobservable thoughts and feelings |
| PSS: Negotiate possession of objects | To determine who is the possessor of an object |

### HOLDING CONVERSATIONS ON NONPRESENT TOPICS

| | |
|---|---|
| DNP: Discuss the nonpresent | To hold a conversation about topics that are not observable in the environment, for example, past and future events and actions, distant objects and persons, abstract matters |

## THE MANAGEMENT OF JOINT ACTION

### NEGOTIATING THE INITIATION OF A NEW ACTIVITY

| | |
|---|---|
| IOQ: Initiate: open-ended question about addressee's wishes | To initiate a new activity while letting hearer propose the activity |
| IPA: Initiate: propose specific activity | To initiate a new activity by proposing a specific activity; to negotiate a proposal |
| IPR: Initiate: propose a preparatory move of a new activity | To initiate a new activity by proposing the performance of a preparatory move of that activity; to negotiate proposal |
| IPM: Initiate: propose performing move | To initiate a new activity by proposing the performance of a move of that activity; to negotiate proposal |
| ICS: Initiate: "come and start" | To get hearer to start a new activity after activity has been negotiated |

### ALLOCATING ROLES, TURNS, AND MOVES IN ACTIVITIES

| | |
|---|---|
| AAH: Offer move, turn, or role in activity to addressee | To negotiate the offer of a move, role, or turn to the hearer |
| AAS: Demand role, turn, or move for speaker | To negotiate the demand for a move, role, or turn to the speaker |

### SETTING UP RULES OF TURN-TAKING IN AN ACTIVITY

| | |
|---|---|
| RTT: Establish rules of turn-taking | To negotiate participants' taking turns in activity |

### RENEWING/REPEATING AN ONGOING ACTIVITY

| | |
|---|---|
| RCN: Renew: propose continuation of activity after a break | To negotiate continuation of an ongoing activity after a break in the activity |
| RRP: Renew: propose repetition of last unit of activity | To negotiate the repetition of the last unit of an activity (or a whole activity) or the continuation of an activity with changes in the roles of the speaker and hearer |
| RNF: Renew: propose a new focus of activity | To negotiate a change in the focus of an ongoing activity, that is, change of object with same action |

(continues)

TABLE 2.2  (continued)

| MOR: Propose addition of a recursive act | To negotiate whether to perform another move of a recursive, unbound activity |
|---|---|

*REGULATING ADDRESSEE'S NEXT ACT*

| RHA: Regulate addressee's acts | To direct the hearer to perform an act; to regulate the way in which he or she will perform an act |
| –RHA: Stop/prevent addressee's act | To stop or prevent hearer's undesirable act |
| MHP: Make addressee pause in action | To make hearer pause temporarily in his or her activity; to wait until resuming activity (including speech) |

*REGULATING SPEAKER'S ACTIONS*

| RSA: Regulate speaker's next act | To talk to oneself; to direct self to perform an act, or to discuss with self ways and means of performing an act by the speaker; to state intent to act; to promise to perform an act in the near future |
| –RSA: Stop/prevent speaker's act | To stop or prevent speaker's undesirable act |
| OHH: Offer to help addressee | To offer help to hearer in his or her actions |

*EVALUATING ADDRESSEE'S AND SPEAKER'S ACTIONS*

| EHP: Evaluate addressee's performance | To evaluate hearer's acts as correct or incorrect or as desirable or undesirable |
| ESP: Evaluate speaker's performance | To evaluate speaker's acts and utterances as correct or incorrect, as truthful or false, or as desirable or undesirable |

*STOPPING, ENDING, AND PREVENTING ACTIVITIES*

| –IPA: Prevent new activity | To prevent the initiation of a new activity by hearer |
| AEA: Attempt to end activity or subunit of activity | To negotiate the ending of an ongoing activity or of its subunit |
| MCA: Mark completion of action | To verbally mark the completion of an activity |

*PERFORMANCE OF VERBAL MOVES IN GAMES AND OTHER ACTIVITIES*

| PR1-PRT: Perform move in social games such as ring-around-the-rosy (each different game a different interchange type) | To perform moves in a game or other activity by uttering the appropriate verbal forms |
| PRO: Perform move in elicited imitation format | To perform moves in an imitation interactive format |
| PRA (P01-P40): Perform move in game of mimicking animal and inanimate noise | To perform moves |

(continues)

TABLE 2.2　(continued)

| MARKING EVENTS: SOCIALLY EXPECTED VERBAL INTERCHANGES | |
| --- | --- |
| MTK: Thank | To politely express gratitude for hearer's past action |
| MPG: Wish a good appetite | To politely wish a good appetite |
| MPS: Bless on sneezing | To politely wish good health on hearer's sneezing |
| MNC: Mark new clothes | To politely bless on wearing new clothes |
| MCN: Congratulate | To congratulate hearer on festive occasions |
| MAZ: Apologize | To apologize for having hurt hearer |
| MEE: Mark exertion of effort | To mark the exertion of effort |
| MEB: Mark swallowing of food | To mark the swallowing of food by hearer |
| MEF: Mark falling of object | To mark the fall of an object |
| MEH: Mark addressee's falling | To mark hearer's falling or stumbling |
| CMO: Comfort | To comfort hearer; to express sympathy for misfortune |
| MRK: Mark events not specified earlier | To mark occurrence of event |

| METACOMMUNICATION: DEMAND CLARIFICATION OR CONFIRMATION OF ADDRESSEE'S MEANING | |
| --- | --- |
| DCC: Demand clarification of verbal communication and wordlike vocalizations | To obtain clarification of hearer's ambiguous verbal communication or a confirmation of S's understanding of it |
| DCA: Demand clarification of nonverbal communication, action, or nonaction | To obtain clarification of hearer's nonverbal communicative acts |

*Source:* A. Ninio and P. Wheeler. 1984. *A Manual for Classifying Verbal Communicative Acts in Mother-Infant Interaction.* Working Papers in Developmental Psychology, no. 1 (Jerusalem: Martin and Vivian Levin Center, Hebrew University), pp. 6–14.

of onomatopoeic mimicking of different animals and so on are considered distinct games.

**Acknowledgments** of past communications are considered expressions of attentiveness and are not distinguished further according to the kind of communication that is acknowledged.

**Metacommunication** is distinguished according to the kind of communicative move that is clarified, namely, verbal or nonverbal communication.

**Text editing** can occur in any kind of talk, irrespective of its interactive arguments, and is considered part of that talk. In consequence, distinctions among different kinds of text editing (e.g., correction or repetition) are seen as determining only the type of the individual utterance, not the type of the talk exchange as a whole.

### 2.4.2 The utterance level of the taxonomy

On the second level of coding, the communicative function of the single utterance is classified within the relevant interchange. For instance, in a verbal exchange composed of negotiation about the next activity, a certain utterance might suggest a specific new activity to be engaged in, whereas another utterance might serve to agree to carry out or reject that suggestion. Although the common business of both turns at speech is the negotiation of the immediate future activity, each utterance has its own unique communicative meaning or contribution to the business of the interchange. This component of utterance meaning is captured in the taxonomy and coding system by speech act category names; we are using mostly the ordinary illocutionary act vocabulary, such as *statement, request/proposal, refusal,* and the like. On an abstract level, the same analysis of decomposing meaning into operations on arguments applies to both speech act codes and interchanges (see Ninio, 1986a). These analyses are not presented here; it is sufficient to note that in general, each ordinary-language speech act term used in the taxonomy represents a unique combination of type of operation and type of argument actually found in the observational database.

The Ninio and Wheeler (1984b) coding system distinguishes 63 categories of speech acts for individual utterances that are moves in interchanges plus two categories for uncodable utterances. Table 2.3 presents them in families according to the major pragmatic force or type of operation on contextual arguments.

## 2.4.3 The discourse level of the taxonomy

Verbal acts within each type of interchange are considered to consist of three types of moves: openers, responses, and elaborations. An *opening move* is one that defines the matter at hand or the business the interchange as a whole is to deal with; it is typically the first turn starting an interchange, but it can also appear at any point in the middle of an interchange, repeating the overture. *Responses* are reactions to openers; the system distinguishes between positive and negative responses whenever the distinction is appropriate, in terms of whether the responder goes along with or opposes the initiative of the first speaker. In terms used by conversational analysts, openers and responses are typically the first and second elements in adjacency pairs (Goffman, 1976). Lastly, *elaborations* are secondary utterances, usually providing explanations or excuses for some opening move or response.

## 2.4.4 Level of detail of the full taxonomy

The final unit of verbal communicative acts in the taxonomy involves speech act–interchange combinations like **Suggest the initiation of a new activity** (e.g., *Let's do a puzzle now*), **Agree to the proposed new activity** (e.g., *OK*), or **Suggest the addressee as the actor to perform the next move** (e.g., *You do it*). Each turn at speech is also coded for its intrainterchange status as opener, response, or

TABLE 2.3   Speech Act Codes, Categories, and Definitions, by Major Pragmatic Force

**Directives and Responses**
- RP    Request/propose/suggest action for hearer; proposed action might also involve speaker
- RQ    Yes/no question about hearer's wishes and intentions that functions as a suggestion
- DR    Dare = challenge hearer to perform action
- WD    Warn of danger
- CL    Call attention to hearer by name or by substitute exclamations
- SS    Signal to start performing an act, for example, to run or roll a ball; pace performance of acts by hearer
- AD    Agree to do = agree to carry out act requested or proposed by other
- AL    Agree to do for the last time
- RD    Refuse to do = refuse to carry out act requested or proposed by other; including refusals by giving excuses and reasons for noncompliance
- CS    Countersuggestion; an indirect refusal
- GI    Give in; accept other's insistence or refusal
- AC    Answer calls; show attentiveness to communications
- GR    Give reason; justify a request for action, refusal, prohibition, and so on

**Speech Elicitations and Responses**
- EI    Elicit imitation of word or sentence by explicit command
- MU    Model utterance for imitation without explicit request
- EC    Elicit completion of word or sentence
- EX    Elicit completion of rote-learned text
- EA    Elicit mimicking of noises made by animals, and so on
- RT    Repeat/imitate other's utterance
- SC    Complete statement or other utterance in compliance with request eliciting completion
- CX    Complete text if so demanded

**Commitments and Responses**
- SI    State intent to carry out act by speaker
- FP    Ask for permission to carry out act by speaker
- PD    Promise
- TD    Threaten to do
- PA    Permit hearer to perform act
- PF    Prohibit/forbid hearer to perform act

**Declarations and Responses**
- DC    Declare = create a new state of affairs by declaration
- DP    Declare (fantasy) = create make-believe reality by declaration
- YD    Agree to a declaration
- ND    Object to a declaration

**Markings and Responses**
- MK    Mark occurrence of event (i.e., thank, greet, apologize, congratulate, and so on)
- TO    Mark transfer of object to hearer
- CM    Commiserate, express sympathy for hearer's distress
- EM    Exclaim in distress, pain
- EN    Endearment = express positive emotion
- ES    Exclaim in surprise = express surprise
- XA    Exhibit attentiveness to hearer
- PT    Polite response to thanking

(continues)

TABLE 2.3   (continued)

**Statements and Responses**
- ST  State = make a declarative statement
- AP  Agree with proposition expressed by previous speaker
- DW  Disagree with proposition expressed by previous speaker
- WS  Express a wish
- CN  Count

**Questions and Responses**
- QN  Wh-question = ask a product question
- YQ  Yes/no question = ask a yes/no question
- TQ  Restricted alternative
- SA  Answer a wh-question with a statement
- AA  Answer in the affirmative to yes/no question
- AN  Answer in the negative to yes/no question
- QA  Answer a question with a wh-question
- YA  Answer a question with a yes/no question
- NA  Nonsatisfying answer to question
- RA  Refuse to answer

**Performances**
- PR  Perform verbal move in game

**Evaluations**
- PM  Praise for motor acts, that is, nonverbal behavior
- ET  Exclaim in enthusiasm = express enthusiasm for hearer's performance
- CR  Criticize = point out error in nonverbal act
- AB  Approve of appropriate behavior; express positive evaluation of hearer's or speaker's acts; approve of hearer's or speaker's acts
- DS  Disapprove, scold, protest disruptive behavior; express negative evaluation of hearer's or speaker's behavior as inappropriate
- ED  Exclaim in disapproval

**Demands for Clarification**
- RR  Rerun request = request to repeat utterance

**Text Editing**
- CT  Correct = provide correct verbal form in place of erroneous one

**Vocalizations**
- VC  Word babble = utter a wordlike utterance without clear function
- XX  Idiosyncratic words

*Source:* A. Ninio and P. Wheeler. 1984. *A Manual for Classifying Verbal Communicative Acts in Mother-Infant Interaction.* Working Papers in Developmental Psychology, no. 1 (Jerusalem: Martin and Vivian Levin Center, Hebrew University), pp. 15–16.

elaboration, but, with rare exceptions, the discourse code is redundant with the communicative act code (e.g., suggestions are typically openers of interchanges), and so the discourse coding is not discussed further here.

The full coding system generates a large number of different types of communicative acts, differing in the type of operation of speech on its contextual arguments, in the identity of these arguments, or in both. The theory underlying the construction of this typology identifies each of these fully detailed categories as a psychologically real, discrete *type* of communicative intent. In other words, each category purports to represent, in Wittgensteinian terms, a unique type of "language game." The category system itself is thus a hypothesis about the organization of the mental representation of communicative intents in the mind.

### 2.4.5 The intercoder reliability of the coding system

To estimate the intercoder reliability of the coding system for detailed speech act–interchange combinations, five 30-minute-long home observations of mother-infant dyads were independently coded by two coders blind to each other's coding. The five sessions included children ages 15, 18, 23, 24, and 27 months. On the 2,934 utterances in the corpus, the overall intercoder agreement was 83.1 percent (*kappa* value 79.1). Maternal utterances were slightly more reliably coded than child utterances (84.1 percent versus 80.0 percent).

## 2.5 Other coding systems derived from the Ninio and Wheeler taxonomy: FCA, INCA-A, PICA-100

The Ninio and Wheeler taxonomy creates coding categories by the cross-classification of communicative intent along several different dimensions. Thus, other category systems can be derived from it in a principled way, either by collapsing distinctions or by making further ones, along one or more of these dimensions. To date, three special or abridged versions of the coding system have been constructed to fit particular research goals: the First Communicative Acts Coding System (FCA), the Abridged Inventory of Communicative Acts (INCA-A), and a parental interview measure called Parental Interview on 100 Communicative Acts (PICA-100). Because results from studies using the three abridged versions are presented in Chapters 3–7, these systems are described here in detail.

### 2.5.1 FCA—First Communicative Acts Coding System.

*FCA—The First Communicative Acts Coding System* (Ninio, 1990b) was developed on the basis of the experience of coding and analyzing very young children's talk with the help of the full Ninio and Wheeler coding system (Ninio, 1985, 1992, 1993b, 1994a). This system is intended for use with children in the single-word period whose repertoire of communicative acts and expressive capacities is restricted. Unlike the full system, FCA does not code separately the interchange, speech act, and discourse functions of utterances. Instead, it defines certain discrete types of speech uses that are, with some exceptions, specific Interchange

× Speech Act × Discourse combinations. Among the very large number of communicative acts the full coding system can acknowledge, those in the FCA were
actually produced by one-word–stage children or their mothers interacting with
them, in a database consisting of close to 50,000 utterances. Some of these moves
were made mostly or only by mothers; including them enables us to estimate
children's productive deficits, as well as their abilities.

The definition of the FCA coding categories followed the principle that a
distinct verbal-communicative act at the single-word stage is one that requires
learning a separate rule of expression as a single-word utterance. To produce
the FCA, several of the original interchange and speech act categories were
broken into sets of more specific coding categories. First, vocal games were
categorized more finely than in the original version of the coding system. The
interchange category **Perform move in game of onomatopoeic mimicking of
animal and other noises** (PRA in the 1984 version) was replaced by 40
categories, each coding for a specific elicitation stimulus—for example, cat, dog,
train, bird, and so on. In a similar move, the original QN speech act code
(**Wh-question** or **Product question**) was replaced in the FCA by 8 specific codes
according to the type of question, namely, questions about the identity of objects
(typically, but not always, *what*), persons (*who*), attribute (*which*), place
(*where*), time (*when*), quantity (*how much*), manner (*how*), and reason (*why*).
The **product-answer** and **refuse-answer** codes were similarly differentiated.
Several other interchange and speech act categories were also elaborated. These
more specific codes make it possible to study, for instance, the differential
developmental course of questions of varying complexity, as well as to give
credit for each type as a separate acquisitional achievement.

On the other hand, several of the interchange and speech act distinctions
of the full coding system were obliterated, grouping together communicative
uses that seemed to be generated by a single form/function mapping rule. This
strategy generated, for example, interchange-independent speech act categories, like a general category **Positive answers to yes/no questions**, including all
such answers regardless of the type of interchange within which the question
was emitted. It also generated a different type of wider category, namely,
"super-speech act" categories—for example, a general **Action-directive** act that
incorporates requests/proposals, countersuggestions, requests for permission,
and questions about hearer's wishes that also function as suggestions. Since
these four are expressed identically in single-word speech, there is no justifica-
tion for differentiating among them at the early stages of development. Another
super-speech act includes **statements and yes/no questions**, which in single-
word speech are distinguished—if at all—only by the employment of falling
versus rising intonation. Super-speech act codes are used in conjunction with
interchange codes just like ordinary speech act codes, creating, for example,
communicative act types like **Action-directive initiating a new activity**.

These modifications were made to make possible the precise quantification
of young children's developmental status in terms of discrete form/function

TABLE 2.4   Interchange Categories of the Abridged INCA-A Coding System

| | |
|---|---|
| NCS | Negotiate co-presence and separation |
| GRT | Greeting on meeting or parting |
| NMA | Negotiate mutual attention and proximity |
| SAT | Showing attentiveness |
| DHA | Directing hearer's attention to objects and persons |
| DJF | Discussing a joint focus of attention |
| DRP | Discussing the related-to-present |
| DRE | Discussing a recent event |
| DNP | Discussing the nonpresent |
| DFW | Discussing the fantasy word |
| DHS | Discussing hearer's nonobservable thoughts and feelings |
| DSS | Discussing speaker's nonobservable thoughts and feelings |
| PSS | Negotiating possession of objects |
| NIA | Negotiating the immediate activity |
| NFA | Negotiating an activity in the future |
| NFW | Negotiating fantasy word activity |
| PRO | Performing verbal moves in an activity |
| MRK | Marking |
| CMO | Comforting |
| DCC | Demanding clarification of verbal communication |
| DCA | Demanding clarification of action |
| TXT | Read written text |
| SDS | Self-directed speech |
| YYY | Uninterpretable utterances |

*Source:* A. Ninio, P. Wheeler, C. E. Snow, B. A. Pan, and P. R. Rollins. 1991. *INCA-A: Inventory of Communicative Acts—Abridged.* Coding manual distributed by Harvard Graduate School of Education, pp. 5–7.

mappings they can control. The resultant FCA coding system consists of 214 discrete communicative acts.

This coding system is clearly inappropriate when the focus of interest is, for instance, the specific social contexts children's speech relates to. The **Positive answers to yes/no questions** code discussed earlier, for example, does not retain information on the type of conversations in which such answers were given. It is, however, well suited for diagnosing developmental delay at entry to speech. In particular, the number of different verbal-communicative acts controlled by children, as measured by this instrument, predicts the size and composition of their vocabularies and the age at which they start to produce multiword utterances (Ninio, 1990a, 1991a, b, 1994a). For some results of a study using the FCA classification, see Section 4.1.

### 2.5.2 INCA-A: Inventory of Communicative Acts—Abridged

An abridged and modified version of the coding system (*INCA-A: Inventory of Communicative Acts—Abridged;* Ninio et al., 1991) was developed for the study of major speech uses in developing children. The INCA-A version groups interchanges into wider categories according to type of speech use, eliminating most distinctions based on type of contextual argument. For instance, all negotiations of immediate action are grouped into a single category, without distinguishing among negotiations of whole activities, of subunits of activities, and of single acts or between negotiating the beginning or ending of activities, repetition or stopping, and so on. Similarly, all marking interchanges (except **Greetings**) are grouped into a single category without distinguishing the event marked (including thanking, apologizing, blessing on sneezing, congratulating, or marking the completion of an action).

On the other hand, further subdivisions were introduced into the interchange code **Discussions of nonpresent topics,** which was not maximally elaborated in the original coding scheme. In INCA-A, this category is separated into three more specific ones: (1) **Discussing the related-to-present,** (2) **Discussing the nonpresent,** and (3) **Negotiating an activity in the far future.** In consequence, INCA-A is better suited to the study of the development of decontextualized language use than the Ninio and Wheeler (1984b, 1988) version.

Table 2.4 presents the 24 Interchange categories of the INCA-A coding system. The speech act categories of INCA-A are identical to those of the full Ninio and Wheeler system. For results of a study using INCA-A, see Section 6.2.


### 2.5.3 PICA-100: Parental Interview on 100 Communicative Acts

The PICA-100 is not a coding system for the classification of utterances but rather is an instrument for interviewing parents about beginning speakers' speech uses (*PICA-100: Parental Interview on 100 Communicative Acts;* Ninio & Goren, 1993). The instrument is based on the FCA—First Communicative Acts Coding System presented in Section 2.5.1, but the super-speech act categories (e.g., statements plus yes/no questions) were disaggregated to their original components. Parents are presented with definitions of 100 different communicative acts and are asked whether their child produces them. All but a few are specific acts from FCA; the rest are open questions about "*other*" communicative acts. The acts queried in PICA-100 were the first 100 produced by a group of beginning speakers in the Ninio (1984) longitudinal observational study reported in Section 6.1. In the same questionnaire, parents are also presented with a list of the most frequently observed early forms of expression for each of these acts. PICA-100 includes 6 items to do with the management of joint and mutual attention, 12 markings of events, 19 types of verbal games, 4 types of exclamations expressing emotions, 28 moves in action negotiations, 28 moves in discussions and conversations, and 3 types of demands for clarification. A detailed list of the communicative act categories contained in PICA-100 is presented in Section 5.2 (Table 5.1) with results from the instrument.

The validity of the maternal reports was tested in a study of 114 mothers of children acquiring Hebrew, between 0;8 and 2;4. The children's verbal-communicative development was independently assessed by 7 items related to language production in the Bayley developmental scales. The correlation coefficient between total number of communicative acts reported by the mothers and a summary score on the 7 items of the Bayley was $r(114)=.85$, $p<.001$, reflecting positively on the validity of the maternal reports.

## 2.6 Central questions about the development of the communicative uses of speech

In Chapters 3–6 we review empirical findings concerning children's acquisition of the communicative uses of speech. The exposition is organized by broad developmental stages and deals with the central questions relevant to each stage.

In Chapter 3 we examine the prelinguistic period, when by definition the only communicative acts that can appear are nonverbal. The question is, are there indeed nonverbal communicative acts? Can children, before the emergence of speech, engage in intentional communication? And if they can, are intentionality and the possession of specific intents antecedents to their verbal expression? Can verbal communication be said to be continuous with preverbal communication, perhaps built on the foundations of nonverbal signaling of intents? And if so, can we distinguish transitional stages and identify transitional phenomena falling between the preverbal and the verbal?

Next, in Chapter 4 we move to the first words children use, asking about the characteristics of the first linguistic productions and what types of pragmatic goals they achieve. We also ask how the entry into communicative use of language can illuminate the process of entry into language itself. We discuss the possibility raised by radical use-conditional approaches: that the mastery of the speech-use system is inherently the mastery of language itself, that is, that the two are identical.

As the initial set of speech uses is necessarily limited in range and character, we go on to ask if there are further developments in the expression of communicative intents within the single-word stage before children start to use structured multiword utterances. In accordance with the radical approach, we ask whether there are any developments in the communicative system that precede and prepare for the entrance into syntax, or connected speech.

Next, in Chapter 5 we map the later development of the speech act system, after children have passed the initial stages of mastery. We ask how many different verbal-communicative acts children control in the initial stages of acquisition and the order in which different types of verbal-communicative acts are acquired. We offer some general principles that determine the order of acquisition of different types of communicative acts on the basis of the detailed examination of the development of several different speech-use subsystems.

In Chapter 6 children's use of speech in interaction is compared throughout development to their mothers' use, and the process of convergence to the mothers' speech is documented. Next, we discuss some developmental trends in children's refinement of verbal communication. We consider how verbal expression becomes increasingly intelligible and interpretable and how nonverbal behaviors (gesture, object use) relate to the development of verbal expression. Lastly, children's gradual mastery of more complex and efficient communication strategies, such as the control of indirect speech acts, is reviewed.

# 3

# Prelinguistic Communication and the Transition to Speech

## 3.1 Prelinguistic development

### 3.1.1 Prelinguistic communicative abilities

For many decades developmental psychologists believed the first period of life was characterized by mental chaos. This view, based in part on the theories of Piaget, has been rejected with the help of methods that provide much more precise information about infants' perceptual and cognitive capacities. We now have evidence that infants are surprisingly mature organisms who perceive the world very much like adults. For instance, newborns exhibit an organization of time that is similar to that of adults; they are able to learn precisely how long to wait between sucking bursts to be reinforced by hearing a singing female voice (DeCasper & Spence, 1991). Further, the visual and auditory worlds of infants are in no sense bizarre. Infants reach for objects they can see (Bower, 1966); they turn their heads to the direction of a sound (Mendelson & Haith, 1976); they even imitate others' facial expressions (Meltzoff & Moore, 1977). They possess, from the first weeks of life, the basic qualifications for constructing a view of the world that fundamentally resembles that of adults.

The cognitive maturity of very young infants is particularly striking in the realm of social interaction. They possess a large repertoire of socially significant behaviors and tendencies, including crying, social smiling (Ahrens, 1954), a preference for the sight of the human face (see Johnson & Morton, 1991, for a review), and a preference for watching human over other types of motion (Bertenthal et al., 1985). Even if these behaviors are the result of very rapid learning rather than of prewired dispositions, human infants are singularly prepared to conduct a social life.

Investigators of early social behavior generally agree that infants' precocious social understanding enables them both to produce intentional communicative signals and to interpret the significance of social signals, actions, and events in their environment well before they can talk or understand speech. This view is shared by those studying the development of verbal communication and language and those concerned with the development of social skills.[1] Although the claim for infant social precocity has generated some skeptics (e.g., Shatz, 1982), it is supported by a wealth of meticulous research into young children's interactive abilities (cf. chapters in Feagans, Garvey, & Golinkoff, 1984; Lamb & Sherrod, 1981; Rubin & Ross, 1982).

Some authorities believe, moreover, that the possession of communicative intents and the interpretation of others' intents are such basic human capacities that they are biological dispositions or universal (e.g., Dore, 1985; Miller, 1970; Trevarthen, 1979). Without adopting this extreme view, we believe the ability to enter and sustain a state of intersubjectivity with others is a very early achievement. Of course, children have not mastered the complete range of interactive moves in early infancy. Like other higher capacities (cf. Fischer, 1980), social abilities are skills that develop gradually (cf. Eckerman & Stein, 1982), requiring at the onset considerable contextual support even for their less complex manifestations.

### 3.1.2 Communicative intents expressed at the preverbal stage

Children pass through a stage of producing expressive vocalizations before they start using sounds for intentional communication. The earliest expressive vocalization is, of course, crying. However, by the middle of the first year infants control an impressive repertoire of expressive vocalizations that are not crying sounds (see Locke, 1993, for a review; also Cruttenden, 1982; Oller, 1981; Vihman & McCune, 1994). These vocalizations are specific in tone and timbre to the infant's emotional state—for example, surprise, frustration, joy at the appearance of a familiar person—or to his or her communicative intents, such as calling someone or demanding an object. These vocalizations are similar enough across normally developing children that mothers can easily identify the situation in which an unknown infant was recorded—even infants from unfamiliar language environments. However, autistic children do not appear to share this repertoire of expressive vocalizations; strangers cannot interpret the "meaning" of their vocalizations, although their mothers can (Ricks & Wing, 1975). The central symptom of autism—problems in interpersonal communication—can evidently be identified even in the system of expressive, pre-intentional communicative vocalizations, which suggests some continuity between the system of spontaneous, "natural," or expressive vocalizations and conventional, cultural, intentional communication.

What is known about infants' intentional communicative abilities? We know that preverbal infants ages 8 to 10 months use intentional vocalizations and gestures, such as pointing, gazing, and giving, for communicative purposes. However, there is little systematic information about the social meanings these acts express. Previous studies fall into three categories.

First, several studies categorized infants' nonverbal illocutionary-type communicative acts produced in dyadic interaction with adult caretakers. Bates, Camaioni, & Volterra (1975) described two broad categories of pre-verbal expressions, both identified as precursors to speech acts later performed verbally. Pointing to objects, giving objects, and other acts designed to direct adults' attention were called *proto-declaratives,* the precursors to statements. Proto-imperatives, the antecedents of requests and other directives, were acts designed to elicit help or obtain desired objects—for example, pointing combined with whining. Coggins and Carpenter (1981) and Carpenter, Mastergeorge, and Coggins (1983), using a more detailed typology, identified the following types of pragmatic behaviors in preverbal children: requesting (object requests, action requests, information requests), greeting, transferring objects, showing off, acknowledging, answering, protesting, commenting on action, and commenting on an object. Interestingly, none of the studies in this group mentioned game-embedded meaningful behaviors of the type documented by Bruner and his collaborators among the preverbal communicative acts infants were able to control.

A second category of studies focused on infants and already-talking toddlers interacting with peers, a situation that generated an expanded list of social meanings expressed by preverbal and early nonverbal communicative behaviors (Bronson, 1981; Dunn & Kendrick, 1982; Eckerman, Whatley, & Kutz, 1975; Lewis et al., 1975). In peer interaction, infants and young toddlers expressed feelings such as sympathy, communicated offers to share objects and activities, expressed compliance and noncompliance or resistance, and engaged in stage setting and pretend games.

Third, investigations have documented preverbal infants' gradually evolving participation in specific interactive formats, such as games of give-and-take and peek-a-boo (Bruner, 1983; Bruner & Sherwood, 1976; Ratner & Bruner, 1978) or joint picture-book reading (Ninio, 1980, 1983a; Ninio & Bruner, 1978;

Snow, de Blauw, & van Roosmalen, 1978; see also Garvey, 1976; Goldman & Ross, 1978; Hay, Ross, & Davis, 1979). Whereas the first group of studies discussed here (e.g., Bates, Camaioni, and Volterra, 1975) sought evidence of children's preverbal mastery of previously defined, context-independent, illocutionary-type communicative acts, studies of infants playing games adopted a form of contextual analysis. In this approach, communicative moves are inherently embedded in a particular rule-governed interactive situation and are meaningful in terms of their role in that situation. Preverbal infants experience a relatively prolonged apprenticeship at such situations, during which they gradually increase their participation in these collaborative activities and perfect the necessary action repertoire (Camaioni & Laicardi, 1985; Gustafson, Green, & West, 1979; Rome-Flanders et al., 1995). Infants' gradual growth in understanding such interactive formats, and their evolving ability to collaborate actively in them, is seen as providing the true foundations of later meaningful verbal communication (Bruner, 1983).

In summary, infants control an impressive array of social meanings and can convey them by nonverbal means. We see the full range of their abilities only by observing them in a variety of settings—with peers as well as adults and in adult-structured activities, as well as in unstructured interaction. These results provide converging evidence that the social capacities underlying communication emerge precociously and open up the possibility, discussed later, that prelinguistic communication may be a crucial precursor of children's entry into language.

## 3.2 The transition to speech

In this section we consider the degree to which the preverbal abilities discussed earlier contribute to the development of language. Within the field, there are many proponents of a strong continuity view, which holds that words come to substitute for gestures or preverbal vocalizations in social interaction. Critics of this view cite a variety of objections: that language has its own organization that must be mastered before intents can be expressed verbally, that early words do not actually express communicative intents, that children undergo a major cognitive reorganization that makes possible novel communicative capacities. We argue here for the view that the social interactions engaged in by children who can talk are continuous with those engaged in preverbally, in that interpersonal intentions are socially constructed by all participants. Furthermore, we argue that the capacities of the older child to express intentions conventionally reflect what he or she has learned in earlier interactions, both about what meanings might be expressed and about how to express them. At the same time, though, we acknowledge that the linguistic expression of communicative intents is qualitatively different from their gestural and behavioral expression, and even if the earliest words are indeed very similar in status to nonlinguistic expressions of intents, their acquisition makes possible further developments in the linguistic domain that have no nonverbal parallels. Linguistic communication thus starts with words substituting for gestures, but the language system, once established, soon diverges from its nonverbal origins.

### 3.2.1 The continuity hypothesis

Some investigators have claimed that children's early language is continuous with their preverbal communicative system, that is, that children acquire early verbalizations by substituting conventional, verbal forms for the nonverbal expressions of their communicative intents (Bates, 1976; Bates, Camaioni, & Volterra, 1975; Bruner, 1983; Carpenter, Mastergeorge, & Coggins, 1983; Carter, 1979; Halliday, 1975; Lock, 1980; Nelson, 1985; Ninio & Bruner, 1978). This view implies that the communicative intents expressed by the first words are identical to those expressed with gestures or vocalizations by preverbal children.

Obviously, those who deny preverbal infants' communicative precocity (e.g., Shatz, 1982) reject the continuity hypothesis. Others (e.g., Dore, 1975, 1978) take a more complex approach. Dore believes preverbal infants can employ a variety of means intentionally to express their wishes and share their inner states with others but does not believe the preverbal and verbal systems form a single, uninterrupted developmental continuum. Dore points out that linguistic expressions operate by two uniquely linguistic mechanisms, reference and predication, that do not exist in nonlinguistic form. Therefore, he claims, the fundamental discontinuity between preverbal and verbal communication is that verbal communication relies on language-specific means to express language-specific contents.

Dore objected to the claim by Bates, Camaioni, and Volterra (1975) that communicative acts children perform nonverbally prior to the emergence of language have essentially the same status as verbal illocutionary acts. His major point of disagreement was with the notion that the later use of verbal expression involved merely the substitution of verbalizations for prior nonverbal behaviors (Dore, 1978). Relying on Searle's (1969) Speech Act Theory, Dore argued that illocutionary acts incorporate a grammatical component that preverbal communicative acts obviously lack. He concluded that prelinguistic communicative skills are necessary but insufficient for the acquisition of linguistic communication and that by themselves developments in the pragmatic domain cannot provide an explanation for the emergence of speech. Dore considers children's gradual mastery of types of communicative intents to be a separate line of development from the development of language proper, neither influencing the other. In fact, Dore dismisses not only preverbal communication as irrelevant to true illocutionary act production but most of single-word speech as well. Even in true verbal utterances of young children, those with illocutionary force, he argues that the illocutionary intent is carried by nonlinguistic means, such as intonation, whereas the words themselves serve only as rudimentary referring expressions naming some random element of the communicative situation (Dore, 1975). Thus, Dore's studies of the development of speech act production, although superficially similar in their subject matter to investigations like Bates's of early pragmatics, actually represent a different viewpoint, one that clearly differentiates between these early pragmatic developments and language acquisition proper.

The view that language represents an emergent novel level of organization qualitatively different from preverbal signaling systems is not inconsistent with the continuity hypothesis. We contend there is considerable continuity, because many of the intents children express with their first words are identical to those previously expressed by nonverbal means. Thus, children can master the principles of intentional communication, as well as the specific social-cognitive concepts underlying some of their earliest verbal utterances, prior to acquiring verbal means for expressing their intentions.

On the other hand, some relatively early utterances express communicative intents that are novel and difficult to express nonlinguistically. For example, how can one make a claim with points, eye movements, or facial expressions? How can a child declare that she is mommy during pretend play? A preverbal child can act out a pretend role, for example, play mommy by mimicking the actions of getting dressed and leaving for work, but cannot announce or declare that she is playing mommy without language.

Many communicative intents are no doubt emergent consequences of learning language, and thus they represent discontinuities between preverbal and verbal communication. However, the acquisition of forms expressing novel intents depends on children's ability to interpret intents they cannot yet produce, which in turn is possible only because of children's sophisticated social capacities at the onset of speech (see Dore, 1975; Nelson, 1978; and Ninio & Snow, 1988, for discussions of this issue). A "weak" continuity hypothesis thus allocates a decisive role to children's precocious communicative abilities in the first stages of language development, regardless of whether the actual verbal forms acquired are directly equivalent to preverbal communicative gestures. We return to this topic in Section 4.1.

### 3.2.2 A particular discontinuity hypothesis

A particular version of the discontinuity hypothesis claims that whereas beginning speakers do possess communicative intents, these are expressed not by what they say but by what they do. Because of the rigid and primitive manner in which early intents are typically mapped to verbal expression, early utterances create the impression of spurious vocalizations merely accompanying what is basically a nonverbal communicative act. Some investigators, such as

Barrett (1986) and Dore (1978), claim that this appearance is reality, that in early utterances the communicative intent itself is carried by the nonverbal action (or the intonation), and the verbalization is just another motor component of an inherently nonlinguistic behavior.

In this model, early speech itself does not have an intentional source, expressing some mental content. Rather, words are "situational," having the characteristics of conditional responses that are elicited by the occurrence of highly specific physical and behavioral situations (cf. Barrett, 1986, 1989; Harris et al., 1988; Harrison, 1972; Lock, 1980; McCune-Nicolich, 1981). The proponents of these ideas do not deny that 10- to 20-month-old children have communicative intents. However, since these intents are not expressed in children's early *words,* they see no continuity between preverbal communication and language.

According to this theory, the concepts underlying early words are representations of external events; from these, "true" word concepts develop through the gradual elimination of spurious situational elements, so the conditions of use are extended to a wider and wider range of situations. Communicative intents have no role in this development; they do not form part of the early event representation underlying the production of an utterance (which consists exclusively of overt actions and objects) nor part of the later decontextualized word meaning (Barrett, 1986). Thus, even though the ability to communicate exists both preverbally and after the onset of language, prelinguistic communication is noncontinuous with the linguistic system proper, which is based initially on situational meanings and develops as a system of decontextualized linguistic signs. Thus, for older children words have a meaning that is independent of their potential occasions of use. In some further unspecified development that is not part of language acquisition, utterances eventually become the true carriers of communicative intents.

This theory has been criticized for serious methodological flaws in the collection and interpretation of the empirical evidence on which it is based (for a detailed critique of the theory see Ninio, 1993a). Yet another type of criticism the theory raises is its conceptualization of adult word meanings as essentially independent of their potential occasions of use. Use-conditional semanticists like Gibbs (1984) would say that words never become decontextualized or use-independent, that their conditions of use are forever part of the concept underlying their meaning. Thus, the developmental process posited in the situational theory of early word meaning does not generate linguistic signs of the kind adults actually possess.

The theory also raises a serious issue about the nature of communicative behavior: How do we know that some particular behavior, verbal or nonverbal, is the carrier of an intent to communicate on the part of whoever produced it? On what grounds can we judge someone's actions or speech as communicative? To answer these questions, we must consider the details of the situational treatment of requests, attention directives, refusals, or calls for help—utterances that seem unequivocally driven by intent rather than situation. Such utterances are independent of the physical situation in which they are produced, since their topic is a potential, rather than the current, state of affairs. Moreover, children give clear nonverbal indications that they possess an intent to communicate such messages and, furthermore, verbalize that intent with an appropriate form. For instance, children who appear to be making a request for an object often say something like *This*. When refusing, children often say *No*. When children appear to want their mother, they often say *Mommy*. It may seem obvious that at the core of these uses of language there is an intent to communicate. The situational model argues that to think so is a mistake, a pragmatic illusion. The child is merely reacting to some external set of stimuli: *No* is a reaction to his own pushing away of the proffered object, *there* to his own pointing, *more* to holding out his empty bowl. The children clearly act out of an intent to communicate, but their intents do not have anything to do with what they *say*. Their intents affect the way they *act*, and speech is a meaningless sensory-motor accompaniment to meaningful nonverbal behavior (cf. Barrett, 1986; Harris, 1993; Harris et al., 1988; McCune-Nicolich, 1981).

Consider one of these situations more closely. A 15-month-old child is offered an apple. She pushes the apple away, saying *no*. A situational analysis, just like a communicative one, would identify this event as the child's refusing the apple, claiming, though, that the refusal is expressed by the hand movement and not by the word—in other words, that the child did not mean anything particular by saying *no*, which is just a word she says when she pushes things away.

The obvious question to ask is how someone decided in the first place that the child intentionally refused the apple. How do we know that the nonverbal action of pushing the apple away *did* carry the child's intent to refuse? The answer, of course, is that it would be ridiculous to claim otherwise; pushing things away is how one refuses objects, and the apple indeed ended up refused rather than in the child's hand. There is no objective basis for this judgment, nor would there be if an adult had carried out the same action in the same circumstances. We can never be absolutely sure that other people are human like us, that they have intentions, that they mean things the way we interpret them. But we proceed on the assumption that they are and that they do if they act as we would in the same circumstances. The child acted exactly like any of us would—maybe slightly less politely—and the episode ended with the apple being refused. These are all the grounds needed or available for recognizing an intentional communicative act.

But how does pushing the apple away differ from saying *no*? In both cases the choice of the appropriate refusal behavior leads to the judgment that the other has refused. Both equally satisfy the only existing criterion for attributing intentional action to the other—*the interpretation makes sense and works in the interactive situation.*

In summary, communication is an interpersonal phenomenon. Whatever its form, verbal or nonverbal, it is built—as theoreticians like Grice, Goffman,

Rommetveit, and Wittgenstein have argued—on subjectivity and intersubjectivity, on assumptions about the other and attributions of shared understanding. Although we can agree on clear cases of intentional communication and clear cases of noncommunication, objective criteria will not help us in the border country of children's early words. All we can rely on there are common-sense formulations—if it communicates it is communicative. Since vocalizations—in particular, conventional words—typically do communicate effectively, we see them as mechanisms for communication and see the communicative intent they express as an important aspect of their meaning. Young children apparently share our view that words can be used to communicate intentions, and that view probably helps them learn more and more elaborate ways of appearing communicative in the eyes of the beholder.

### 3.2.3 Transitional phenomena: phonetically intermediate signals

The hypothesis of continuity between preverbal and verbal communication is supported by findings about children's gradual mastery of the conventional phonetics of their language. In particular, various transitional communicative signals have been identified that combine preverbal and verbal features. Carter (1979), Dore and colleagues (1976), and Halliday (1975) have documented an intermediate developmental stage where partly conventionalized vocal signals ("vocables") or proto-words were used. This phase considerably overlaps the first stage of real language use (Vihman & McCune, 1994).

David, a child acquiring English observed by Carter between ages 12 and 16 months, systematically emitted vocalizations starting with a particular consonant on similar communicative occasions. For example, vocalizations beginning with *m*, like *mama*, were generally accompanied by a reaching gesture and expressed a request for an object, whereas vocalizations beginning with a *d* sound, like *dede*, were accompanied by pointing and served to direct the hearer's attention to an object the child did not want. Vocalizations beginning with *l*, like *lala*, were expressions of sadness and were usually precursors of crying. With time, these semibabbling vocalizations came increasingly to resemble regular English words. For example, the various *m*-type vocalizations specialized into two distinct forms: *mow*, indicating recurrence, and *moin*, indicating possession. At the last phase, these forms came to be indistinguishable from normative English words—the former *more*, the latter either *my* or *mine*.

Carter suggests that the relevant set of words, also including *mommy, this, that, there,* and the like, apparently developed through some process of **environmental shaping** from spontaneous expressive vocalizations and idiosyncratic communicative signals of the child. As a consequence, these initially expressive vocalizations underwent a process of first partial and then full phonetic consolidation, so that they gradually approximated the conventional verbal forms used by adults for the expression of communicative intents similar to the child's.

Other researchers interpret this phenomenon somewhat differently. Halliday (1975) treats the functionally consistent almost-words preceding full conventionalization as the child's spontaneous invention, which owes nothing to the models in the linguistic environment. Halliday's theoretical commitment to child autonomy does not seem to be supported by the empirical data; many of his child, Nigel's, proto-words at 9 to 16 months were clear approximations of ordinary English expressions, such as *bird* or *what's that*. Whatever the origins of such expressions, they had certainly undergone environmental pressure to resemble conventional forms existing in the child's language community for the same communicative intents (see also Ingram's [1989] discussion of Halliday's findings).

Regardless of the controversy about their origin, the existence in children's language of these *phonetically consistent forms* (Dore et al.'s [1976] term) suggests that the entry into language use, from the phonetic point of view, is a gradual and relatively protracted process rather than a sudden all-or-none phenomenon. As we shall see in Section 4.1, this is true of early speech in other respects as well.

## 3.2.4 Is there a special preverbal stage of imitation?

Tomasello, Kruger, and Ratner (1993) claim children undergo a stagelike development in their capacities for social learning, development driven by their changing concepts of other persons and their skills in perspective-taking. The earliest stage is characterized by an exclusive reliance on imitation of others as the mechanism of learning. In the second stage, children are capable of "instructed learning." The most advanced form of learning from the social environment, called "cultural learning," is collaborative, resting on a fully evolved concept of others as "reflective agents." In this view, metacognitive skills and concepts—such as the ability to reflect on others' and one's own behavior and express these concepts in language—underlie children's later abilities to engage in social learning.

This proposal is relevant to pragmatic development because it highlights the ambiguous status of imitated verbalizations as meaningful communicative behaviors. A significant proportion of very early utterances consists of imitations of previous utterances (e.g., Bates, 1979). There is, however, little consensus in the literature as to whether imitations should be included as speech acts in investigations of pragmatic development (see Section 4.1). If Tomasello, Kruger, and Ratner (1993) are correct, imitations cannot be treated as intentional verbal behaviors just like requests or statements. Rather, imitation has to be seen as a primitive behavior predating the achievement of mature intersubjectivity in children and thus certainly does not qualify as one of the interpersonal, intentional verbal-communicative acts, glossable as expressing some communicative intent like "speaker intends to be interpreted as intentionally imitating addressee's utterance for the sake of language practice" or "for the sake of making a joke."

We argue against excluding imitations from the child's communicative repertoire or treating them as primitive behaviors reflecting a lack of intersubjectivity. We believe (together with other adherents of Cultural Psychology) that children start the process of enculturation already endowed with a precocious capacity to establish intersubjectivity with other persons (see DeHart & Maratsos, 1984; and Trevarthen, 1979, for explicit formulations of this hypothesis). Our view of imitation as communicative derives from the commitment of Cultural Psychology to a "constructivist" conception of meaning—that all meaningful participation in the social life of a group, and all meaningful use of language, involves an interpersonal, intersubjective, collaborative process creating the shared significance.

If all learning is to be construed as social learning, and all social learning is to be construed as collaborative, this means that what may appear at first sight to be imitative or instructed learning is also in effect a collaborative endeavor that is dependent on the achievement of intersubjectivity between the participants. The essential nature of the interaction is not affected by the participants' abilities to reflect on the collaborative encounter.

The research program of Cultural Developmentalists could be summarized as an attempt to show how early behaviors and learning involve the child's collaborating in the creation of shared meaning with the adult. Much research since the 1970s has been devoted to the reevaluation or "upgrading" of children's early behaviors. For example, very young infants have been described as engaging in mutual and collaborative synchronization of attentional states with their mothers (Brazelton, Koslowski & Main, 1974; Stern, 1974). Dore (1983) has proposed that emotional, symbiotic intersubjectivity between an infant and its mother is the carrier wave through which the maternal "voice" is internalized by the child.

Toddlers in apparently imitative-learning contexts (during their first attempts at joint play or during joint picture-book reading when language instruction is taking place) have been shown to be able to learn novel linguistic forms because they understand the scripts or interactive formats in which the novel words are embedded as meaningful moves (Bruner & Sherwood, 1976; Nelson, 1978; Ratner & Bruner, 1978; Snow, Dubber, & de Blauw, 1982). Whether children actually imitate the adult in these contexts has no notable effect on their learning a new word, demonstrating that imitation has no special status among other meaningful interactive moves in these contexts, such as answers to questions or requests for labels (Ninio & Bruner, 1978). Similarly, Eckerman and Stein (1982) construe imitation between unfamiliar toddler peers as a way—a rather primitive way, to be sure—of signaling intersubjectivity to each other rather than as a mechanical copying of behavior. Toddlers in their second year exhibit empathy to their siblings, suggesting they can take the other's perspective (Dunn & Kendrick, 1982).

Preverbal or barely talking children are sensitive to signals of noncomprehension on the part of their interactional or conversational partners and engage in repair of failed messages (Golinkoff, 1983). And conversely, very young children can signal their own noncomprehension and thus control the level of complexity of their caretakers' speech (Bohannon & Marquis, 1977).

The attribution of precocious social understanding to young children may seem to ignore the evidence that person-concept-related skills undergo substantial changes throughout early childhood. But developmental change is not inconsistent with precocity. Cultural Developmentalists do not see cognitive abilities as something a child either has or does not have. Rather, such abilities are thought of as schemata constructed for operating within specific contexts. These schemata undergo gradual development over the years: The tasks children can handle using the schemata become more complex; the schemata become gradually "decontextualized," that is, freed from the context of acquisition and applicable to a wider range of contexts (Bates, 1979; Bruner, 1983; Halliday, 1975; Nelson, 1985); and their operation requires decreasing support or "scaffolding" from the environment (Bruner & Sherwood, 1976; Kaye & Charney, 1980; Vygotsky, 1978). For clear statements of this conception of cognitive abilities, see Bidell and Fischer (1992), Fischer (1980), and Fogel and Thelen (1987).

As Tomasello, Kruger, and Ratner (1993) state, metacognitive skills and concepts and the language that is used to verbalize them do develop considerably over the first years of life. However, metacognitive abilities are a separate skill, not something underlying cognitive or social functioning in general. An infant smiling and raising her arms to be lifted up cannot utter the sentence "*my parent is a reflective agent*," even if she does believe at some vague level of cognition that the parent will understand her need to be picked up; she would not make a similar complex of gestures to a coat tree or a Saint Bernard. It takes hard work to understand Grice's (1957) definition of nonnatural meaning as a set of reflexive intents, and it takes a Grice to write it. But ordinary human beings possess those very same intents when they use language meaningfully.

Tomasello, Kruger, and Ratner in effect take metacognitive abilities as the criterion for the existence and operation of full intersubjectivity. We argue that metacognition is a late achievement irrelevant to everyday, procedural, social-cognitive concepts and functioning. These "practical concepts" are much too vague and unformed to be real verbal concepts; we may even lack the vocabulary for talking about them coherently. They involve procedural knowledge rather than reflective knowledge, and we argue that very young children possess considerable procedural sophistication in social interaction and intersubjectivity.

In summary, we argue that there is no separate and more primitive imitation stage in children independent of an understanding, however vague, that repeating someone else's words or actions constitutes engaging in an interpersonal exchange with that person. Imitation is simply another type of communicative behavior, with the advantage of reduced processing demands, whose development and uses are part of the larger picture of the acquisition of verbal-communicative acts.

---

## Notes

1.  For example, Acredolo & Goodwyn (1988), Antinucci & Parisi (1975), Bates (1976), Bronson (1981), Bruner (1983), Carpenter, Mastergeorge, & Coggins (1983), Carter (1979), Chapman (1981), Collis & Schaffer (1975), Dore (1974, 1975, 1978), Eckerman, Whatley, & Kutz (1975), Edwards (1978), Golinkoff (1983), Harding (1983), Harding & Golinkoff (1979), Lewis et al. (1975), Lock (1980), Moerk (1975), Ninio & Bruner (1978), Ninio & Snow (1988), Rheingold, Hay, & West (1976), Ross & Kay (1980), Scoville (1984), Snow (1979), Snow, Dubber, & de Blauw, (1982), Snyder (1978), Sugarman-Bell (1978), Vandell (1977), Zinober & Martlew (1985).

—

# 4

—

# The First Stage of
# Speech Use

## 4.1 The characteristics of early single-word utterances

$A$ priori, it should be easy to answer the simple question of what communicative acts children can control at the onset of speech. Children's earliest speech uses have been extensively investigated (cf. Antinucci & Parisi, 1973; Barrett, 1981; Bates, 1979; Camaioni & Laicardi, 1985; Carpenter, Mastergeorge, & Coggins, 1983; Dale, 1980; Dore, 1974; Greenfield & Smith, 1976; Griffiths, 1985; Gruber, 1973; Halliday, 1975; McShane, 1980; Wells, 1985, and more). Even if individual variation and limitations as a result of the typically small sample sizes are taken into account, these various studies should have produced a common list of universally observed early communicative acts.

However, there is a surprising lack of agreement among the different investigators about the nature of the earliest speech uses. For example, Camaioni and Laicardi (1985) report that *all* of their subjects' first linguistic utterances were produced within game formats, whereas Barrett (1981), Dale (1980), Dore (1974), Griffiths (1985), and McShane (1980) report no verbal moves in games among the early speech behaviors they observed. Similarly, Dale (1980) reports **Naming** as the earliest-appearing speech act, but Halliday (1975) has no such speech behavior among those he reports for his subject, Nigel. Of course, it is possible that the children observed by these various investigators differed enormously in their early speech uses; before making this assumption, though, we must carefully consider the methodologies employed. Two findings emerge.

First, as discussed in Chapter 2, the studies use disparate systems for categorizing speech act types or functional uses, with categories of widely varying scope. For example, McShane (1980) acknowledges an early speech act he names **Giving**, consisting of the utterance of, for example, *here* and *there* to accompany the giving of an object. Other investigators, for example, Wells (1985), do not have such a specific speech-use category; the closest category in Wells's system is the much broader **Verbal Accompaniment to Behavior**, part of his **Expressive** subsystem, and it is not known whether he included in it *here* and *there* accompanying giving if it occurred in his observations. Such differences in the way observations are categorized and reported in the different studies make comparison and generalization perilous and perhaps impossible.

The variety of the coding systems employed reflects, furthermore, basic theoretical disagreements about which early speech uses should be considered bona fide communicative acts. Research, as a rule, begins from a particular theoretical approach; in this case, not all investigators share a definition of meaningful communication. In consequence, different investigators select different subsets of early child vocalizations as representing true communicative utterances. Each investigator has a set of pretheoretical assumptions that generate a criterion of meaningfulness or communicativeness; vocalizations that fail this criterion are excluded from consideration.

The vocalizations excluded vary from study to study, because the field has no clear definition of the boundaries of meaningful and conventional language use. Because of the varying exclusion criteria, each study ended up describing a different subset of early speech behaviors. Some investigators excluded utterances others found central. The resultant generalizations about the nature of early speech are thus different and sometimes explicitly contradictory. The utterances excluded in these various studies demonstrate conflicting views about the criterial features of meaningful speech acts; in addition, they reveal a fundamental characteristic of children's early speech uses—that they are all marginal examples of true verbal communication.

Five types of early speech use emerge as problematic in conforming to criteria of meaningful communicative acts. These are (1) labeling and other "language practice" utterances; (2) speech addressed to the self; (3) the performance of moves in games, for example, saying *boo* in peek-a-boo; (4) expressive exclamations, for example, *eh!* expressing surprise; (5) imitated rather than spontaneous utterances.

*Labeling.*     Halliday (1975), a linguist working within the tradition of Functional Grammar, excluded all utterances used for object labeling and other forms of language practice from consideration in his functional categorization of the early speech uses of his son, Nigel. In Halliday's approach, learning a system does not qualify as using that system, and thus "practice utterances" cannot be categorized as language uses in the strict sense. Halliday views it as paradoxical to treat learning language as one of the proper functions of language.

Halliday is the only investigator who excluded labeling, as well as questions about names (and answers to such questions), from his corpus of analyzed early speech uses. However, treatment of these behaviors by others is by no means straightforward; for example, Dore (1974) has a specific category for **Labeling** and another category called **Practicing**, neither of which he considers "acts addressed to other people" (p. 350).

*Self-addressed speech.*        Wells (1985), who carried out an extensive investigation of the development of pragmatic abilities in a large sample of children, made a clear distinction between speech addressed to the self and speech addressed to another person. He placed all "self-talk" in a separate category from the "interpersonal uses" he analyzed for pragmatic meaning. Thus, in determining order of emergence of communicative meanings, Wells excluded utterances addressed to the self from the database. For example, a child giving herself directions for performing a task was not coded as producing a directive, and a child labeling referents for herself was not coded as labeling; these utterances were thus excluded when computing the order of emergence of requests or of labeling. This restriction to interpersonal speech acts in the literal sense reflects the criterion that "true" communicative language must have an addressee who is different from the self.

Similarly, Barrett (1981) acknowledged as separate categories of speech use **Private self-guiding** and **Private labeling**; these categories were not subdivided further, although for interpersonal speech Barrett distinguished, for example, object requests from action requests. That is, the utterance *teddy* produced by a child instructing himself as to which object to pick up was not distinguished from the utterance *put* used in telling himself to perform some action, although if addressed to others these would have been categorized as two different speech uses.

*Verbal moves in games.*        As mentioned previously, several investigators (Barrett, 1981; Dale, 1980; Dore, 1974; Griffiths, 1985; and McShane, 1980) did not report the production of verbal moves in interactive games, such as peek-a-boo or patty-cake, in any of their subjects at any of the ages studied. Indeed, they did not have this category in their coding systems.

Coding categories were also unavailable for moves in vocal games eliciting the onomatopoeic mimicking of prototypical animal and machine noises, for example, *miauw*, *brmm-brmm*, or *tick-tock*. Typically, such mimicking is elicited by adults with questions such as *How does a cat go?* to which the child is to respond *Miauw*. The studies referred to earlier did not have coding categories for either the eliciting moves or the game-embedded verbalizations.

Others, chief among them Bruner and his colleagues (e.g., Bruner & Sherwood, 1976; Ninio & Bruner, 1978; Ratner & Bruner, 1978), have extensively documented the presence of game-embedded verbal behaviors among the earliest speech uses in young children from cultural backgrounds similar to those in the studies discussed here; the absence of this type of speech use in their findings thus almost certainly represents a systematic exclusion rather than individual differences or sampling variation. Apparently, the production of verbal moves in games was not considered true language use, because such utterances do not possess symbolic or propositional meaning and are more similar to social acts than to communicative acts in the strict sense. Although it is harder to document, other "pure performatives" (Greenfield & Smith, 1976), that is, speech uses without propositional meaning that constitute purely socially defined acts, have probably been omitted from analysis in these and other studies as well.

*Expressive exclamations.*      These are not reported either by Barrett (1981) or by Dale (1980). The category system used by Dore (1974) includes only one entry, **Protesting**, that could refer to a type of exclamation. By contrast, for example, in the work of Leopold presented by Griffiths (1985), the category **Expressives**, an early-appearing speech use, includes a varied set of utterances expressing disapproval, admiration, greetings, pleasure, disgust, excitement, action completion, endearment, and more. Apparently, exclamations and other expressives were excluded by some investigators because the language forms used are semiconventional rather than fully conventional.

*Imitations.*      The fate of imitations is particularly illuminating. Whereas Camaioni and Laicardi (1985), Dore (1974), and Wells (1985), for instance, have Repeating or Imitating as a type of speech act or interpersonal speech use, others studying the communicative or pragmatic meanings expressed in early speech (e.g., Barrett, 1981; Dale, 1980; Greenfield & Smith, 1976; Griffiths, 1985; Halliday, 1975) have explicitly excluded imitations from their database. According to Greenfield and Smith (1976), imitations do not qualify as true meaningful speech uses, because they can be performed without comprehension. Thus, the exclusion of imitations from studies of the pragmatics of early speech relies on the criterion that the speaker has full control of the semantic content of the utterance and the ability to produce the relevant utterance spontaneously.

Many investigators have failed to distinguish *the speech act* of Imitating (which is probably only used in normal populations by persons engaged in learning a first or second language, as a means of language practice) from repetitions of a previous utterance used *to carry out a communicative intent,* for example, agreeing or disagreeing with a proposition, answering in the affirmative to a yes/no question, answering a restricted-alternatives question, agreeing to do as requested, acknowledging the interlocutor's utterance, and so on (see Keenan, 1977). Although this distinction is clearly made in the coding system of communicative acts developed by Ninio and Wheeler (1984b), in other systems all repetitions are treated as a single speech act of Imitation (e.g., Wells, 1985) or are separated from spontaneous utterances and treated as speech uses with special immature characteristics (Bates, 1979).

In each of the studies discussed here, good reasons were given for excluding a subset of early vocalizations; the exclusions were justified by various deficits of the excluded speech use relative to some ideal or norm of full-blown language. If we wished to be very strict in our definition of what true speech is and to adopt every exclusionary criterion used by any of our colleagues, we would end up excluding *practically every utterance beginning speakers make*. Of course, it is not by chance that most early utterances risk exclusion. On the contrary, the very defining characteristic of early speech uses is that they fulfill only partially the criteria for prototypical meaningful communicative acts (see Ninio, 1993b). Early utterances are borderline cases on several grounds:

1. The meanings they express tend to be social rather than, properly speaking, illocutionary, that is, they are mostly nonreferential, playful, or ritual speech uses (e.g., Bates, 1979; Braunwald, 1978; Bruner, 1983; Camaioni & Laicardi, 1985; Greenfield & Smith, 1976; Lucariello, Kyratzis, & Engel, 1986; Ninio, 1992; Vihman & McCune, 1994).

2. The expressions used tend to be marginal linguistic forms, such as vocatives, exclamations, or interjections, rather than members of major word classes, such as verbs, nouns, or adjectives (Benedict, 1979; Dore, 1985; Nelson, 1973; Ninio, 1993b).

3. Moreover, even when they do express genuine, pragmatically central meanings, such as requests, using real words rather than semi-conventional vocalizations, beginning speakers generally use the most general pro-words, such as pronouns, deictic locatives, pro-verbs, and the like (Barrett, 1981; Clark, 1978b; Greenfield & Smith, 1976; Griffiths, 1985; Ninio, 1993b; Weisenberger, 1976). In linguistic terms, such expressions are **unmarked** options for expressing the relevant contents as opposed to **marked** expressions that encode specific alternatives.

4. Some children use conventional lexical items with very limited, underextended meanings. For instance, Halliday's son, Nigel, had a word approximating *syrup* that he used exclusively for requesting maple syrup on his pancakes at breakfast, but that he did not use in any other sort of reference to maple syrup.

5. Rather than being interpersonal, early meaningful speech uses are often directed at the self rather than at another person (Piaget, 1926; Vygotsky, 1978; Wells, 1985).

6. Children's utterances are much more limited in semantic content than adult speech. For example, most early statements concern the immediately observed rather than the distant or the abstract; most arguments regarding the truth of propositions concern correct names for referents rather than more complex issues.

7. Lastly, a significant proportion of early utterances are imitations of previous utterances by an interlocutor, rather than spontaneous pro-

ductions (e.g., Bates, 1979). These imitations can be seen as scaffolded by the conversational context in which they occur and thus as evidence that young children need more social support than older ones to express their communicative intents (as they do for other challenging cognitive tasks).

Children start to use speech meaningfully by first learning those form-meaning pairings that do not require simultaneous control of many different novel principles. These speech uses tend to be supported by familiar interpersonal contexts, such as games; they involve unmarked general forms with a wide range of applicability; and they involve types of speech uses appropriate for a novice user of the verbal-communicative medium, for example, imitations, language practice, and self-directed speech.

The transitional nature of early utterances may be a logical necessity: Children must start to acquire the linguistic system by learning *independent* linguistic signs; they cannot start with signs whose meaning depends on their relation to other signs, because those other signs have not yet been acquired (Ninio, 1993b). What characteristics follow from starting with independent linguistic forms? Early signs must be meaningful on their own terms rather than by contrast; they must be discrete rather than part of a system; they must be inherently intransitive rather than relational, isolated rather than connected, independent and unrelated rather than part of dependency relations, self-sufficient rather than embedded in a larger unit. They do not belong to any set, class, network, field, or hierarchy nor constitute one of a set of alternatives. Above all, each sign is significant because of its own individual "language game" and not because of the comprehensive language game that is the whole of language. The various, apparently unrelated "deficits" of very early speech uses relative to some norm of full-blown language all derive from this single principle of *system independence.*

A study of the characteristics of the speech uses of 16 Hebrew-speaking children, 10 to 12 months old (Ninio, 1993b), demonstrated system independence. The children were videotaped in a 30-minute free-interaction session with their mothers at home (see Section 6.1 for details). Utterances were analyzed for the communicative intent expressed using the First Communicative Acts Coding System (FCA) (see Section 2.5.1). The children produced a range of one to nine different speech uses, defined as unique form-function combinations. Table 4.1 presents some examples.

Most of the linguistic forms acquired by the children consisted of expressions lacking syntactic combinatorial properties in adult language. Table 4.2 presents the frequency of the different types of linguistic expressions used: interjections, vocatives, moves in rituals and in games, and unmarked and marked forms expressing specific communicative intents.

About 93 percent of all utterances produced were either syntactically isolated signs or unmarked general forms for the expression of various commu-

TABLE 4.1    Examples of Communicative Intents Verbally Expressed
by 10- to 12-Month-Old Children

| Communicative Intent | Form of Expression |
|---|---|
| Answer affirmatively | Repeat |
| Answer affirmatively | *ken*    yes |
| Answer in the negative | *lo*    no |
| Answer where-question | *hine*    here |
| Call addressee's attention | *ima*    mommy |
| Direct attention to focus | *hine*    here |
| Exclaim in surprise or enthusiasm | *ai* |
| Exclaim in surprise or enthusiasm | *eh* |
| Mimic cat noise | *miau* |
| Mimic goose noise | *gah* |
| Perform moves in tickling game | *dag* |
| Perform moves in other games | *hau* |
| Propose new activity | *et-ze*    this |
| Propose object to act on | *et-ze*    this |
| Refuse proposal to do | *lo*    no |
| Statement on joint focus of attention | *doda*    auntie |
| Statement on joint focus of attention | *ze*    this |
| Statement on joint focus of attention | *buba*    doll |

*Source:* A. Ninio. 1993. "On the Fringes of the System: Children's Acquisition of Syntactically Isolated Forms at the Onset of Speech." *First Language* 13: 300–304.

nicative intents. About 7 percent were marked forms. As expected, marked forms were "semantic isolates"; no child used more than a single marked form for the expression of a given type of communicative intent.

**Imitations** were included in the database of this study as a type of gamelike or performative speech use. They were considered meaningful language uses, as they were in all cases amenable to interpretation by their addressee, either as a verbalization produced in compliance with a request to imitate or, in the spontaneous case, as an intentional act of language practice.

Imitation, elicited as well as spontaneous, was among the earliest-acquired speech uses observed, that is, it was used by children with the smallest repertoires. The circumstances in which children imitated spontaneously made it clear that this was a reaction to some linguistic problem they were having: They either imitated elements of questions they were apparently unable to answer, or they repeated answers their mothers gave to questions the children had failed to answer. Mothers requested imitations in similar circumstances as a reaction to children's inability to label a referent or to pronounce a word correctly. Some of the imitated words were also used by the same child in spontaneous productions.

Among the syntactically isolated signs observed, **vocatives** were most frequent. In 12 of 13 utterances, the child summoned an addressee by calling out his or her name. One child also used a vocative interjection, *eh!* Vocatives were used mostly to solicit the addressee's attention or physical proximity, but

TABLE 4.2　Distribution of Children's Utterances According to Type of Speech Use, by Number of Children and Tokens Produced

| Type of Speech Use | Number of Children (n = 16) | Number of Tokens in Sample |
|---|---|---|
| Imitation | 10 | 38 |
| (Elicited | 6 | 23) |
| Vocatives | 6 | 13 |
| Moves in games | 5 | 16 |
| Interjections | 4 | 8 |
| Onomatopoeic | 3 | 8 |
| Social rituals | 2 | 3 |
| Unmarked forms[a] | 12 | 48 |
| Marked forms[b] | 5 | 10 |
| Total | | 144 |

[a]Used in communicative acts: Direct attention to focus, Statement on joint focus of attention, Answer where-question, Answer affirmatively, Answer in the negative, Propose new activity, Propose new focus of activity, Propose object to act on, Agree to proposal, Refuse proposal to do, Forbid, Request further communication.

[b]Used in communicative acts: Statement on joint focus of attention, Answer what-question, Statement on the nonpresent.

*Source:* A. Ninio. 1993. "On the Fringes of the System: Children's Acquisition of Syntactically Isolated Forms at the Onset of Speech." *First Language* 13: 301.

in some cases they were appeals for help, for example, when a child got stuck under some furniture.

*Verbal moves in interactive games* were also relatively frequent and were probably among the earliest forms acquired, judging from the fact that children who had very few form-content combinations produced them. The early-occurring forms were part of simple idiosyncratic games, apparently well established in the dyad, like swinging the arms and saying *di-dah*. The game "words" produced by the more advanced children in the dyads were moves in conventional children's games, like the Hebrew version of ring-around-a-rosy (*uga-uga*).

Of the relatively few *interjections* produced, all were exclamations of surprise, like *oh! Onomatopoeic* forms mimicking animal sounds were relatively infrequent in this sample. Only the three most advanced children produced such utterances, among them *hau, miau,* and *gah* for dog, cat, and goose sounds, respectively. Children produced these sounds as part of a question-and-answer game, in response to the parent asking, for example, *How does a dog go?*

*Markers,* utterances embedded in *social rituals or formats,* were almost nonexistent; two children marked the transfer of objects by the expressions *ze* (this) and *toda* (thanks), once each.

*Unmarked forms* were used by the sample for 12 different types of communicative intents. They included attention directers or markers, such as *ze* (this) or *hine* (here) in both discussion contexts and action-negotiation contexts; other generalized request forms, such as *ima* (mommy); *ken* (yes) as a positive answer and *lo* (no) as a negative answer and as a form of refusal; *ma?* (what?) as an answer to a call, a request for further communication, and the like. Five children used *here* or *this* in discussing a joint focus of attention *after* the two participants had already established joint attention—in other words, at precisely the point in labeling routines where older children would produce individual labels. These uses exemplify children's appropriate participation in interaction formats before acquiring the necessary knowledge for the production of specific labels.

The *marked forms* used by the sample were almost without exception object labels produced in discussions of a joint focus of attention, that is, labeling routines, either spontaneously or as answers to a what-question. The words produced were popular targets for language instruction among Hebrew-speaking mothers, such as *or* (light), *doda* (auntie), or *buba* (doll). In all cases, the referents were concrete objects attended to by the dyad during the talk.

As mentioned before, no child used more than a single marked form for the expression of a given communicative intent. Children did not yet use these expressions contrastively; not only did they not produce any other labels, but even the production of these unique forms required much maternal scaffolding. Apparently, these children were on the verge of acquiring their very first common-noun vocabulary items and were demonstrating the isolated exemplars of this class in their repertoires.

These results confirm that young children cannot yet learn linguistic signs integrated into a general linguistic system by a complex network of interrelationships. Rather, they are limited to forms sustained by discrete language games that specify both the interactive formats for use of the form and the linguistic form to be used, independent from other speech uses.

## 4.2 The pragmatics of early speech

Children's earliest speech repertoire is limited, transitional, and imperfectly languagelike on a number of counts. In fact, children's earliest utterances are more like key words for certain interactive moves than fully specific speech acts. Thus, the *social* functions of children's earliest utterances are more salient than their *pragmatic* functions. How do children use this novel channel of social behavior?

The utterances produced by the 10- to 12-month-olds in the observational study reported earlier (Ninio, 1993b) were used mostly for the attainment of two fundamental interactive goals: first, to make it possible for the children to *participate* as equals in some meaningful social endeavor; and second, to ensure a state of *intersubjectivity* with others, namely, a state of mutual attentiveness, proximity, "togetherness." The first goal was attained with utterances best categorized as context-construing or context-embedded speech uses. These utterances, sometimes called pure performatives (e.g., Greenfield & Smith, 1976), are context-appropriate vocalizations consisting of game sounds, onomatopoeic mimicking sounds, imitations, exclamations, and so on.

Context-embedded utterances are equivalent to nonverbal interactive acts: Their meaning depends on their role as social moves in social-interactive contexts. They convey no linguistic meaning other than as moves in the game. They certainly do not qualify as symbolic speech use; rather than reflecting on or representing some piece of reality, they *are* pieces of social reality. Therefore, their interactive significance resides solely in the child's making use of speech to participate in some joint encounter with others.

The specific game sounds individual children acquired were rather varied and even idiosyncratic. For instance, some children learned to emit stylized barking sounds when asked *How does a dog go?* whereas others learned cat, goose, or rooster noises in a similar game. One child learned a "word" approximating a piece of text from a dancing song similar to ring-around-a-rosy, whereas another played a simple tickling game in which you touch someone's side and say *dig-dig.* Since all these speech uses serve the goal of allowing children to participate in interactive routines, their specific identity is unimportant; the expressions acquired depend on the idiosyncratic preferences of the children and parents. These games, like many adult games, are fairly "pointless," that is, they have no function beyond providing a context for playful interpersonal activity. One might think animal-noise games teach children something about animals, but in fact the sounds produced are language-specific and unlikely to help in identifying or communicating with real animals. For these urban children who had never seen a real rooster or goose, emitting a ga sound when asked *How does a goose go?* is as absurd as any Zen exercise. In fact, though, young children have no problem learning to produce these linguistically meaningless sounds as long as their social significance is clear.

The speech act coded as **Statement about joint focus of attention**, like responses to animal-sound questions, often consisted of little more than signals of participation, such as *this* or *here.* Even the sporadically produced object-name responses to labeling routines should probably be classified as simple signals of participation, since their status as true labels is questionable. The children only produced a single object name each, which they, moreover, used exclusively in the labeling format; these were probably acquired in a game routine much like the mimicking game and do not function as true names.

The second major interactive goal was to establish mutual and joint attention between child and mother. This goal is more serious and could be considered truly pragmatic, in the strict, utilitarian sense of the word. By contrast to the variability of expressions acquired in the game-sound category of speech uses, children produced a small, widely shared set of specific communicative acts for establishing mutual attention: **Calling hearer's attention** and **Directing hearer's attention to focus.** Since the occurrence of face-to-face interaction depends on establishing shared and mutual attentiveness, this interactive goal is fundamental.

We could include in the category **Establishing mutual attention** much that passes as a request in this age group. Almost without exception, children got their mothers to start a new activity, to shift the focus of an activity, or to perform an action by directing their attention to an object, using pro-words like *this* and *here*. In other words, a child could ensure the adult's *action* by directing her *attention* to a joint focus.

In summary, it seems as if children start acquiring the pragmatic use of speech by establishing verbal control over two types of speech uses: a participant-act type (for various interactive formats set up as a rule by the adult) and a mutual–joint attention regulator, taking care that the fundamental condition for intersubjectivity is fulfilled. The participant-act type has been previously described as the first to emerge, for example, Greenfield and Smith's (1976) claim that the earliest speech uses are pure performatives. The present results suggest that the joint attention–ensuring function emerges equally early.

These two speech functions are among the very simplest on the two dimensions of complexity suggested in Sections 2.3.2 and 2.3.3. The social concept underlying the regulation of mutual attention involves a differentiation between mutual attentiveness and the lack of it; this is a single dichotomous discrimination between the two most fundamentally different interactive states. The performance of verbal moves in game-type formats involves the simplest and most direct mode of relating speech to its interactive context: enacting the interaction rather than conversing about it. Apparently, both the simplicity of the social concepts underlying speech and the directness of the relation of talk to the context determine the ease with which the relevant speech uses are acquired.

Deciding which of these speech uses emerges earliest is not easy. The data presented here from Ninio (1993b) do not help, because both attention directing and game sounds were produced by the youngest children observed, so ordering them relative to each other is impossible. We have already seen (Section 4.1) that differences in observational setting and in pragmatic taxonomies make the synthesis of past findings nearly impossible. Thus, some researchers like Wells (1985) report **Call** among the earliest speech acts acquired (around 1;3), concurrent with his categories **Ostension, Exclamation,** and **Wanting,** whereas others like Barrett (1981) place it among later ones (between 1;6 and 1;10). Still others, for example, Dale (1980), have no speech act like **Call** in their category system, although Dale does report that a speech act he called **Attention-seeking** emerges after **Naming** and **Greeting** and **Ritualized** forms. McShane (1980) places **Directing attention** among the earliest speech acts, but he, like Barrett and Wells, does not have a category for game sounds, so it is not clear how these two speech uses are ordered relative to each other.

A parental interview study (Ninio & Goren, 1993) using the PICA-100 instrument described in Section 2.5.3 helps to resolve questions about order of emergence. The study included 114 Hebrew-speaking mothers of children ages 0;8 to 2;4; the mothers were asked whether their children spontaneously produced the described speech acts, and what kind of expression the children used for each speech act. According to their answers, the communicative acts included in the questionnaire formed a 33-step developmental scale, ranging from verbal acts produced by children who had no other meaningful speech to speech uses produced only by children with a repertoire of 90 or more types. Table 4.3 presents the first 10 steps, covering children's development more or less up to their first birthday.

The results of the parental interview study clearly support the findings of the observational study. Strikingly, children begin by acquiring no fewer than four different communicative acts to do with the establishment of joint and mutual attention. Other types of speech uses—even the most primitive imitations, game sounds, exclamations, and simple event markers—appear only after both **Calling hearer's attention** and **Directing hearer's attention to focus**. Answers to what-, who-, and where-questions appear at steps four through six, in a period dominated by verbal game sounds. They precede statements on a joint focus of attention, which in these young children were mainly demonstrative pronouns or perhaps a few proper nouns and object names. The earliest statements and answers to questions are indeed evidently produced within gamelike object-labeling formats.

At the sixth developmental step, moves in action negotiations appear. Children learn how to respond to others' proposals and actions and how to propose a new activity, an object to act on, and a new object as the focus of an ongoing activity. Toward the end of this period, a further type of answer to questions is acquired, as well as the first question; the rest of the responses are more game sounds, markers, and attention regulators. Utterances acquired after this very early set are discussed in Chapter 5.

To recapitulate, these beginning speakers are mostly using speech simply to ensure the basic interpersonal achievement of intersubjectivity. Speech is not used at this initial stage for anything truly pragmatic, such as making requests more intelligible, bringing inner states or emotions to the knowledge of the interlocutor, or telling a story about a personal experience. The major motivation for early utterances is not, as is often thought, to improve clarity of communication. Early speech is used for something much more important and fundamental: Like smiling and crying, it is used to bring the other into a state of togetherness with the child, and, if possible, to keep her there.

The first use of speech helps us understand why children bother to learn pointless "words," such as game sounds like *boo,* redundant polite greetings, such as *hi,* or onomatopoeic imitations of the noises airplanes and donkeys make at this stage when the learning of any new word costs so much effort. Frame-appropriate speech, even if meaningless, produces intersubjectivity and generates a large gain in "personhood": Children can be speaking participants in a joint endeavor on equal terms with adults and can demonstrate to others and themselves their full-fledged membership in human society—all this without having to deal with complex concepts.

TABLE 4.3   First 10 Steps in the Acquisition of Communicative Intents
According to the Parental Interview Questionnaire

| Order | Communicative Intents |
|---|---|
| 1 | Call hearer's attention |
| 2 | Direct hearer's attention to focus |
| 3 | Call hearer to approach speaker<br>Acknowledge call or being spoken to<br>Exlcaim in distress<br>Exclaim in surprise<br>Mark effort<br>Mark—other events |
| 4 | Imitate<br>Mimic cat<br>Mimic—other<br>Answer what-question<br>Answer who-question |
| 5 | Thank<br>Mark fall of object<br>Mimic dog<br>Perform verbal move in game of peek-a-boo<br>Perform verbal move in telephone game |
| 6 | Greet on meeting<br>Mark eating or swallowing<br>Perform verbal move in tickling game<br>Perform verbal move in games—other<br>Answer where-question<br>Refuse to do<br>Agree to do<br>Request/propose a new activity<br>Request/propose an object to act on<br>Request/propose new focus for activity |
| 7 | Name objects at joint focus of attention |
| 8 | Answer call by question<br>Perform verbal move in honking game |
| 9 | Mark object transfer<br>Answer in the affirmative<br>Ask what-question |
| 10 | Mimic donkey |

*Source:* A. Ninio and M. Goren. 1993. *PICA-100: Parental Interview on 100 Communicative Acts* (Jerusalem: Department of Psychology, Hebrew University).

We now understand as well why children start to speak at all when they get on so well without it. Speech is more efficient than nonverbal communication in achieving the fundamental interpersonal aim of children, to gain and keep the attention of another person. If we want to speculate about the nature of biological preparedness for acquiring speech, its efficiency in producing intersubjectivity is a good candidate. Just as we are almost certainly prewired for the precocious development of several socially fundamental behaviors, such as an interest in faces, smiling, crying, and the like, humans may be prewired to learn quickly *any* behavior that increases their chances of being in a state of intersubjectivity, including the odd behavior of emitting phonetically restricted, contextually specified vocalizations.

## 4.3 Developmental trends in the expression of communicative intents

The earliest meaningful speech uses, which we are informally calling key words for particular communicative situations, are typically defined by individual language games and serve some fundamental interactive goals. But are all early utterances of this kind? Are there subtypes of such key-word expressions? In this section we look more closely at the ways in which children express communicative intents in single-word utterances and trace the development of the expressive means at their disposal.

When we talk about any speaker "expressing a communicative intent" with an utterance, we are claiming that the utterance *can be interpreted* as the expression of the intent. This is so for adults, as well as for young children's early single-word utterances. Even adults rarely express their intents in fully explicit performative sentences (Austin 1962), such as *I hereby order you to open the door*. An addressee can attribute communicative intent to the speaker only by a process of interpretation based on the assumption that they share an interpersonal code tying intents to expressions. This is true for any linguistic sign and its meaning—we have to assume we mean the same thing by the word *chair* or *honesty* to use those words communicatively.

We assume that people use a set of implicit encoding principles in mapping their communicative intents onto verbal expressions and in interpreting others' intents. How do children learn this system of mapping rules?

As soon as children can produce speech that carries meaningful messages, they must know some of these coding rules. Their utterances are amenable to interpretation because they conform to encoding principles, that is, they fall within the range of options acknowledged by the interpersonal code. In the case of single-word utterances, these regularities consist of the strategies available for packaging communicative intents into single words in a way that makes it possible to recover the speaker's intent without recourse to the much larger measure of explicitness offered by multiword sentences.

Two major developmental trends can be identified in the expression of communicative intents in the single-word period. The first consists of children's moving from a constant to a variable style of mapping between their intents and verbal expressions. The second consists of moving from one-to-one mappings of communicative intents of utterances to the many-to-many mapping characteristic of adult systems.

### 4.3.1 Constant-to-variable mapping

As we have seen in Section 4.1, at the onset of speech children typically use a constant, key-word type of expression to express a certain type of communicative meaning. For example, saying *this* often serves as the form for requesting any kind of object. During the single-word stage children come to learn other, more elaborate packaging strategies that verbalize the specific details of their communicated intents.

Children's early mapping style has sometimes been described as holistic, namely, a style in which the complete communicative event is packaged into words in an unanalyzed and undifferentiated fashion (cf. Barrett, 1986; Griffiths, 1985). According to one approach, young children are limited to this kind of mapping, because they are unable to represent situations and events except as holistic complexes whose component parts are fused to an inseparable whole (e.g., Nelson, 1985, 1986; Nelson & Lucariello, 1985). Analysis of communicative events into their component parts—objects, persons, locations, social moves—and the selective mapping of such components onto verbal expressions are thought to be beyond the cognitive capacities of very young speakers.

However, children's early utterances do not point to a general inability to analyze situations into their component parts or to use any but a strictly holistic strategy of mapping intents to speech. Even during the first period of speech use, mappings of intents to utterances are basically analytic (Ninio, 1993a). The earliest utterances, for example, *bye-bye* and *ta* (Greenfield & Smith's [1976] pure performatives), are used generally and appropriately from the beginning, rather than like forms embedded in unanalyzed situations. From its first use, *bye-bye* is said to different persons in different physical circumstances, the communality being that all of the addressees are about to leave, and *ta* is said to mark the transfer of objects from hand to hand, involving different objects, persons, and settings (Barrett, Bates, 1986; Camaioni, & Volterra, 1975; Bruner, 1983; Greenfield & Smith, 1976; Lock, 1980). Even for these early utterances, children can isolate from the total event on varying occasions the relevant, invariant feature that constitutes its condition of use. Were events represented as unanalyzable wholes, such abstractions would be impossible, and we might expect some difficulty in generalizing *bye-bye* from daddy's leaving, where it is learned first, to situations where grandma, Auntie Vi, and the milkman are leaving. The fact that such generalizations are not problematical suggests that children understand the communicative generality of *bye-bye* and from the first separate the core event of leave-taking from its specific circumstances, such as the persons involved, the location, the time of day, and so on.

Nevertheless, it is clear that children's treatment of the separated-out components of communicative situations changes during development. During the first period of speech use, the specific details of situations are separated from the core event only to *ignore* them as irrelevant to the verbal expression of the communicative meaning. With further development, children learn how to *express* these very same specific details in words.

In other words, during the course of development children learn more analytic strategies for the *verbal expression* of communicative meanings. If early on children tend to use general, unmarked, nonspecific terms (such as pronouns and other pro-forms) for the expression of particular communicative functions, later they use a host of more specific terms (such as common nouns and verbs) in the same communicative circumstances (cf. Barrett, 1981; Bloom, 1973; Clark, 1978b; Griffiths, 1985; Halliday, 1975; Weisenberger, 1976). The developmental phenomenon could be summarized as the abandonment of the key-word type of expression as the sole mapping principle and the mastery of the principle that communicative intents can be mapped to speech by expressing their specific details.

In a study of children's mastery of mapping principles at the single-word stage, Ninio (1990a, 1991a, 1994b) found that the transition from unmarked, key-word mapping to marked or selective mapping occurred around the middle of the second year. The subjects were 10- to 22-month-old children acquiring Hebrew. Some of the results of the youngest subjects were presented in Section 4.1. For a considerable period after the onset of speech the children expressed most intents by mapping the intent to a constant, fixed expression, ignoring variation in the specifics of the intent. Such realization rules were of three types:

1.   The message is holistically mapped onto a word, for example, marking action completion with *here* or performing a move in a pretend telephone game with *hello*. A similar principle operates in the case of exclamations expressing distress, such as *ai, oh,* and the like.
2.   A word expresses a fixed element of the message. For example, the word *more* is used to express the communicative intent glossed as **Speaker proposes that speaker (and/or addressee) repeat previous action;** *more* encodes the element of continuation, but the elements speaker, addressee, directive force, or specific action are not expressed. The component of the message expressed is a "fixed element" in that it remains the same whether the action requested is drinking, eating, being given Lego pieces, or being tickled, and the form of expression is similarly constant across the different activities. Saying *no* as a refusal or as a negative answer to a yes/no question has the same character.
3.   A word expresses a variable element of the communicative intent by a constant form, like a pronoun or prolocative, for example, uttering the word *this* with an intent glossed as **Speaker suggests the initiation of a joint activity, possibly focused on an object.** In this case, the

TABLE 4.4   Examples of Constant-Type Mapping Rules

| |
|---|
| Exclaim in distress → say *oy, vay, oh* |
| Mark object transfer → say *here, this* |
| Perform verbal move in peek-a-boo game → say *boo* |
| Answer in the affirmative → say *yes, OK, ahem* |
| Greet on meeting → say *hi* |
| Direct attention to a focus → say *here, this, look* |
| Propose new activity → say *this* |
| Statement discussing joint focus of attention → say *here, this, there* |

*Source:* A. Ninio. 1991. "The Expression of Communicative Intents in Single-Word Utterances and the Emergence of Patterned Speech." Paper presented at the Biennial Meeting of the Society for Research in Child Development, Seattle, Washington, April.

component object selected for verbalization is variable—balls on one day, blocks on another. However, the word indicating the relevant object, namely *this*, is a fixed pro-form that never changes. Other formally constant deictic utterances often occurring in early single-word speech are *here, there,* and *that,* which typically constitute fixed forms expressing some communicative intent. Other examples of constant-type mapping rules employed by children in the Hebrew-speaking sample are presented in Table 4.4.

Children in the first period of speech also use several other, relatively simple mapping principles to generate single-word expressions of communicative intents. These are:

1. Realizing an intent by lexicalizing the element *addressee* of the message, for example, *mommy*. This strategy is intermediate between constant and variable mapping. On the one hand, the particular addressee is a variable element of the communicative. On the other hand, the element addressee is constant across all different communicative intents. The verbalization of this element, common to all communicative intents, conveys no information about the kind of communicative intent expressed but is considered a nonspecific, fixed expression of the intent to communicate. Mappings of this type were used to express the communicative acts **Calling, Proposing turn for hearer, Proposing repetition of act, Proposing object to act on, Proposing an act on a known object, Proposing a new activity,** and the like, as well as **Answering in the negative, Marking the transfer of an object, Performing a move in a telephone game,** and so on.

2. Realizing an intent by lexicalizing the element *speaker* of the message. This strategy is used, for instance, for realizing the communicative act **Demanding a turn for speaker.**

3. Realizing an intent by repeating or rephrasing in a single word all or part of a previous utterance. Such a communicative strategy is often used for

realizing **Affirmative answers to yes/no questions, Agreeing with a proposition,** *Disagreeing* **with a proposition** (if said in a questioning intonation), **Agreeing to perform as requested, Pointing out the whereabouts of an object asked about, Acknowledging a communication,** and, obviously, in spontaneous and elicited **Imitation.**

4. Realizing an intent by reciting a single word of a rote-learned text. Such a communicative strategy was used, for example, for realizing the communicative act **Recite text of songs** or **Complete incomplete text if so demanded.**

At the onset of speech, mapping to a constant expression and these other simple mapping strategies predominated in children's speech. Since most of their active vocabulary was generated by such rules, it was heavily biased toward demonstrative pronouns, prolocatives, exclamations, proper names used as vocatives, game words, and other transitional linguistic forms (Section 4.1). Common nouns and verbs constituted a small part of the children's vocabulary.

Around the middle of the second year, children apparently master the principle of mapping selective elements of their intents to *variable* expressions that encode the specifics of the communicative situation. Formally, mapping rules like these consist of the following principle: *"Realize an intent by a variable expression that selectively expresses an element of the communicative intent that covaries with circumstances."* For instance, in the utterance *ball!* expressing the communicative intent discussed earlier, **Speaker suggests the initiation of a joint activity +/- focused on an object,** the element object is selected for encoding, and what is said changes with the specific object suggested as the focus of activity. Table 4.5 presents examples of variable-type mapping rules used by the sample.

The novelty in the use of these mapping rules resides not in the capacity to extract a particular element of the communicative intent but in the ability to express such an element with a systematically varying verbalization. Apparently, children initially find it much too complicated to relate a set of changing expressions to communicative messages whose pragmatic point is essentially unvarying.

The transition from key-word mapping to selective or variable mapping is both abrupt and prolonged. At one particular point in development, children suddenly acquire a large number of these variable mapping rules, and they continue to acquire them for a considerable time. However, the use and further acquisition of nonselective mapping rules continue. Even the mothers in the study produced a large proportion of their single-word utterances with key-word principles (Ninio, 1985). Nevertheless, mastery of the principle of variable mapping at around 18 months transforms the earliest key-word speech into the core of a true linguistic system; words are no longer embedded in their individual language games but can serve flexibly as expressions of *components* of many different types of intents.

TABLE 4.5  Examples of Variable-Type Mapping Rules

---

Propose new activity +/− focused on object or person →
    Verbalize object (e.g., Lego, water, pacifier, ball)
    Verbalize activity (e.g., walk, dance, build)
    Verbalize person to play with (e.g., daddy, Johnnie)
Request object, action is known, for example, give, put, bring →
    Verbalize object (e.g., wheel, book, pencil)
Request for action, object is known → verbalize action (e.g., put, open)
Answer what-question → satisfy wh-element (e.g., flower, nose)
State intent to act → verbalize object of action (e.g., block)
    Verbalize location of action (e.g., in the box)
Statement describing recent event → verbalize event (e.g., fell, broke)
Statement describing past event → verbalize person involved (e.g., grandma)
    Verbalize location involved (e.g., train)
Statement describing joint focus of attention →
    Verbalize entity at focus (e.g., shoe, daddy)
    Verbalize action at focus (e.g., eat)
    Verbalize attribute of entity at focus (e.g., red, big)
    Verbalize state of entity at focus (e.g., asleep)
    Verbalize number of entities at focus (e.g., two)
    Verbalize location of entity at focus (e.g., in bed)

---

*Source:* A. Ninio. 1991. "The Expression of Communicative Intents in Single-Word Utterances and the Emergence of Patterned Speech." Paper presented at the Biennial Meeting of the Society for Research in Child Development, Seattle, Washington. April.

## 4.3.2 Unique-to-multiple mapping

The second developmental trend transforming single-word speech is children's mastery of the principle of many-to-many mapping of communicative intents to verbal expressions. At the onset of speech, children tend to use a given verbal expression in a single functional context; only later do these forms get defunctionalized (Barrett, 1983; Bates, 1976; Dore, 1985; Greenfield & Smith, 1976; Halliday, 1975; Ingram, 1971; Menn & Haselkorn, 1977; Nelson & Lucariello, 1985). Conversely, beginning speakers apparently operate with a uniqueness principle specifying that each speech function or communicative intent is mapped onto one verbal expression (e.g., Halliday, 1975). The acquisition of multiple mapping rules for the same intent, characteristic of adult speech, is thus a later development. Until about 16 months children tend to use a single realization rule for expressing a given intent, but after that they realize intents increasingly by multiple rules (Ninio 1990a, 1994a).

    The uniqueness principle is limited in two ways. First, the realization of a particular communicative intent is limited to a single fixed form but not to a single rule. For instance, in the one-word expressions by 18-month-olds of the communicative intent **Agree to a request**, one fixed form (*yes*) was over-represented, whereas other modeled forms (*all right, OK, good,* and *right*) were not acquired. However, an alternative realization rule was acquired—that repeating part or all of the request counts as an agreement to comply. Children in general had a single realization as well for **Agree with the proposition expressed in hearer's previous statement, Answer in the affirmative a yes/no question, Grant permission for hearer to carry out action for which permission was requested, Refuse to comply with request,** and so forth. Children at this age tend to learn a single fixed form to express these intents, ignoring other fixed options, but they might have alternative forms operating on a different principle. It appears that at around 18 months the uniqueness principle reflects some mutual exclusivity bias that rejects alternative mappings to two different *words* for a given intent. It does not seem to apply to multiple mappings in general as long as they involve two different types of expression, for example, a specific key word, as well as the use of repetition.

Second, the uniqueness principle is asymmetrical, that is, it does not limit children to a single intent per verbal form. The same words (e.g., *yes*) appear as legitimate expressions of several different intents in the same children. Children by this age have mastered the principle of one-to-many mapping of forms to intents but not the principle of many-to-many mapping characteristic of adults' speech.

Multiple rules appeared after a child had mastered 9 to 13 verbally expressed communicative intents, about the same time as the mastery of the variable mapping principle discussed earlier (Ninio, 1994a). These two trends—defunctionalization of given expressions and the acquisition of two or more forms of mapping for the same type of speech function—lead children from an initial one-to-one mapping of meanings to forms to the full many-to-many mapping characterizing the adult linguistic system.

The mastery of variable mapping and multiple mapping occurs at a period in children's language development characterized by rapid changes on a number of dimensions. The rate of acquisition of novel vocabulary items sharply accelerates, resulting in the so-called vocabulary spurt in most (Benedict, 1979; Nelson, 1973), even if not all, children (cf. Goldfield & Reznick, 1990). Within a short time, multiword utterances begin to be acquired, signaling the onset of syntax (e.g., Ninio, 1991a). These developments are often thought to be the result of general cognitive rather than communicative advances; in particular, the vocabulary spurt, characterized by the acquisition of many novel object labels, is thought to be the result of the development of stable object concepts (Corrigan, 1978) or of changes in object classificatory skills (Gopnik & Meltzoff, 1986).

However, the vocabulary spurt is less strongly related to object naming than is sometimes assumed; apart from learning novel object labels, children also acquire at this time a novel vocabulary referring to acts, activities, events, and locations. It is possible that the accelerated vocabulary acquisition is the result of language-internal developments, chiefly the mastery of variable mapping (see Ninio, 1994a). The principle that communicative intents can be expressed by terms specifying their details is more general than the idea that nominals may be used to name objects. Indeed, children begin to use variable-type expressions at the same time for many different communicative acts apart from object labeling, such as requests of various kinds, statements of intent and statements about recent and past events, refusals, corrections, and disagreements. The vocabulary spurt appears to be part of a general, wide-range reorganization of children's word use in various different communicative circumstances.

The trends identified earlier, holistic to selective and singular to multiple mappings, are visible in lexical and grammatical acquisition as well (e.g., in the use of the grammatical resources available in a language for recounting events in a narrative; Berman & Slobin, 1994; and see Markman & Wachtel, 1988). The evidence from pragmatics supports the notion that these are general trends in language acquisition.

## 4.4 Learning to express communicative intents in the single-word stage

Are children's early production rules learned from the linguistic input, or do they emerge from children's cognition? Empiricists claim that the ability to communicate verbally is learned in the context of interaction and that children learn how to express their intents verbally by following the realization rules modeled in the speech addressed to them by competent speakers of the language (cf. Bateson, 1975; Bruner, 1983; Ninio, 1983b; Ninio & Snow, 1988; Snow, 1979, 1983b). Empiricists assume that children's utterances mirror those of adults in the same communicative circumstances to the extent memory, cognition, and linguistic resources permit.

Rationalists, of course, make the contrary assumption. For instance, Leonard and Schwartz (1978) concluded that children's single-word utterances after the onset of combinatorial speech were completely dissimilar to those of adults. They claimed that after excluding answers to questions, "inspection of the resulting [child language] data revealed virtually no instances of these utterances that would be produced in the same manner by adults in these contexts" (p. 154). Because Leonard and Schwartz did not actually compare children's speech to adult single-word speech, this claim reveals more about their theoretical presuppositions than about the relationship between child language and the adult input. Underlying such claims is a perception of early child language as an invention or reinvention by the child, an outcome of internal cognitive processes in which the role of the linguistic input is minimal (cf. Lock, 1980; Pinker, 1984). For instance, Greenfield (1980) claimed that young children, unlike adults, select words for the expression of a given communicative intent aimed at being informative from the child's own point of view rather than from the point of view of the addressee: "[The] child basically produces messages which resolve his or her own uncertainty" (p. 219). Others (e.g., Bates, 1976; Bates & MacWhinney, 1979; Snyder, 1978; Weisenberger, 1976; Wieman, 1976) claimed that the child selects what is to him or her the most important novel or attention-getting element of the situation, regardless of the communicative needs of the listener. Utterances produced by such rules obviously differ from what an adult would consider utterance-worthy in a similar communicative situation.

Diversity of opinion on the nature of early language can only be resolved by data about what adults and young children say in similar communicative circumstances. In fact, children's single-word speech is strikingly similar to that of adults. Ninio (1992) compared the single-word speech of 24 18-month-old children acquiring Hebrew to that of 48 Hebrew-speaking mothers. On average, 94.6 percent of all realization rules employed by children and 97.0 percent of all utterance tokens produced by them conformed to maternal models. In addition, the relative frequency of the different maternal models for realizing a given communicative intent predicted the likelihood that the children would use the same realization rules. The rule most frequently modeled by mothers was most likely to be adopted by children, and the children were much less likely to use less frequently modeled rules. These results suggest children acquire their initial linguistic expressions as means of expressing specific communicative intents following the rules for verbal realization of intent modeled by competent speakers.

These findings also support the view that early pragmatics plays a role in children's entry into language "proper" (see Section 3.2.1). Use-conditional or functionalist theories of acquisition for early speech have been suggested by several investigators (e.g., Antinucci & Parisi, 1975; Bates, 1976; Bruner, 1983; Halliday, 1975; Nelson, 1978; Ninio, 1992, 1994b; Ninio & Snow, 1988; Ninio & Wheeler, 1984a). For example, Ninio and Snow (1988) proposed that novel linguistic forms are acquired at the onset of speech through pragmatic (rather than semantic) matching, that is, that children pair an unknown verbal string in the speech addressed to them with their interpretation of the speaker's intended communicative effect. At some point in development, pragmatic matching may well become unable to account for language acquisition, but that point occurs after the single-word stage.

# 5

# The Acquisition of a Verbal-Communicative Repertoire

Children's verbal communicative skills, of course, continue developing beyond the level achieved at the very early period discussed in Chapter 4. Very young children's use of language is rudimentary and inefficient; it needs to undergo considerable expansion and refinement to reach the level of proficiency exhibited by adults with even average pragmatic skills. Developments during the childhood years include expanded range and variety of verbal-communicative acts, increased interpretability of communicative acts, decreased reliance on nonverbal means to express intents, expanded mastery of a variety of mapping rules and encoding strategies, and increased effectiveness of speech act use resulting from more flexible use of pragmatic resources, greater conventionality of expression, and improved politeness. We elaborate on these developments in this and the next chapter.

We draw on two types of research in discussing these developments: observational studies and parental interviews. Observational studies sample children's verbal communicative behavior in a home or laboratory setting, in a free or an experimentally imposed interaction context, in a session typically between 5 and 30 minutes long. A particularly interesting version of this method was employed by Wells (1985), who sampled 24 90-second intervals throughout the day at each observed age, aiming to arrive at a total observation time of 27 minutes but eventually analyzing only 100 utterances per observation point.

The location of the observation sessions, their duration, the instructions given to participants, and the number of utterances analyzed obviously influence the findings.

In general, observational studies cannot provide information on absolute competence. A typical observation session is of limited duration and offers a limited array of possible interactive activities, making it ecologically impossible that the participants will display their entire verbal-communicative repertoire within its limits. The nonoccurrence of particular communicative acts does not necessarily imply that either of the participants, child or adult, is unable to emit them. Certain types of talk may not be observed simply because the contexts in which they would normally emerge never arise during the observation session rather than because they fall beyond the child's competence.

To return to an example mentioned earlier, in Wells's (1985) naturalistic home observations made throughout the day, **Calling** was one of the very earliest communicative acts observed, significantly preceding functions such as **Greeting** and **Statements other than naming**. In the children observed by Dale (1980), the communicative act he called **Attention seeking** emerged later than **Greetings and ritualized forms** and coemerged with **Nonlabeling comments and descriptions of attributes of objects**. This difference stems in all probability from Dale's use of an experimenter-equipped laboratory setting for his observations rather than a home setting like Wells. In Dale's study, the child's mother stayed in the room with the child throughout the observation, so there was no occasion for the child to call her to achieve co-presence. Furthermore, mothers were instructed to play with the children as they would normally; although this instruction seems nonrestrictive, in fact it requests that the mothers spend the time playing with the children. In these circumstances it is unlikely that the parent would spend any time not attending to the child and therefore create a need or opportunity for the child to demand attention.

Some communicative acts children can produce simply do not occur during particular observation sessions. Similarly, some acts are fairly infrequent, not because they are complex but because of biases arising from the interactive business undertaken. Nonoccurrence and low frequency cannot be interpreted as indicating lack of competence or relative difficulty.

Observational studies can be reliable sources of information about relative order of acquisition, although not about age of acquisition. If children are observed over several months in similar settings, communicative acts consistently produced in earlier observations can safely be assumed to have been acquired earlier than acts observed only at a later session (although actual age of acquisition cannot be inferred).

Observational studies are, however, extremely useful in exploring children's ability to participate as equals in whatever interactive events occur during the observed encounter. Children's talk is thus best assessed in comparison with the adult partners' verbal-communicative behavior in the same session.

In summary, given the context dependency of the estimates derived from observational studies, such studies seldom provide accurate estimates of children's overall verbal-communicative repertoire, whether for communicative intents, lexicon, or grammar. A much better research instrument for assessing competence is an interview to elicit from parents information about children's language. Parents draw on information from a wide variety of settings in which they have interacted with or observed their children. Of course, parental reports can be inaccurate, are subject to social expectancy bias, and may reflect differences in the ways parents and psychologists analyze language. Parents are, however, fairly accurate in reporting their children's language abilities, at least during relatively early stages of development, producing reports generally consistent with contemporaneous observational estimates (see Section 2.5.3; Dale et al., 1989).

In this chapter we present data from parental reports and observational studies concerning age and order of emergence of communicative intents. In Chapter 6 we turn to children's use of their communicative repertoire.

## 5.1 The size of children's verbal-communicative repertoire in the first two years

Children's increasing mastery of different types of verbal-communicative acts reflects the most fundamental developmental process involved in the construction of the speech-use system. The first question of interest is the size of children's verbal-communicative repertoire, that is, how many different communicative acts are children able to express verbally at various ages? This question makes sense only at those stages of development when, apparently, children are acquiring communicative acts in a piecemeal or discrete manner, that is, when they need to learn how to produce each speech act separately in the environment of each talk interchange. At this period, for instance, they learn separately how to make a request to begin an activity and another request to end one. At some point the system becomes generative, and speakers have the competence to express practically any type of communicative message, representing a conjunction of speech act and interchange type, without having to learn specifically how to produce each of them.

For beginning speakers, however, the question is a reasonable one. It can be answered with the PICA-100 parental interview (see Section 2.5.3), which asks about the first 100 discrete types of communicative acts that appear in young children's speech.

In our discussion of children's earliest speech uses in Section 4.2, we presented the first 10 steps in children's acquisition of a verbal-communicative repertoire, based on a study (Ninio & Goren, 1993) using PICA-100. In the present section, we discuss the further growth of the verbal-communicative repertoire as it emerged from the results of that study. The mothers interviewed had children ages 0;8 to 2;2. Figure 5.1 presents the distribution of the number of different communicative acts as a function of age for the 114 children in the sample.

Mothers report that children start to produce intentional verbal communicative acts at about age eight-and-a-half months at the earliest. By two years, children have mastered between 70 and 90 different communicative acts. There is considerable individual variation in the size of children's verbal-communicative repertoires across this age range; the variation peaks at around 18 months when the reported repertoire sizes range from 30 to 70.

## 5.2 General trends in the order of acquisition of communicative acts

In what order do communicative acts emerge? Table 5.1 presents the first communicative acts children acquire with the onset of speech, between 8 and 24 months. To present the full picture, the first 10 steps of development presented in Table 4.3 are also included in this table.

Table 5.1 is organized according to major types of speech uses, following Goffman's (1964) conceptualization of the ways to achieve intersubjectivity (see Section 2.3.3 and Figure 2.2). Goffman's original scheme was modified slightly to suit the young subjects. All types of discussions were placed together, and exclamations expressing emotions were made a separate category. This presentation highlights the finding, reported in Section 4.2, that the very first speech uses acquired are the achievement of mutual attentiveness and markings of participation in gamelike interactions. Other types of speech uses appear only after children have had a period of apprenticeship in the verbal performance of these simplest interactive moves.

After the participant or performative speech uses, the next major accomplishment is the mastery of the moves involved in action negotiations and discussions. In this stage children turn their attention to the two central adult uses of talk—first, the interpersonal consolidation of plans of action through directives and responses to them, and second, the production of statements and questions about some state of affairs and responses to these. Beginning at about the tenth step of acquisition, the major developments in children's communicative act repertoires involve the refinement and expansion of these two types of speech uses. Performative acts continue to be acquired throughout this period, but new performatives are scarce compared to new negotiations and discussions. The composition of children's speech, in other words, becomes much less esoteric relative to that of adults over this period.

The last major type of speech use to be mastered, and the most complex in terms of pragmatic function, is request for clarification of the other's communications. Such moves represent a meta-communicative function in which speech does not relate directly to the interactive context but relates reflexively to communication itself. Clarification questions appear only at step 28 of the developmental

FIGURE 5.1   Distribution of Number of Different Communicative Acts as a
Function of Age

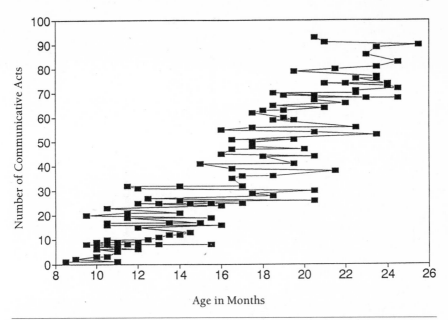

*Source:* A. Ninio and H. Goren. 1993. *PICA-100: Parental Interview on 100 Communicative Acts.* (Jerusalem: Department of Psychology, Hebrew University).

sequence (see Section 7.4 for additional discussion of children's and parents'
clarification sequences), after performatives (moves that are direct components of
the interactive context), meta-interactive acts (negotiations and evaluations of
immediate actions), and descriptions and discussions, mainly of the here and now.

The first verbal moves to appear are those that merge completely with the
interactive context of talk—they *are* the context; they *enact* the context rather
than using it as a background for talk. Verbal moves in games are clearly context
enacting, but so are the very earliest calls, responses to calls, and attention
directors. Consider the situation that occurs when you lose track of a friend in
a crowd: He calls your name, and you answer *Here;* this interaction is rather
different from what we would call a negotiation of mutual attentiveness. Your
friend's call and your own response directly establish your renewed togetherness; they do not discuss the possibility of co-presence, they create it.

The next communicative acts to appear involve some withdrawing or
distancing from the present situation. These include descriptions of the immediate physical context or negotiations about the immediate future course of
the interaction. Meta-communication, yet further removed from the ongoing

TABLE 5.1 Order of Acquisition of the First Communicative Intents Between 8 and 24 Months, According to the Parental Interview Questionnaire

| Step | Attention Negotiations | Express Emotions | Marking Events | Perform Games | Discussions | Action Negotiation | Clarification |
|---|---|---|---|---|---|---|---|
| 01 | Call attention | | | | | | |
| 02 | Direct to focus | | | | | | |
| 03 | Call to approach | Surprise | Mark effort | | | | |
| 04 | Acknowledge call | Distress | Mark—other | Imitate<br>Mimic cat<br>Mimic clock<br>Mimic—other | Answer what-question<br>Answer who-question | | |
| 05 | | | Thank<br>Mark fall of object | Mimic dog<br>Peek-a-boo<br>Telephone game | | | |
| 06 | | | Greet on meeting<br>Mark swallowing | Tickling game<br>Games—other | Answer where-question | Refuse to do<br>Agree to do<br>R/p (request/propose) a new activity<br>R/p object to act on<br>R/p new focus for activity | |
| 07 | | | | | Describe joint focus | | |
| 08 | Answer call by question | | | Honking game | | | |
| 09 | | | Mark object transfer | | | | |
| 10 | | | | | Answer in the affirmative<br>Ask what-question | | |
| 11 | | | | Mimic donkey | | | |
| 12 | | | | | Answer in the negative | R/p repeating activity<br>Forbid action<br>Warn to direct action<br>R/p preparatory action<br>Give information for act | |
| 13 | | | Greet on parting | Mimic telephone | | | |
| 14 | | Disapprove | | | | | |
| 15 | | | | | Discuss feelings | | |

| No. | | | | | |
|---|---|---|---|---|---|
| 16 | | Dancing game | | R/p continuation | |
| 17 | Mark action completion | | Answer restricted-alternative question | R/p ending activity<br>R/p act on object | |
| 18 | | Mimic train | Discuss recent event | R/p more of an action | |
| 19 | | | Agree with proposition | | |
| 20 | Respond to thanking | Mimic rooster | Complete utterance | | |
| 21 | | | Answer which-question | | |
| 22 | | Recite songs | | R/p location for act<br>R/p actor role for hearer | |
| 23 | Polite—other | | Disagree with proposition | R/p actor role for speaker | |
| 24 | | | Count | Explain reason for prohibition<br>R/p starting act | |
| 25 | | Complete text | Discuss the nonpresent<br>Ask where-question | | |
| 26 | Apologize | | | R/p pausing<br>Pretend roles | |
| 27 | | | | Praise act | |
| 28 | | | Ask yes/no question | Ask for permission | Request repetition |
| 29 | | | Ask who-question | Grant permission | |
| 30 | | | Answer how-many question | | |
| 31 | | | | R/p manner of act | |
| 32 | | | Correct addressee<br>Answer how-question<br>Answer why-question | | |
| 33 | | | Ask why-question | | Ask yes/no question |

*Source:* A. Ninio and H. Goren. 1993. *PICA-100: Parental Interview on 100 Communicative Acts* (Jerusalem: Department of Psychology, Hebrew University).

action and requiring reflection on the communication occurring and not just on the physical or activity context, emerges even later.

In other words, the degree of *context embeddedness* or, conversely, *context independence* is a decisive factor in the ordering of acquisition of different types of communicative acts. *The more closely they are related to the immediate context, the earlier communicative acts appear.* Similar findings emerged from observational studies (see Sections 6.1 and 6.2).

We now examine the specific communicative acts acquired before the age of two years within each major type of speech use to consider other factors that might affect order of development. We start with elicited speech and markers of events, two nonreferential, nonsymbolic speech uses that are among the most "primitive" communicative moves possible. Developments within these primitive systems are easier to interpret than those occurring within the more complex discussion and action-negotiation systems, but the principles illustrated here are generally applicable.


## 5.3 Developments in the elicited verbal behavior system

Speech acts designed to elicit both specific verbalizations from the addressee and responses to these are common and widespread in adult-child talk, although they are rare in adult-adult discourse (limited perhaps to language classrooms). Four types of speech-elicitation formats can be distinguished. First, eliciting moves include requests for imitation, either explicitly expressed (e.g., *Say "daddy"*) or consisting only of the model with imitation-eliciting intonation (e.g., *daddy!*). The second type includes requests for onomatopoeic sounds (e.g., *How does the clock go?* or *What does the birdie say?*). Since these sounds are language-specific and conventional, we categorize this question-answer format as a stimulus-response game rather than the exchange of a sincere request for information and response.

A third game-type speech-elicitation format involves requests for the completion of texts of songs and poems (e.g., *Pat a ...*, waiting for *cake* or *ring-a-round-a ...*, waiting for *rosy*). A related subtype, requests for the completion of words and sentences (e.g., *This is the kitty ...*, waiting for cat), is coded in the **Discussions** subsystem, because such requests, rather than being part of a game, typically occur during discussions—for example, book reading—when the child's response is delayed. All four subtypes are similar in that correct responses do not require control of the semantics of the words produced; it is sufficient for the respondent to come up with the correct sound pattern.


### 5.3.1 Responses before elicitation requests

Two phenomena are documented in Table 5.1. First, children learn to emit *responses* to speech-elicitation moves within their first two years, but they do not learn to emit the *requests* eliciting speech until later. Children obviously understand the requests as soon as they start to respond correctly to them; clearly, though, comprehension requires less than the active procedural knowledge necessary for production, which children acquire much later.

Why this developmental asymmetry between requests and responses in the speech-elicitation system? First, there are clear differences between the status or social roles of adults and children in interaction. Adults are typically the ones to make requests of children, and children, ideally, are the ones who comply. Adults are the experts, children the apprentices; these elicitation requests form part of adults' didactic efforts to get children to talk. Since children do not have to teach their mothers to name things or to pronounce words correctly, they do not learn to produce the relevant requests. Development is driven by the interactive needs of children at a particular stage in their lives.

In addition, children do not learn to emit the elicitation requests they can respond to because of a real difference in the linguistic complexity of requests and responses. Speech-elicitation requests are typically multiword utterances; responses are typically single words. Apparently, with a great deal of contextual support, children can get enough of the sense of a two-word request like *Say "daddy"* to respond by saying *Daddy* or of a query like *What do doggies say?* to respond *Hau*. But to produce the request utterances requires a type of syntactic knowledge children simply do not have at this stage.

Do children learn to produce these elicitation requests at an age when their mothers still play these games with them? Bruner and his colleagues have shown that children gradually take over the adult speech role modeled in repeated interaction formats, e.g., peek-a-boo and joint picture-book reading (e.g., Ratner & Bruner, 1978s; Section 3.1.2). Does this happen also in the case of the speech-elicitation games examined here? In the Ninio (1984) observational study (presented in detail in Section 6.1), all four types of elicitation requests did occur in children's speech by the age of 32 months (the end of the study). However, only two—**Elicit completion of rote-learned text** and **Elicit completion of word or sentence**—were produced by at least 20 percent of the sample at any one age. The text-completion request reaches this criterion for onset at 26 months; the word-completion requests elicit completion at 28 months. The other two speech acts, **Elicit imitation of word or sentence by explicit command** and **Elicit mimicking of noises made by animals, and the like,** did not reach even this liberal criterion for onset, although children did produce them sporadically between 26 and 32 months.

To summarize, responses precede elicitation requests and are used more often and more consistently by children in this period of development. However, children also learn to play the eliciting role typically taken by adults in these formats, although with a developmental lag. As we shall see, this pattern of findings recurs in the Discussions system with questions and answers to questions.

### 5.3.2 The effect of phonological complexity

The acquisition of **elicited imitation** and **onomatopoeic sounds** (at step 4) considerably precedes the acquisition of the two types of **completion** (at steps 18 and 25). According to the observational study, this represents at least 6 to 8 months of lag for **completions**. The study also showed that **spontaneous** **imitation** and **onomatopoeia** are acquired as early as their elicited counterparts.

Why are **completions** acquired so late (about 18 months)? Their interactive and cognitive demands appear similar to those of **imitation** or the **production of animal sounds**, but in fact **completions** require a sophisticated control of the sound structure of words, the ability to segment a word into at least two pieces. The earlier-appearing acts require only a much more approximate mastery of phonology; in **imitations** the model is provided, whereas the **onomatopoeic forms** have simplified "baby-talk" phonology and are less strictly defined in their phonological features than full-fledged lexical items.

The child's phonological system undergoes a reorganization beginning at around 12 months, probably as a result of the growth in vocabulary occurring then. Whereas the first 30–50 words can evidently be stored as individual articulatory-semantic items, increased vocabulary size forces a systematic re-structuring of phonotactic rules, basing speech perception and production on phonemic contrasts (Shvachkin, 1973). This phonologizing of the production system may be a prerequisite to the analysis needed to produce text or word completions but not to the simpler, unsystematized imitated and onomatopoeic forms of the earlier period.

## 5.4 Developments in the marking system

**Expressive exclamations** and **markings of events** are, like **game verbalizations**, nonsymbolic, nonpropositional speech uses, context-construing or performative in character. Although they are clearly meaningful speech uses, they are rather like conditional responses; whenever a certain class of event occurs, it is appropriate, perhaps obligatory, to produce the related verbalizations. As we have seen, markings are among the earliest-acquired speech acts.

As shown in Table 5.1, children under two years acquire many of these very simple forms of speech. However, many types of **exclamations, markings of events**, and **politeness formulas** are not acquired by children in their first two years. Even if we consider only the subset of **markings** mothers use in interaction with young children rather than the whole range of **politeness forms** used in a language community, it is obvious that children are very selective in the **exclamations** and **markings** they acquire. Turning back to the Interchange and Speech Act codes of the Ninio and Wheeler coding system (Tables 2.2 and 2.3), which includes only forms actually used in the mother-child context, we find many are not included in the repertoire of two-year-old children (see also Ninio, 1988, for a detailed discussion of this finding).

**Markings, exclamations,** and **politeness formulas** acquired by 24 months probably constitute children's complete repertoire for the next year. In the Ninio (1984) observational study, children did not acquire any **markers** to criterion between 18 and 32 months. A few children used **apologies** at the 22-month observation, but this and other novel forms were used by far fewer than 20 percent of the children. These rare forms constitute the two "other" categories in Table 5.1 (**Mark-other** and **Polite-other**), each of which represents a highly heterogeneous collection of rarely used forms.

Examining the difference between the **exclamations** and **markings** that are adopted by children and those that are not, it appears that two different factors determine the acquisition of speech uses in this communicative subsystem. One is the role appropriateness of the relevant communicative move for young children. The other is the complexity of the social concept underlying the communicative act.

### 5.4.1 The effect of role appropriateness

Children learn conventional exclamations expressing their **distress or disapproval** and their **surprise at, or enthusiasm for, some event in the environment.** These are very similar to the two earliest-produced acts, **calling** and **attention directing,** in their interactive purposes. Young children's signals of distress, protest, and surprise are, of course, entirely role appropriate.

Children in this age group, however, have not learned some exclamations expressing positive emotions toward another person, such as conventional **endearments** or expressions of **comforting and commiseration,** although these forms are used frequently by their mothers. Children acquire egocentric exclamations, those that reflect their own needs and interest, but not other-oriented exclamations used to please, comfort, or calm the addressee. These concerns are apparently beyond the social duties of young children.

Children also learn the markings that draw the others' attention to themselves and to their acts—**Mark transfer of object to hearer; Thank,** used most often upon being given an object; **Mark completion of action; Mark exertion of effort**—or to surprising events that have attracted their own attention (**Mark fall of object**). Children do not learn markings, modeled frequently, of events to do with the other person, for example, **Politely wishing a good appetite, Politely blessing on sneezing, Mark addressee's falling, stumbling, and so on** (e.g., *Oops!*), or **Exhibit attentiveness to hearer in the absence of any event** (for instance, *Yes*), an act that prevents dissolution of intersubjectivity because of an extended silence. Once again, these acts are other-oriented, and their function is to help the addressee or the dyad to deal with some situation; the more mature participant takes responsibility for producing them.

### 5.4.2 The effect of complexity of the underlying social concept

Young children also do not acquire politeness routines or culturally specific, socially required markings that require an understanding of culturally valued events or rituals. The social/cultural underpinnings of these markings are apparently too complex. Many do not even occur in mother-child interactions with children this young, although some mothers make half-hearted teaching efforts to introduce the concepts or the formulas to the children. These include **Congratulations,** for example, wishing someone a happy birthday or a happy anniversary; various religious salutations and formulas, like greetings specific to holidays or saying grace; specific greetings for parts of the day, like *Good morning, Good evening,* or *Good afternoon;* special-occasion politeness formulas, like **Wishing that addressee enjoy new clothes,** and so on.

The children acquired only five politeness formulas: **Thanking** and **Polite response to thanking, Greeting on meeting** and **on parting,** and, at the end of this period and with a much lower frequency, **Apologizing.** These formulas have much more transparent conditions of use than congratulations, religious salutations, or special-occasion greetings and probably start as primitive event markers rather than polite acts. **Thanking** occurs in this age range exclusively as a response to the transfer of objects to the child; children do not thank people who provide other types of services, like buttoning a coat, putting them in a high chair, or helping them to solve a problem. Bruner (1983) pointed out that children initially use *thank you* or *ta* indiscriminately to mark passage of an object between another person and themselves, that is, for both giving and receiving. **Responses to thanking** are used by these children in the very same circumstances, with the Hebrew form identical to the object transfer marker *please.* **Thanking** and **response to thanking** in young children are probably simply markers of object transfer rather than anything to do with polite behavior.

In the same vein, **Greetings** are essentially markings of transition between separation and co-presence. **Greeting on meeting** is probably a conventionalization of an expressive surprise response to the appearance of another and **Greeting on parting** the conventionalization of a distress response on being left alone. These changes in state are obvious, as well as crucial, in human interaction, so it is not surprising that young children can learn to mark them verbally.

In summary, factors affecting the order of emergence of the simplest communicative acts—namely, elicited verbalizations, exclamations, and markings—include the pragmatic importance of the act for the conduct of interaction and communication, the role appropriateness of the act for young children, the centrality of the child in the event being marked by the act, the relative complexity of social concepts underlying the act, the phonological skills necessary for the act, and the linguistic difficulty of the expressions used in producing the act. Next we turn to developments in the two central and much more complex subsystems of verbal communication, namely, discussions and action negotiations, where these same factors also play a role.

## 5.5 Developments in the discussion system

Discussions are topic-specific exchanges of representations of some state of affairs, consisting of statements, questions, and replies. Children master the most basic speech acts used for the conduct of discussions relatively late (see Table 5.1). Statements and questions barely appear in the first 10 steps of acquisition; agreements and disagreements with someone else's statements, as well as corrections, are particularly late. Children control the central moves of the apparently more fundamental attention-negotiation, exclamation, marking, and game-sound systems and many acts within the action-negotiation system well before they start to produce statements about a joint focus of attention. Exchanging descriptions is apparently not among the most natural pragmatic uses of speech. Development in the discussion system gains momentum after the tenth step of development, in the middle of the second year, when children start acquiring the full variety of speech acts out of which discussions are built and begin using them for a variety of topics.

### 5.5.1 Contextualized discussions appear earlier

The column labeled Discussions in Table 5.1 presents four categories of statements discussing various topics in order of appearance: **Statements discussing a joint focus of attention**, **Statements discussing feelings and inner states of the speaker** and **of the addressee**, **Statements on a recent event**, and lastly, **Statements discussing nonpresent topics**. This developmental progression reflects the main organizing principle of the speech-use system, namely, degree of context embeddedness (see Sections 2.3.3 and 4.2). The more a discussion is contextualized or built on a joint perceptual focus, the earlier it is participated in verbally by young children. Thus, perceptually present external objects and events are talked about earlier than perceptually present but internal events; internal events are discussed earlier than immediately preceding or recent events, which in turn are discussed before invisible or absent objects, events in the distant past and future, or hypothetical or abstract states of affairs. The ordering is rather obviously determined by the conceptual and linguistic complexity of introducing the relevant topics; achieving convergence on an internal state or a distal topic is a much more difficult matter than reaching convergence on a perceptually salient object.

At the earliest stages, rather primitive speech uses qualify as "statements" in discussions. Thus, children's first **Discussions of a joint focus of attention** consist of object labeling, the earliest of which are pro-forms, like *this* and *there*, rather than true names (see Sections 4.1 and 4.2). Similarly, early **Discussions of nonobservable inner states and feelings** consist of a few stock expressions, like *hot* and *cold, afraid, sad, angry,* and the like, all related to children's states and feelings, not the mothers' (Ninio, 1984). Even when children took part in conversations coded **Discussions of addressee's inner state**, their participation consisted of answers to inquiries mothers made about how the *children* felt. As with markings, the forms acquired to discuss internal states express meanings in which the children themselves are central. **Discussions of a recent event** also involve a limited set of expressions, mostly describing negative events involving objects, like *broke, fell,* and *spilled* (see Ninio, 1988, for a more detailed treatment). **Discussions of the nonpresent** are limited to concrete objects and events and often rely on a shared experiential, if not physical, context (e.g., a child saying *Grandma* in the discussion of a past shared train trip). Young children do not engage in discussions of hypothetical or abstract topics. Despite these cognitive and communicative limitations on children's participation in discussions, they can nonetheless participate in all major types of discussion by the age of two years, demonstrating their understanding that speech can be used to react to, reflect on, or describe objects and events.

### 5.5.2 The acquisition of questions and answers

In addition to statements, discussed earlier, the major constituents of discussions are questions and answers. For all types of question-answer pairs, answers are consistently acquired before the matching questions. In a sharp contrast, statements emerge before the matching agreements and disagreements or corrections.

The answer-question lag may, like the elicitation-response lag for speech elicitations, reflect effects of role-appropriateness, conceptual, and syntactic difficulty. Children learn to ask most kinds of questions before they begin to request completions or imitations, perhaps because questions can be expressed in single-word utterances and speech elicitations cannot. More fundamentally, though, speech-elicitation requests demonstrate possession of knowledge, whereas questions are procedures for acquiring knowledge. Children are understandably less motivated to play elicitation games with their mothers than to acquire new knowledge.

So why do responses to statements appear later than statements, when children produce responses to questions before questions? The reason is that the two types of response have a different status. Questions are requests and as such demand a response, whereas statements do not. Speech acts, like agreement and disagreement, are optional rather than obligatory responses to statements. Furthermore, mothers interested in conversational interaction exploit questions to generate responses from their children (Snow, 1977a), so children have ample opportunity to produce answers if they know how. Since statements do not require a response, they are less effective conversation starters. In addition, children may not really grasp at first that a statement has truth conditions, that it can be true or false, agreed to or disagreed with. Their own earliest statements, indeed, are mostly indicators of interest and participation (e.g., *here* or *this* during labeling routines) rather than true and thus debatable naming expressions (see Section 4.1). The late emergence of responses to statements strengthens the impression that early statements (as well as answers to the initial what-, who-, and where-questions) are performative in character, elements of labeling games rather than predication. Furthermore, statements appear at exactly the age when various other game sounds are being acquired. If we shift the first four entries in the Discussions column of Table 5.1 to the left, they blend nicely with the block of performative speech uses characterizing steps three through seven of the developmental timetable.

Logicians would say that children do not have genuine predication until they understand that a statement can be false. By this criterion, children do not produce true statements until the twenty-third step of pragmatic development, when **Disagreements with propositions** appear, sometime between 18 and 20 months for most children (Ninio, 1984).

The acquisition of questions and answers to questions takes many months (see Table 5.1; Ervin-Tripp, 1970). The first questions to be asked or answered are **What-questions; Yes-no questions** and their **Answers** are mastered much later. **Where-questions** and **Who-questions** and various types of **Answers** precede **Why-questions**. Wells (1985) also found that most **Content (wh)-questions** appeared before **Yes-no questions**, with **Why-questions** acquired considerably later. Mothers reported, however, that **Why-questions** preceded **Which-questions, When-questions**, and **How-many questions**, a finding confirmed in observations (Ninio, 1984). **Restricted-alternative questions** were not produced at all by the children, even at 32 months when the study ended. Wells (1985) followed children to 5 years but unfortunately did not mention this type of question, so we do not know when children start to produce them.

Semantic-cognitive factors clearly influence the order of emergence of these questions and answers; for instance, children at this age have a very hazy grasp of time, quantity, and causality but a fairly good understanding of objects, persons, and space (Snow & Winner, 1994). Linguistic complexity also influences the acquisition sequence. **A Restricted-alternative question** (e.g., *Do you want tea or coffee?*), although apparently rather simple to answer, in fact requires an understanding of the use of the logical connective *or*.

Even though children acquire a wide range of speech acts for use in discussions before age two, by 32 months they have not mastered even some relatively simple discussion acts used by mothers. Some speech acts modeled by mothers in discussions (**Asking a how-much question, Asking a restricted-alternative question**, or **Expressing a wish**) were practically never produced by the children. Later developments in children's capacity to converse using the discussion system are discussed in Chapter 7.

## 5.6 Developments in the action-negotiation system

The second central subsystem of communicative acts is the negotiation of immediate action. Children use 25 discrete communicative acts within this class before two years of age (see Table 5.1).

The PICA-100 questionnaire includes 28 items that are individually defined moves in action negotiations. Requests relating to whole activities were separated into several distinct subtypes, distinguishing among requests for initiation, continuation, repetition, ending, and so on. Similarly, requests relating to individual acts were differentiated according to the specific point of the request: directives specifying the object to be involved in the act, the act to be carried out on a known object, the desired location or positioning of the act, the manner in which it was to be carried out, and directives concerned with beginning some act otherwise agreed on by the participants. In consequence, simple communicative acts like **Make a request** or **Direct addressee's action** do not appear. Such distinctions were not, however, made in the parental questionnaire for responses, so, for example, **refusals** made to any of these types of requests were all coded the same. Second, no general distinction was made between a certain type of directive addressed to the interlocutor and the same type addressed to oneself. (See Sections 2.5.1 and 2.5.3 for further explanation of the categorization system.)

In the development of this communicative subsystem it is possible to distinguish three broad stages, defined by their clustering in acquisition.

### 5.6.1 The first stage of development: recruiting attention-directing skills

The first stage of the development of action negotiations consists of the acquisition of types of communicative moves that are mastered in the sixth step of the developmental timetable presented in Table 5.1. According to the Ninio (1984) observational study, this step is completed at 12–14 months. At this stage, children learn to express six fundamental moves verbally: **agreeing to** and **refusing someone else's proposals for action, initiating a novel activity +/- focused on an object, changing the object at the focus of an ongoing activity**, and **proposing objects to act on.** Children build their verbal action-management skills from the bottom up, starting with the most crucial functions.

The initial stage of action negotiations closely follows the acquisition of the very early communicative acts negotiating mutual and joint attention. Apparently, the initial action-negotiation system is a direct extension of children's attention-negotiation skills. A detailed analysis of children's early communicative moves within the four action-negotiation interchanges acquired the earliest revealed that except for agreements to and refusals of the mothers' proposals, in the vast majority of cases these consisted of indications of objects the children wanted to be given to play with, elected as the next focus of an activity, wanted the addressee to act on within an ongoing activity, or intended to act on themselves. In other words, children's initial participation in action negotiations consists of their using their attention-directing skills to regulate joint activities.

### 5.6.2 The second stage: regulating joint activities

The second stage of development, extending from step 12 to step 18 of the developmental timetable in Table 5.1, includes types of speech uses children started to produce between 14 and 16 months but that did not reach criterion until 18 months (Ninio, 1984). The novel functions that emerged included five that relate to the conduct of joint activities: **suggesting the continuation, repetition, recursive extension,** and **ending of activities** and **proposing a preparatory move to an activity.** Other functions that emerged at this stage were **providing information necessary for the conduct of actions, warning against dangers in action, forbidding the addressee to perform an action,** and **specifying the action they want the addressee or themselves to perform.**

The five activity-managing requests represent basic interpersonal intentions relevant to the regulation of joint action: CONTINUE/DON'T STOP, DO IT AGAIN, DO IT MORE, ENOUGH, and PREPARE ACTIVITY. Except for the initiation of novel activities (acquired in stage one), these are the most basic moves in the conduct of joint enterprises, such as games, meals, or getting dressed.

CONTINUE/DON'T STOP redirects the interlocutor's attention to some joint activity that he or she has stopped attending to, repairing a break in intersubjectivity. Mothers most often use this function with young children, but according to the observational study, by 16–18 months children also produce many requests to continue an interrupted game.

DO IT AGAIN requests the repetition of complete activities or self-contained subunits of activities. For example, mother and child are playing a game in which the child is helped up to the table, then jumps off as mother says *Hoppa*. After completing several jumps, child turns to mother and says in an insistent tone: *Hoppa!* The unit of joint action whose repetition is demanded here is a complex whole, made up of several different moves in sequence. It is the *game* and not one particular act whose repetition is being requested.

DO IT MORE is related to both AGAIN and CONTINUE/DON'T STOP. For example, a child being pushed on a swing might, if the adult stopped, say *more!* meaning "keep pushing me." Or a child being fed spoonfuls of baby food is asked after every few bites, *Do you want more?* and answers, *Yes.* This interactive function involves both the continuation of an ongoing activity after a temporary break and the repetition of actions carried out before, making it apparently more complex than AGAIN; MORE is acquired on the eighteenth step of development, whereas AGAIN is acquired on the twelfth step. Activities like being pushed on a swing are made of a single act repeated until the participants have had enough, with no structure, goal, or natural end point. The MORE negotiation is about whether to add another recursion to a chain of identical acts.

ENOUGH is a negotiation about ending an ongoing activity. When the mother playing *Hoppa* finally refused to lift the child onto the table again, she used this speech function. Children used it when they wanted adults to stop feeding, dressing, or grooming them. As soon as children started using the ENOUGH function, they produced both responses and initiations within it.

PREPARE ACTIVITY consists of proposals to perform some preparatory move before starting the main business of a novel activity. Such preparatory moves involve the interactants' location, for example, sitting down side by side before reading a book; preparing a surface appropriate for the new activity, such as clearing the table before laying out a puzzle; locating objects required for the activity; and other moves that are prerequisite to the actual joint activity. A child may tell the mother *There!*—and, at a later age, *Move!*—when he or she wants to sit down with her on the sofa after the two have agreed they will look at a book together. Children in the observational study produced requests to prepare activity at 18 months, as well as agreements, refusals, and questions within prepare-activity negotiations.

Apart from these clearly activity-related interactive functions, at the relevant stage children also mastered the REQUEST ACT, ASK/GIVE INFORMATION NECESSARY FOR ACTION, FORBID, and WARN WHILE ACTING functions. The first of these—REQUEST ACT—is the only one of this group to deal with individual acts, whereas the other three are used to regulate both single acts and complete activities.

REQUEST ACT is used to specify the action to be performed when other parameters of the act (e.g., the object involved) are already established. For example, a child might say *Put!* to her mother who is holding a puzzle piece. Children first produced these kinds of requests addressed to their mothers and to themselves at around the same age, the self-addressed requests being true directives aimed at themselves rather than informative statements addressed to the mother about what they were about to do. Children at first expressed this intent with a very restricted set of verb forms, the imperative or (single-word) infinitive of the Hebrew verbs for *open, close, put, take out, bring, get up, get down* (Ninio, 1984). Although the forms grew more varied between 18 and 32 months, they initially resembled a collection of key words for requesting specific actions rather than anything like a true verb vocabulary.

The ASK/GIVE INFORMATION NECESSARY FOR ACTION function was a discussion-type move—a statement, a question, or an answer to a question—emitted in the context of action negotiation. Children asked their mothers' help or guidance in some action they were engaged in or gave them advice; they also asked themselves, out loud, the same types of questions and gave themselves advice.

A child with a piece of puzzle in her hand might, for example, hesitate about where to put it and, choosing an empty position, ask her mother, *Here?* The first expressions used in this interchange, as in others, were linguistically very simple.

FORBID is a negotiation to block action. Unlike the ENOUGH function, which consists of attempts to end an activity being engaged in, FORBID negotiations are attempts to prevent the relevant act or activity from being performed in the first place. Children initially used some constant form such as *No!* to express this function.

The last function acquired during the second stage is WARN WHILE ACTING; it is not a prohibition but rather a caution to the addressee (who can be the speaker him- or herself) to be careful in carrying out some act. In the initial phases of producing this act, children used some variant of the imperative *be-careful,* a single-word expression in Hebrew.

The interactive functions mastered at the second stage cannot, like those of the first, be accomplished by indicating a particular object to focus the activity on. The new functions are no longer an application of attention-directing skills but constitute a true action-management system.

Significantly, in the majority of cases the unit of interaction to which children's talk related and which it attempted to regulate was the *activity* rather than some single, discrete behavior. We saw that pragmatic development started with children bringing under verbal control the most fundamental interpersonal transition, from lack of mutual attentiveness to mutual/joint attention (Section 4.2). The first stage of action negotiation still belongs to this level of interpersonal control; the verbal-communicative moves acquired at the first stage consist of children's effecting a transition from *not* jointly attending to an object to jointly attending to it. The second stage is an advance in the level at which the interactive state is brought under control: The *definition of the situation* implied by these communicative moves increases in complexity (see Section 2.3.2). For example, the CONTINUE function implies some concept like the following:

> I suggest the continuation of a temporarily interrupted joint activity consisting of the game of ball tossing/catching while in focused interaction with my mother in each other's presence.

In terms of the model of interactive states presented in Figures 2.1 and 2.2, children advance from verbally controlling the entrance to focused interaction to verbally controlling transitions much more deeply embedded in the hierarchical definition of the situation. The novel interchange types reflect children's greatly enhanced understanding of the range of interactive functions that can be achieved by talk and, probably, of the structure of joint action itself.

In terms of social cognition, these communicative acts are built on the grasp of relatively sophisticated concepts, such as continuation, repetition, preparation, and ending of activities. These concepts represent the contextual arguments that speech operates on; in the case of action negotiations, children need to advance in their social cognition to a considerable level before they are able to produce directives that relate to these relatively complicated aspects of joint behavior.

Children can only produce these novel action-negotiation moves because of the cognitive advances of the second year. For example, PREPARE ACTIVITY requires some understanding of means-ends relations, which in the Piagetian framework emerges around the middle of the second year. Such specific cognition-language coemergence phenomena have been documented for the semantic content of children's utterances (e.g., Gopnik & Meltzoff, 1987; Tomasello, 1992); now it appears that they occur in the case of pragmatic intents as well.

Finally, such interactive intents can only be expressed if children go beyond the initial stock of semiwords used for playing games and indicating interesting objects and events. The speech forms used to express requests for continuation, repetition, actions, and the like represent a considerable advance in children's vocabularies.

### 5.6.3 The third stage: the emergence of sophisticated interactive goals

In the third stage of development in action negotiations, 11 somewhat heterogeneous speech uses emerge (the twenty-second through the thirty-first step of the developmental timetable). Newly emerging functions, in order, are **Request/propose a location for an action; Offer next move, turn, role to addressee; Demand role, turn, or move for speaker; Explain reason for prohibition; Request/propose to begin an action at once; Request that addressee pause in action; Declare pretend roles and identities; Praise addressee for correctness of acts; Ask for permission to carry out action; Grant permission to perform action; Request/propose manner of action.**

These functions emerged rather suddenly at 18 months, appearing only sporadically before then (Ninio, 1984). Moreover, an unusually high percentage of children produced each of them at the point of onset. In other words, the onset of these speech-uses was atypically abrupt and reflected a discontinuous leap of speech-use abilities between the 16-month and the 18-month observations. For most of the children in the sample, this was the age at which they abruptly reorganized the system of principles by which they mapped their communicative intents to verbal expressions, moving from fixed to variable mapping and from primarily singular to primarily multiple realization rules for the same communicative intents (see Section 4.3). These novel principles for packaging messages into words constitute a considerable advance in children's linguistic ability; variable realization rules mean the acquisition of a noun and verb vocabulary, and multiple mapping rules prepare for the onset of multiword utterances and syntax (see Ninio, 1990a, 1991a, 1994a).

These linguistic advances also appear to have a direct effect on children's ability to participate in more complex talk interchanges, probably because of their enhanced capability to interpret utterances addressed to them. The 10 types that emerged in the third stage of action-negotiation development expressed more sophisticated interactive goals than those acquired previously. Children were newly able to make proposals specifying the location, timing, and manner of single acts and thus to direct action with considerably enhanced precision.

Expressions for offering and demanding moves, turns, and roles emerge during the third stage—the YOU DO IT and I DO IT functions. Children can now negotiate who is to hold the book and who will turn the pages; who will tell the story, draw the picture, or dress the doll; and who will be the passive participant. Early in this period children use *You* or *Mommy* to make these kinds of demands of the mother; they also agree to or refuse such suggestions on the part of the mother.

The I DO IT function is used when the speaker wants to perform an act by him- or herself, without assistance. Children most often initiate I DO IT negotiations: English-speaking children said something like *Me* or *Myself;* the Hebrew-speaking children observed typically said *levad,* literally "alone." The emergence of self-consciousness around 18 months no doubt helps to explain children's contemporaneous insistence on autonomous action.

Negotiations about who will perform an act reveal that the child can now separate the actor from the act; the negotiation takes the action as given. In stage two children manage to isolate actions and the objects involved in performing them; in this third stage they can also separate the location, the timing, the manner, and the actor from the act itself.

Two developments occur within prohibitions. First, children now provide reasons for their objection to some act rather than just prohibiting it. Second, children can now direct the addressee to pause temporarily, as well as to stop entirely.

Evaluations are an important part of the action-control system, providing feedback to an actor on the success of his or her acts. At this stage, rather than merely exclaim in enthusiasm or disapproval, children begin to evaluate actions in words. At first, they are limited to **praising** (acquired at 20 months); **criticisms of incorrect acts** reach criterion 4 months later, at the 24-month observation (Ninio, 1984). **Evaluations of the other's and the self's acts** appear at about the same time; in general, communicative acts dealing with the regulation of the other's and the self's actions develop side by side at this stage of development.

Around this age children also start to engage in pretend play. In the action-negotiation system the relevant communicative moves appear: **declaring make-believe identities for objects** and **declaring make-believe roles for themselves.**

Finally, directives, the foundation of action negotiation, undergo considerable refinement during stage three. In addition to producing basic requests and agreements to requests, children acquire the complexities of **asking for** and **granting permission.**

In addition to the stage-three acts appearing in Table 5.1, around this time children also begin to participate in yet another novel verbal interchange dealing with the initiation of joint activities, **Initiate activity: Open-ended question about addressee's wishes** (IOQ). In this type of negotiation, one participant asks the other what he or she wants to do next. Eighteen-month-olds typically do not ask, but do answer, such questions, for example, producing responses like *Record, Biscuits, Story,* or *To see.* To participate in this kind of talk, children have to understand questions like *What do you want to do now?* and then to name their desired activity—possible only with their emergent ability to use content words, like nouns and verbs, *to specify varying elements of intents.* Naming for your interlocutor the activity you want to be engaged in next is, of course, a prototypical use of the variable mapping principle; the novel activity chosen varies with the speaker's momentary wishes from one situation to the next, and if the answer is to be informative, it must change accordingly. Although children begin to produce answers to **what-questions** as early as the fourth step of the developmental timetable, these very early answers tend to be constant expressions, like *this,* or at the most to consist of a single object name a particular child acquired as part of a performative labeling game (see Section 4.1). The emergence of open-ended negotiations about novel activities has to wait until children control the provision of *varying* answers to **what-questions**, in the middle of the second year.[1]

### 5.6.4 Developments past two years

Immediately following the period covered by Table 5.1, two novel types of verbal evaluations reached criterion, the negative **Criticize addressee for incorrectness of acts** and **Disapprove of hearer's or speaker's inappropriate behavior** (Ninio, 1984). The last speech act of this group, **Approve of hearer's or speaker's behavior**, was not used at all by children within the period of development covered by this observational study.

At 28 months, children mastered the **Give in: accept other's insistence or refusal** function. **Promises** started to be used consistently at 30 months. Communicative intents used by a few children, such as **Threatening** or **Setting rules of turn-taking**, did not reach the criterion for general onset by 32 months. These speech acts were relatively infrequent in maternal speech as well. Finally, children never used the speech acts **Agree to do for the last time, Dare/challenge hearer to perform action,** and **Approve of hearer's or speaker's behavior as norm appropriate** (rather than as correct for problem solving), perhaps because these moves are role inappropriate for young children. Except for the four speech acts **Criticize, Disapprove, Give in,** and **Promise**, relatively little new was learned about action negotiation between 24 and 32 months. The rapid expansion of the action-negotiation repertoire that characterized the second half of the second year slowed to a trickle in the following eight months, because children were already producing most of the speech acts mothers used to regulate activity.

Wells's (1985) study, the only description of speech act development beyond age three, found very few new communicative acts after 32 months. The only ones whose onset occurred past 32 months were **Blame** and **Tale-tell** in the Expressive subsystem; **Social explanation, Moral explanation,** and **Psychological explanation** in the representational system; and **New topic marker** in the Procedural subsystem. Except for the last, these categories distinguish statements according to content, not on illocutionary characteristics. Their appearance thus represents an advance more in children's cognitive and semantic range than in their control of types of communicative acts proper. Wells's study suggests that during the 32–60-month period, children do not significantly enlarge their communicative repertoire; instead, they learn the lexicogrammatical means for the full verbal realization of previously acquired communicative intents (pp. 209, 224; see also Brown, 1973; Slobin, 1973). The Wells study employed home observations; outside the home environment children do learn new communicative moves, some of which are documented in studies by Dore and McDermott (1982) and Streeck (1983), on the pragmatics of classroom speech. At home, though, children appear to have acquired most of the interpersonal speech uses they will need by age two and a half.

## 5.7 Summary: order of acquisition of communicative acts

The verbal-communicative system undergoes rapid, although somewhat uneven, growth between ages 0;8 and 2;8. By two years children have mastered most of the basic moves of the central communicative uses of speech, namely, discussions about various topics and the negotiation of action. After age two they turn to acquiring the more complex, infrequent, and specialist speech uses and to developing skill at deploying in a variety of situations the basic repertoire acquired in parent-child dyadic interaction (e.g., Ervin-Tripp, 1980).

The first period of speech use is characterized by a focus on the acquisition of the pragmatic system of communicative acts. As has been pointed out by Ingram (1974), at this stage a child's development may be manifest more by the number of communicative intents he or she can express verbally than by either lexical or syntactic advances (for a similar point, see also Carpenter, Mastergeorge, & Coggins, 1983; Dore, 1975). Starting at about two years, the major acquisitional task appears to be perfecting the linguistic means by which familiar communicative acts are expressed. Children's language increases rapidly in syntactic and morphological complexity, but their communicative repertoire does not change much. This continuity in communicative functions during a period of enormous change in form of expression is reminiscent of the transition between preverbal and verbal communication; at both periods radical changes in children's linguistic forms occur, whereas their speech functions remain constant. As has been suggested by Brown (1973), Bruner (1983), Slobin (1973), and Wells (1985), broad phases consisting of the acquisition of either novel functions or of novel forms of expression appear to alternate in language development.

A second conclusion to emerge from this detailed review of development is that the verbal communicative system expands in an orderly fashion, with separate stages and substages characterized by distinct levels of organization. In the first stage children acquire verbal control of the attention-directing system and learn to participate verbally in interactive games. Further stages are built on these foundations; discussions grow from performative moves in labeling games, and the action-negotiation system is built on the attention-direction system. As these more adultlike and serious speech uses are acquired, the more primitive and playful markers, exclamations, and game moves come to make up less and less of children's talk.

Third, the order of acquisition is determined by the joint effect of the importance of the act for the achievement of children's interactive and communicative aims and the relative complexity of the act in its conceptual and formal features. Seven factors affect the order of emergence of communicative acts:

1. The pragmatic importance of the act for the conduct of interaction and communication: Acts that help children achieve their most basic interactive goals are acquired earliest.
2. The role appropriateness of the act for young children: Child-role acts, like requesting and responding with verbal moves in a game, are acquired before maternal-role acts, like comforting and reprimanding.
3. The relative complexity of general cognitive prerequisites for the verbal acts: Acts that require taking the others' perspective are acquired later than acts performed from an egocentric perspective, as are acts involved in the discussion of abstract rather than concrete topics.
4. The directness of the relationship of talk with the interactive context: Context-construing game verbalizations are acquired before context-managing action directives, which, in turn, are acquired before metacommunicative clarification requests.
5. The relative complexity of the social concept underlying the verbal act, that is, the depth of embedding in some hierarchically organized definition of the social reality: Speech acts dealing with simple state changes, like that between inattention and mutual attentiveness or between co-presence and separation, are acquired before acts dealing with changes in some specific aspect of an agreed-on activity, such as the assignment of roles to participants in a game.
6. The phonological skills necessary for the act.
7. The syntactic or formal complexity of the language needed to express the communicative act.

Pragmatic skills are not easily separable from social-cognitive skills or from formal linguistic skills. The speech-use system interacts with the linguistic system proper, for example, when children's strategies for mapping communicative intents to words are reorganized in the middle of the second year. Children's mastery of variable or selective mapping of intents to words has a deep impact on both their linguistic abilities and their pragmatic capacities. Selective mapping brings in a new vocabulary of nouns, verbs, adjectives and adverbs, a group of word forms that could not be learned until their role in the expression of communicative intents became clear. Such words form the backbone of the linguistic system; their acquisition is the crucial prerequisite for the emergence of syntax and morphology.

Changes in the linguistic system have, in turn, a considerable effect on the verbal-communicative system. The onset of variable mapping, coinciding with steps 13–24 of the developmental timetable, constitutes a watershed in all of the various communicative systems: markings, games, attention direction, discussions, and action negotiations. Children at this point no longer rely exclusively on their attention-directing and participant skills to achieve interactive goals, and they stop rapidly acquiring markers, exclamations, and other semilinguistic forms. Their statements become real truth-carrying propositions; their action-negotiation strategies become much more complex. Thus, the revolution in children's intent-mapping strategies not only changes the ways in which existing communicative acts are expressed in words but also triggers a widening of the verbal-communicative repertoire itself.

The interface between the pragmatic system and social cognition is also crucial for the development of both. Verbal-communicative acts relating to fundamental contrasts between interactive states, such as between mutual attentiveness and the lack of it, are acquired much earlier than those relying on more subtle concepts, such as the repetition or the continuation of an activity. Development appears to proceed from the more fundamental and thus simpler functions to the ones more deeply embedded in a multilevel, hierarchical definition of the situation (from the outside in, as shown in Figure 2.2). Acts embodying truly complex concepts, such as promising—taking on a commitment to perform an action in the future—are not mastered until very late.

On the other hand, whereas developments in the social-conceptual system drive pragmatic development, the mastery of verbal-communicative acts also drives the social-cognitive system. A concept such as giving permission or promising has no existence outside the speech-use system; acquiring the speech act introduces these concepts to the cognitive apparatus of children. How do children develop social-cognitive skills sophisticated enough to permit mastery of this kind of speech use by 30 months? As in other domains of cognitive development, the accumulation of a critical mass of simplex concepts is probably one necessary precondition.

## Notes

1. These data on the emergence of IOQ negotiations come from the Ninio (1984) observational study, as the PICA-100 instrument did not distinguish among answers to questions according to the talk interchanges in which they were embedded.

# 6

# Participation in Verbal Interaction

In this chapter we describe how one- to three-year-old children use their communicative abilities in face-to-face interaction with their mothers, drawing on two longitudinal observational studies. Observational data can provide estimates of children's verbal-communicative competence but are most informative about children's developing ability to use their competence in verbal encounters with others. Comparing mothers' and children's speech uses in the same interactive sessions tells us how well children participated in the various kinds of talk that actually occurred during the observed interaction.

## 6.1 The Ninio longitudinal observational study

Ninio (1983b, 1984) followed a group of 24 Hebrew-speaking children between the ages of 12 months and 32 months, in a staggered longitudinal design. Eight children were observed between 12 and 22 months, eight between 18 and 28 months, and eight between 22 and 32 months. They were videotaped every two months. Half of the mothers in each group had postsecondary education; half had secondary education or less. In each of the subgroups, half of the children were males, half females. All of the children were normally developing firstborns living in two-parent families. (The communicative development of the 12-month-olds in this sample was described in Section 4.1, along with that of another sample of 10-month-olds.)

The children were videotaped in a 30-minute unstructured, free-interaction session with their mothers at home. Mothers were asked to do what they normally did at that time of the day and to select the room for the recording. They were asked to stay in one room as much as possible because of the video equipment. If one member of the dyad left the recording room temporarily, the recorder continued to focus on the other. If both members moved, the equipment and cameraperson followed the dyad. Mothers were told that we wished to obtain a naturalistic sample of infants' interaction and were not interested in any particular behavior. They were told only at the end of the study that maternal and child language would be the special focus of analysis.

All utterances were categorized for communicative intent, using the full Ninio and Wheeler (1984b) coding system. We present the results of interchanges and speech acts separately, as they present slightly different developmental pictures.

### 6.1.1 Changes in the range of the interchange repertoire used in interaction

One of the measures of the mastery of the pragmatic system is the range of the verbal interchange types children participate in during an observed interaction session. Table 6.1 presents the mean and standard deviation of the number of different types of verbal interchanges the children and their mothers took part in during a 30-minute observation session, at the different observational points. The mean values as the function of age are also presented in Figure 6.1, for easier inspection of the developmental trends. The number of different verbal interchange types mothers generated is the upper limit for what children can be expected to produce in the same communicative circumstances. The coding system used distinguishes 70 different interchange types, each of which was used at least once in this study. This number represents a maximal repertoire of verbal interchange types; only a subset is expected to occur in any 30-minute interaction.

Mothers engaged in a remarkably constant number of interchange types throughout most of the period studied, about 28–29 different interchanges (or a bit below one per minute) in 30 minutes; the absence of child-age–related changes was confirmed for rather different observational circumstances by Snow and colleagues (1995; see Section 6.2.1). Interacting with 12-month-olds, mothers participated verbally in 31.4 different types of interchanges, and the 12-month-olds participated in an average of 5.0. Children's participation increased steeply for the next 10 months, reaching a value of 21.3 different interchanges at 22 months, which was then maintained—with very slight increases—for the next 10 months. During the first months of speech use, the children had many more opportunities to participate in talk exchanges than they could take advantage of, but by 2 years of age the children were using only 5–6 fewer interchange types than the mothers, a gap that held steady until 32

TABLE 6.1   Number of Different Talk Interchanges Participated in by Children and by Mothers in a 30-Minute Interactive Session, by Children's Age

| Age in Months | N | Children | | Mothers | |
|---|---|---|---|---|---|
| | | Mean | SD | Mean | SD |
| 12 | 8 | 5.0 | 3.6 | 31.4 | 5.5 |
| 14 | 8 | 8.9 | 3.7 | 32.6 | 3.4 |
| 16 | 7 | 13.9 | 7.1 | 37.1 | 3.8 |
| 18 | 16 | 16.0 | 7.2 | 33.0 | 4.3 |
| 20 | 15 | 18.1 | 5.9 | 31.1 | 3.3 |
| 22 | 24 | 21.3 | 6.7 | 31.1 | 4.7 |
| 24 | 16 | 20.2 | 4.7 | 28.3 | 5.4 |
| 26 | 16 | 22.3 | 4.8 | 27.9 | 3.8 |
| 28 | 16 | 22.8 | 3.4 | 28.2 | 3.8 |
| 30 | 7 | 22.1 | 4.3 | 28.4 | 3.0 |
| 32 | 8 | 23.6 | 2.0 | 29.5 | 2.9 |

*Source:* A. Ninio. 1984. "Functions of Speech in Mother-Infant Interaction." Final Science Report to the U.S.-Israel Binational Science Foundation, Jerusalem, Israel.

FIGURE 6.1   Mean Number of Different Types of Verbal Interchanges in Which Children Took Part in a 30-Minute Interaction, by Age

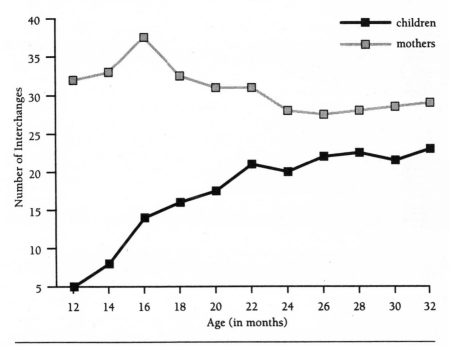

*Source:* A. Ninio. 1984. "Functions of Speech in Mother-Infant Interaction." Final Science Report to the U.S.-Israel Binational Science Foundation, Jerusalem, Israel.

months. Mothers' asymptotic value of 28–29 represents about a 43 percent use of the total interchange repertoire in a 30-minute session, whereas children's asymptote of 22–23 is about 34 percent of the same maximum. In other words, by 24 months children already exhibit a range of participation in verbal interchanges that is almost like that of their mothers in the same type of interpersonal circumstances.

The children had probably not, however, mastered the same absolute range of verbal interchange types as their mothers. The mothers were obviously capable of producing all 70 different interchanges included in the coding scheme, so the 28–29 they produced is merely a sample of a much larger repertoire. Eventually, the children produced almost the same number, but they might well have been sampling from a smaller total repertoire. These statistics simply do not answer the question of how large children's overall interchange repertoire is. We do know it reaches at least 22–23 interchanges at around 2 years; this is the lower limit of their interchange-type competence.

The increase from 5 to 20 observed interchange types between 12 and 24 months probably reflects a real widening of the children's verbal interchange repertoire, but the asymptote between 24 and 32 months does not imply that learning has ceased (see Section 5.6.4 for evidence of emergent capacities in this later period). Instead, this plateau suggests the children have acquired the means and the procedural knowledge to conduct adultlike talk with their mothers—to match their own range of interchanges to that of the adult. It is tempting to speculate that the asymptote of about one interchange type per minute represents some optimal constant of unstructured face-to-face interaction, at least with young children; this constant value holds despite considerable changes during the same period in the types of talk the mother-child dyads engage in (see Section 6.1.3). Parenthetically, the tendency of mothers in the earlier observations to use more interchange types may represent a relative failure to find activities and topics that could be shared with the children. Thus, children's catching on to an asymptotic value close to the maternal optimum by 24 months is a real developmental accomplishment.

### 6.1.2 Changes in the range of the speech act repertoire used in interaction

Speech acts characterize the contribution of individual utterances to the ongoing verbal interchange. Sixty-two speech acts are distinguished in the coding instrument (see Table 2.3 for list), excluding as before codes for uninterpretable utterances. As in the case of the range of interchanges, mothers keep to a constant value of 37–39 different speech act types per 30 minutes of interaction with children 16 months and older (see Table 6.2, Figure 6.2). However, mothers' variety of speech acts is *greater* with older children than with 12- to 14-month-olds, the opposite of the trend found for interchanges (see Section 2.1, Table 6.4, for contrasting findings in a laboratory setting).

TABLE 6.2  Number of Different Speech Acts Used by Children and by Mothers in a 30-Minute Interactive Session, by Children's Age

| | | Children | | Mothers | |
|---|---|---|---|---|---|
| Age in Months | N | Mean | SD | Mean | SD |
| 12 | 8 | 3.8 | 2.3 | 32.0 | 2.0 |
| 14 | 8 | 8.0 | 3.2 | 34.0 | 3.0 |
| 16 | 7 | 11.1 | 4.7 | 37.7 | 4.5 |
| 18 | 16 | 15.2 | 4.9 | 39.2 | 3.9 |
| 20 | 15 | 18.6 | 5.9 | 38.8 | 5.8 |
| 22 | 24 | 20.7 | 5.7 | 37.6 | 5.7 |
| 24 | 16 | 22.1 | 4.9 | 36.6 | 5.1 |
| 26 | 16 | 22.4 | 5.5 | 36.6 | 5.2 |
| 28 | 16 | 25.8 | 4.3 | 36.6 | 5.0 |
| 30 | 7 | 27.4 | 5.1 | 38.7 | 3.8 |
| 32 | 8 | 27.2 | 2.7 | 38.1 | 3.2 |

*Source:* A. Ninio. 1984. "Functions of Speech in Mother-Infant Interaction." Final Science Report to the U.S.-Israel Binational Science Foundation, Jerusalem, Israel.

FIGURE 6.2  Mean Number of Different Speech Acts Produced by Children in a 30-Minute Interaction, by Age

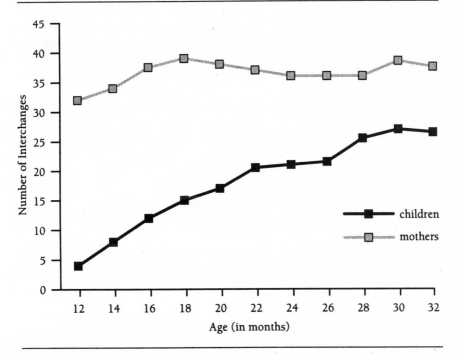

*Source:* A. Ninio. 1984. "Functions of Speech in Mother-Infant Interaction." Final Science Report to the U.S.-Israel Binational Science Foundation, Jerusalem, Israel.

Children's use of their speech act repertoire in interaction, like their use of the interchange repertoire, grows faster between 12 and 22 months of age than between 22 and 32 months, as shown by fitted growth curves for the three subsamples (Ninio, 1989). However, variety in children's speech act repertoires continued expanding throughout the age range studied and did not plateau like interchanges. Even so, at 32 months children's range and variety of speech acts were considerably below those of their mothers, with a wider gap than that for interchange repertoires. By 32 months children used about 44 percent of the 62 speech act types in a 30-minute session, whereas the mothers used about 60 percent (recall that for interchanges the comparable figures were 34 percent and 43 percent). Children probably do not yet know at 32 months how to express enough different verbal speech acts to approximate the variety employed by the mothers.

In summary, mothers maintain a remarkably constant level of speech use regardless of their children's ability to participate verbally in the relevant conversations. They do not limit their repertoire to their children's productive abilities, for example, matching children's circumscribed range at the earliest observations. For communicative intents, as for mean length of utterance and vocabulary, mothers do not simplify their speech below a certain level even with very young infants. Rather, they create a stable verbal interactive frame for children to grow into, just as they do with formats like peek-a-boo or joint picture-book reading: The adult keeps the game constant, and the child's contribution increases dramatically over time (Bruner & Sherwood, 1976; Ninio & Bruner, 1978). The mothers' asymptotic value of about 30 different interchange types and about 37 speech act types per 30 minutes probably represents some minimal range of communicative acts necessary for conducting face-to-face interaction of the type appropriate to children under three. The children become fairly adept with this range of speech uses by about two, although even by 32 months they have evidently not mastered it completely.

### 6.1.3 Developments in the distribution of major speech uses in interaction

The next question to be asked is how children's speech in interaction is distributed according to the major types of speech uses. Table 6.3 presents the mean proportion of children's utterance tokens belonging to seven major categories of speech use, as well as the distribution of maternal utterances addressed to 32-month-old (m32 in the table). At the earliest ages, about half of children's utterances consists of **game verbalizations**; the other half is distributed across **discussions of a joint focus of attention, action negotiations,** and the **management of joint and mutual attention.** Children neither initiate nor respond in **clarification episodes** and barely engage in **discussions of the nonpresent** or **markings of events.**

TABLE 6.3   Distribution of Utterances Emitted by Children in a 30-Minute Interactive Session, by Type of Major Speech Use and by Children's Age

| Age | N | Number of Tokens | | Relative Frequency of Tokens by Major Speech Use (means and SD) | | | | | | |
|---|---|---|---|---|---|---|---|---|---|---|
| | | Mean | (SD) | Verbal Moves in Games | Discussions of a Present Topic | Attention Negotiations | Action Negotiations | Discussions of the Non-Present | Markings and Polite Routines | Clarification Episodes |
| 12 | 8 | 11.4 | (8.7) | 49.6 (31.1) | 26.5 (33.8) | 6.1 (6.7) | 15.1 (19.5) | 1.7 (3.3) | 1.0 (2.7) | 0 (0.0) |
| 14 | 8 | 40.0 | (26.8) | 24.7 (20.7) | 43.6 (24.9) | 3.3 (6.2) | 24.5 (16.6) | 0.7 (1.9) | 0.3 (1.0) | 2.9 (3.8) |
| 16 | 7 | 57.1 | (37.9) | 25.2 (14.4) | 40.9 (31.0) | 5.2 (5.6) | 18.4 (13.7) | 2.6 (3.3) | 2.0 (2.6) | 4.8 (3.7) |
| 18 | 16 | 92.8 | (60.5) | 14.4 (12.7) | 36.4 (14.6) | 3.2 (2.4) | 36.4 (13.5) | 4.0 (4.5) | 1.7 (2.2) | 3.9 (3.2) |
| 20 | 15 | 138.7 | (73.8) | 12.0 (8.4) | 38.2 (13.0) | 2.7 (3.4) | 34.1 (12.5) | 4.5 (5.1) | 3.2 (4.3) | 5.4 (3.5) |
| 22 | 24 | 186.8 | (96.1) | 13.7 (12.3) | 39.2 (10.6) | 2.7 (2.8) | 31.4 (12.5) | 5.0 (4.6) | 2.7 (4.0) | 5.3 (3.6) |
| 24 | 16 | 219.3 | (79.0) | 7.7 (11.1) | 35.6 (13.8) | 2.5 (2.8) | 39.3 (16.3) | 6.4 (5.8) | 1.0 (1.0) | 7.5 (5.3) |
| 26 | 16 | 257.6 | (100.8) | 9.8 (12.1) | 39.6 (8.9) | 1.6 (1.9) | 36.2 (13.0) | 3.9 (3.8) | 2.1 (3.0) | 6.8 (3.1) |
| 28 | 16 | 261.4 | (95.9) | 5.7 (7.8) | 35.1 (12.4) | 1.8 (2.3) | 41.4 (14.5) | 8.0 (11.0) | 1.4 (1.4) | 6.5 (2.6) |
| 30 | 7 | 267.9 | (63.6) | 7.7 (11.8) | 31.1 (6.6) | 2.4 (1.1) | 43.3 (17.1) | 7.9 (7.3) | 1.1 (1.0) | 6.5 (2.9) |
| 32 | 8 | 295.6 | (49.3) | 4.5 (4.5) | 30.7 (10.7) | 2.4 (1.2) | 43.0 (14.8) | 7.6 (4.5) | 1.2 (1.2) | 10.6 (9.9) |
| M32 | 8 | 556.0 | (71.2) | 0.7 (1.3) | 28.8 (9.2) | 2.7 (2.0) | 50.3 (11.1) | 8.7 (4.8) | 1.1 (0.5) | 7.7 (1.8) |

Source: A. Ninio. 1984. "Functions of Speech in Mother-Infant Interactions." Final Science Report to the U.S.-Israel Binational Science Foundation, Jerusalem, Israel.

This distribution undergoes a gradual but consistent change, so that by 32 months it closely resembles the distribution of the speech of mothers (see Table 6.3 for distribution of maternal acts [m32]). The convergence is not total; even at this age children engage more frequently than their mothers in the production of game sounds and less frequently in action negotiation. But relative to the total picture of convergence, these are marginal phenomena. Changes in the children's speech uses are gradual, and it is hard to pinpoint where the distributions become more similar than different. Perhaps 24 months is the best approximation of a turning point, as there is a striking decrease in the proportion of game sounds and an increase in action negotiations, clarification moves, and discussions of the nonpresent, relative to previous observation points.

In Figure 6.3 we can see children's speech uses converge on the maternal distribution simultaneously for each type of major speech use, although with different profiles of convergence. For **performative or game verbalizations** (including imitation and onomatopoeic mimicking), which are early-appearing speech uses, mothers maintain a low level throughout development, and convergence consists of children gradually reducing their proportion of this speech use until it matches the mothers' use at about 28 months (Figure 6.3a). Figure 6.3a also presents the children's proportions of game-verbalization utterances, excluding imitation, to make maternal and child categories more comparable (mothers do not engage in imitation for imitation's sake). A similar picture emerges.

Of course, mothers do emit many game verbalizations—in fact, more than twice as many as the children in the 12–16-month period, even including imitation by the children. But since mothers use speech for many other purposes as well, whereas children are restricted to simple uses like game sounds, the proportion of mothers' total speech devoted to this use is very small. The reduction in proportion of performative utterances in children's speech between 12 and 30 months is thus a good diagnostic of their overall increased sophistication in speech use.

**Discussions of present topics** present a different picture (see Figure 6.3b). Included in this superordinate category are **Discussions of a joint focus of attention, of a recent event, of addressees' and speakers' inner states and feelings**, as well as **Negotiations of possession** and **Comforting**. However, the great majority of utterances fall into a single interchange type, namely, **Discussions of a joint focus of attention**, and as a consequence the figure mainly represents developments in this type of talk.

As with **Moves in games**, **Discussions of present topics** constitute a consistently higher proportion of children's talk than of mothers' talk. After a relatively slow start at 12 months (when, as we know, much of children's talk consists of game vocalizations), by 14 months there is a very large gap between the two distributions. However, unlike the case of **game sounds**, convergence is achieved by children gradually lowering, and by mothers gradually increas-

FIGURE 6.3    Relative Frequency of Utterances Produced by Mothers and Children, by Type of Major Speech Use and by Age

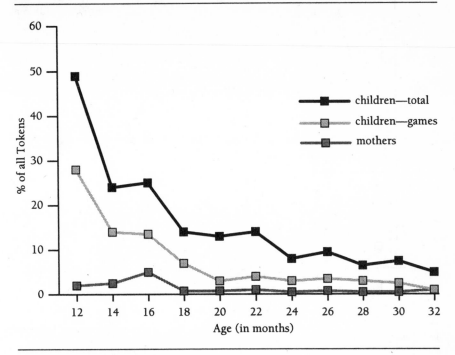

a: Performative or Game Verbalizations

ing, the proportion of utterances devoted to this type of speech use. By 32 months the two distributions almost reach a common value, a compromise between the children's and the mothers' starting points at 14 months. In contrast to game sounds, mothers adapt their rate of engagement in discussions to child age, ability, and interest in this type of talk.

Action negotiations (Figure 6.3c) present a mirror image of the previous pattern. Development starts with a very large discrepancy between the mothers and the children; this time mothers produce the larger proportion of utterances. Mothers talking to 12-month-olds devote 60 percent of their utterances to **action negotiation** and decrease to 50 percent by the time their children are 32 months old. This appears to be the most dominant type of speech use of mothers in interaction with children under three. Children already employ speech for action direction by 12 months, but they start with only 15 percent of their tokens allocated to this interactive goal, increasing gradually to a high of about 43 percent at 30–32 months. The disparity still existing at 32 months may reflect asymmetrical social roles, that is, greater maternal responsibility to organize action, rather than children's still incomplete competence to engage in action-negotiating talk.

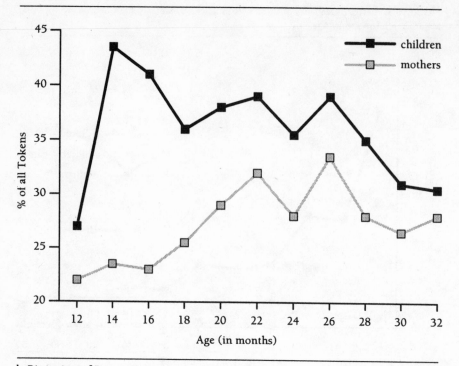

b: Discussions of Present Topics

There is one subtype of **action negotiation** in which no role asymmetry is expected: **self-directed action directives.** Children engage in this type of talk more frequently than their mothers after 16 months (see Figure 6.3d), suggesting that role specificity does explain children's lesser engagement in other **action negotiations,** as reflected in the aggregates of Figure 6.3c.

**Attention negotiations,** including calls and attention-directing and attentiveness-signaling speech uses, are used fairly comparably by mothers and children (Figure 6.3e). The two distributions are rather similar at 12 months, with mothers slightly higher, and they decrease to an identical value by 22 months. One might expect mothers to be more responsible for keeping the dyad in focused interaction, but children clearly acquire the verbal means necessary to take a role in attention negotiation very early (Section 4.1); the present results indicate that they spend about the same portion of their speaking time on this interactive function as mothers do, practically from the onset of speech.

The last three major speech uses start off at an almost null level in the speech of children at 12 months. These are **markings** (Figure 6.3f), **clarifications** (Figure 6.3g), and **discussions of nonpresent topics** (Figure 6.3h). Despite

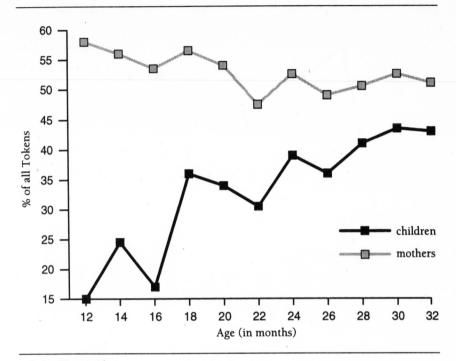

c: Action Negotiations

these similar beginnings, however, they show different patterns of convergence of maternal and child proportions of uses.

**Polite and other markings of events** are, interestingly, a relatively infrequent speech use by mothers as well as children. Children do produce small numbers of such utterances from the start of speech, but only by 16 months do they approximate their mothers' level of use. The proportion of markings decreases steadily in mothers' speech over the 12–32-month period, and children's use parallels mothers' usage except for the two earliest observations. Children do have an early and fairly extensive repertoire of markers of all sorts, according to parental reports (see Section 5.4). Their low frequency of use thus does not represent a competence limitation. The avoidance of this speech use is especially striking given the background of children's very extensive employment of other kinds of performative speech, uses such as verbal moves in interactive games. Perhaps the difference is in the much stronger interpersonal buildup of joint games than of the events that serve as the context for markings. Games are proposed, prepared, and their details explicitly negotiated; there is a very strong expectation that children will actually perform the relevant moves.

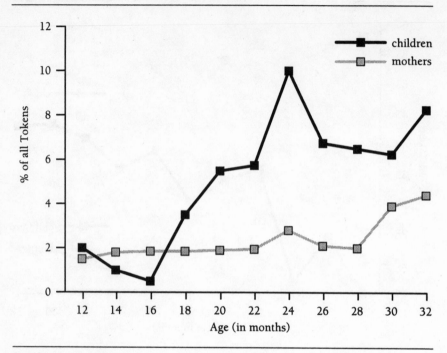

d: Self-Directed Action Directives

Events to be marked, like a toy falling to the floor, simply *happen,* and marking them by a vocalization is apparently optional.

Mothers devoted an increasing proportion of utterances to **clarifications of communication** as their children got older. Children started to participate in clarification episodes at 14 months, and the proportion of their utterances dealing with clarification remained very close to that of the mothers thereafter. Clarifications and markings started out at the same level (4.5 percent) in mothers' speech, but subsequently clarifications increased and markings decreased. Children seemed *to join* the mothers' trend after the first months for both markings and clarifications.

It seems as if mothers' proportions of talk devoted to these two interactive functions, and the age changes in these proportions, are determined by factors independent of children's ability to produce these types of utterances. Markings are among the most primitive types of speech uses; like games, they are nonpropositional and performative in character. Mothers may produce them before children do as a type of verbal game to fill in the interactive time. Clarifications are highly important procedural speech uses, and mothers use

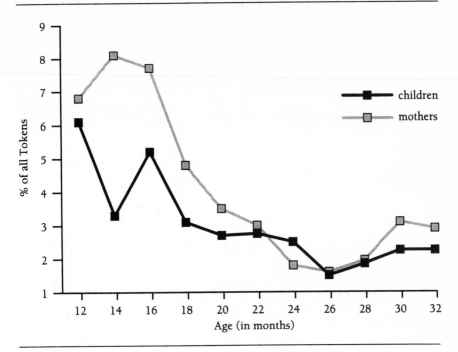

e: Attention Negotiations

them in real attempts to clarify what children mean in their communications and actions, even before the children can answer them verbally. For these reasons, mothers devote about 4 percent of their utterances to these uses in the 12–14 month period despite the children's lack of participation in the relevant interchanges (see Section 7.4 for a more detailed discussion of clarifications).

By contrast, **Discussion of the nonpresent** shows an almost perfect match of mother and child distributions throughout the period studied. In contrast to markings and clarification episodes, mothers devote no more of their talk to this speech use than their children do in the first months after the onset of speech in children. This pattern of convergence probably does represent pure fine-tuning by the mothers, namely, an adjustment of the content of their talk to the children (see Sachs, 1982). Topics related to the nonimmediate past or future and to hypothetical and abstract matters are largely beyond children's cognitive and linguistic capacity at the start of this period; only very gradually do children become able to process utterances dealing with such topics. Mothers do not engage in one-sided conversations or monologues with children on

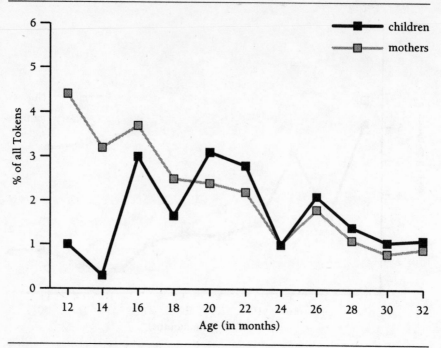

f: Polite and Other Markings of Events

subjects the latter cannot follow, but as soon as the children signal comprehension they start including nonpresent topics in their discussions.

In summary, mothers and children gradually become similar in the proportion of their utterances devoted to the major types of speech use. Convergence occurs for each type of speech use; however, the process by which mothers and children come to resemble each other in speech-use patterns is specific to each major type of speech use. In addition, for each type the two distributions reach a comparable value at a different point in development.

In some cases, the convergence reflects children's developing abilities to participate in maternal-initiated interactions and in others mothers adapting their speech to their children's capacities. Because the different uses of speech make varying cognitive and linguistic demands on children, some reach maternal values before others.

The convergence described here is in proportional use. Children produce many fewer utterances per observation than their mothers, and a higher relative frequency on their part does not necessarily mean a higher absolute frequency. A comparison of the absolute frequencies would show a very different picture.

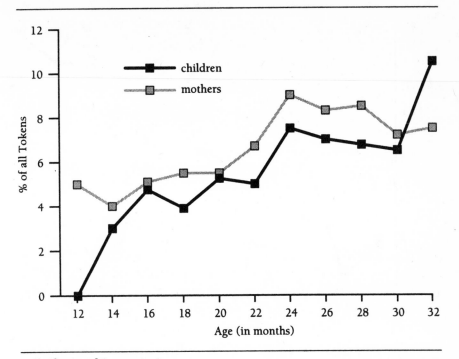

**g: Clarification of Communication**

The particulars of the convergence patterns for token proportions relate to the developmental ordering of these different speech uses (see Section 5.2). **Game sounds, markings,** and **attention directors,** whose use decreases with age in both mothers and children, represent early acquired speech uses more appropriate for younger than for more mature children. These nonsymbolic, nonpropositional speech uses, directly embedded in the interactive context, give way to more sophisticated speech uses as children get older. **Discussions of the nonpresent** and **clarification episodes,** whose use increases with age, are late-acquired, complex speech uses that require the speaker to distance her- or himself from the ongoing interactive or physical context, something very young children cannot do.

**Action negotiations** and **discussions of present topics** are intermediate between the previous two classes in their being related to, but not fused with, the context of speech. Their convergence patterns are the most complex: Action negotiations show a decreasing use by mothers and an increasing use by children, whereas discussions of present topics show the opposite pattern. These are early-acquired uses, but the specific communicative acts embedded

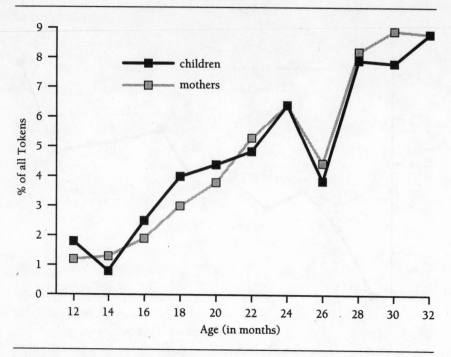

**h: Discussions of Nonpresent Topics**
*Source:* A. Ninio. 1984. "Functions of Speech in Mother-Infant Interaction." Final Science Report to the U.S.-Israel Binational Science Foundation, Jerusalem, Israel.

in them change and become much more sophisticated as children get older (see Section 5.6). Thus, the convergence in proportion of use reflects not only a growing correspondence between mothers' and children's investment in these verbal interactive functions in general but also an increasing similarity in the particular communicative acts used to negotiate action and conduct discussions. We shall explore some of these more detailed convergence patterns in four interchange types belonging to the family of **Action Negotiations**.

### 6.1.4 Developments in the distribution of subtypes of action negotiations

As we saw, mothers start with a very high proportion (60 percent) of their utterances in the general **Action-Negotiation** category, which they gradually lower to 50 percent by the end of the period covered by the longitudinal sample. Children, on the other hand, begin with a relatively low percentage (15

FIGURE 6.4   Distribution of Four Types of Action-Negotiation Interchanges in Maternal and Child Speech, by Age

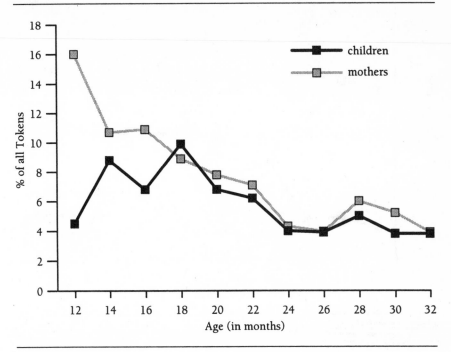

a: Initiate a New Activity

percent), which they increase—almost monotonically—to the high value of 40 percent by the end of the period (Figure 6.3c). Are these patterns repeated for four subtypes of action negotiation—**Initiate a new activity, Regulate hearer's acts, Attempt to end activity,** and **Propose addition of a recursive act**—representing kinds of speech uses acquired at different stages of development?

The developmental change in the proportion of utterances used to negotiate the **initiation of a new activity** (IPA) (Figure 6.4a) does not mirror the totals. First, the use of this interchange type declines in frequency in mothers' speech much faster than **Action Negotiations** overall. Second, children's use up to 24 months parallels the action-negotiation totals (of which IPA constitutes about 50 percent of all utterances during that period), but by 26 months the IPA proportion declines for children as for the mothers. Children's overall proportion of **Action-Negotiation** utterances is *increasing* during this period, so **Initiation of a new activity** constitutes a sharply decreasing proportion of **Action Negotiations**. Finally, children apparently already control this type of talk at a very high level by 18 months when they first use it as much as their mothers, a phenomenon that does not occur with other types of action negotiations.

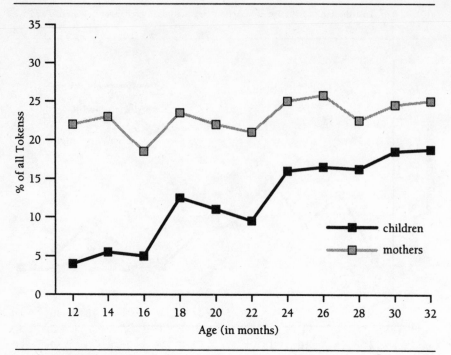

b: Regulate Hearer's Acts

**Regulate the hearer's acts** (RHA) shows a very different pattern (Figure 6.4b). Children start at a very low level, continue to increase the proportion of their use throughout the period observed, but do not reach the mothers' level even by 32 months. The distribution strongly resembles that for the **Action-Negotiation** totals (Figure 6.3c) after 24 months, once again because in this period about half of all **Action-Negotiation** talk is concerned with the regulation of individual acts.

By contrast, mothers' proportion of act-regulatory talk is dissimilar to the totals proportion; their proportion of RHA tokens does not decrease (as their totals do) but even increases somewhat during this period. Children's increasing use of RHA thus mirrors the maternal trend for this subtype of negotiations.

Children do not participate in the next interchange type, **Attempt to end an activity** (AEA, Figure 6.4c), until 16 months, but from then on children's distribution is nearly identical with that of the mothers, a constant low percentage of all utterances. **Attempts to end an activity** neither increase in children's talk nor decrease in mothers' talk, as do **Action Negotiations** in general; rather, they show no age-related changes.

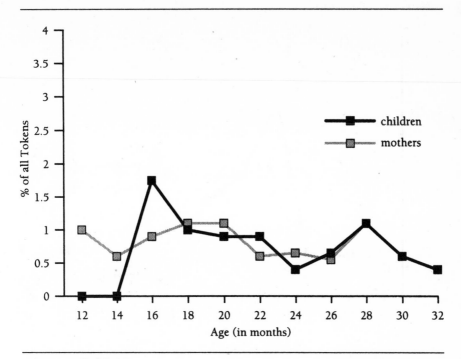

**c: Attempt to End Activity**

**Propose addition of a recursive act** (MOR, Figure 6.4d) is somewhat more central than AEA—at least for 6 months after emergence. Children do not participate in this kind of action negotiation before 18 months, but for the 6 months thereafter it is rather popular with children, who produce a much higher proportion of such utterances than their mothers. By 24 months this short-lived interest is over, and children, like their mothers throughout the period, devote a constant 1 percent or less of their utterances to this interactive function. This is one of a group of action-negotiation interchange types children show a tendency to over-use right after acquisition; others exhibiting this phenomenon include **Requesting the repetition of an activity** and **Requesting the continuation of an activity**. These interchange types are relatively late-acquired, "specialist" action-negotiation moves; apparently their acquisition involves an unusually intensive period of practice.

In summary, children's **Action-Negotiation** talk systematically changes in composition as children grow older and bring increasingly refined types of action negotiation under verbal control. There is a general pattern of convergence on the maternal proportion of use for **Action Negotiations**, but it reflects

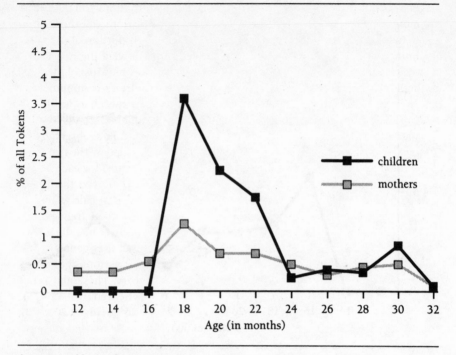

d: Propose Addition of a Recursive Act
*Source:* A. Ninio. 1984. "Functions of Speech in Mother-Infant Interaction." Final Science Report to the U.S.-Israel Binational Science Foundation, Jerusalem, Israel.

an average of several different developmental trends characterizing this heterogeneous system.

To summarize the findings regarding participation in verbal interaction, children gradually establish a substantial verbal-communicative repertoire that they come to use in much the same way as their mothers. The distribution of utterances produced in 30 minutes of free interaction over the major categories of speech use is radically different for mothers and 12-month-olds but is fairly similar for mothers and 32-month-olds. Children become equal partners in the interactions they conduct with their mothers.

The process of convergence is, however, specific to each major type of speech use, as well as to narrower categories of speech uses. Mothers use some categories, such as the initiation of new activities, frequently before children can take more than minimal part; in these cases children rise to maternal levels, learning to produce the communicative acts mothers have been consistently modeling. In other cases, for example, discussions of nonpresent topics, convergence between the two participants is the result of fine-tuning on the part of the mothers. In yet other cases, such as game verbalizations, mothers never match in relative frequency young children's very high proportion of use at the beginning of the period. They do not, in other words, "lower" their speech to mostly *boos* and *hau-haus* of imitations and semivocalizations. Most of the time, mothers talk like adults throughout the period; as children's communicative repertoires increase, game talk becomes marginal in their speech as well.

In spite of the considerable similarity in the developmental trends we have obtained on the basis of parental interviews and the longitudinal observational study, it is worth noticing the differences between data yielded by the two types of instruments. In the interviews, parents were asked to report for each of 100 verbal-communicative acts whether their child actually produced them. The developmental order of acquisition presented in Table 5.1 is a scale generated by these reports of absolute competence, without regard for the frequency at which the various acts may have been used by the children in interaction. Observations, by contrast, constitute samples of speech use; they generate data on the proportion of children producing particular acts at various ages or the frequencies of utterance tokens in each speech-use category. These may relate to developmental ordering, but the frequency of use is influenced by interactive agendas, as well as by speaker competence. Thus, high frequencies of use do not necessarily mean the relevant acts were acquired early or that they are simpler than other acts, and low frequencies do not mean late acquisition.

This is most clearly observed for markers. Even though, according to the parental interview study, many of these are acquired at an early age, in the observational study markers as a group do not constitute more than 3 percent of the utterances produced by children at any of the observational ages. If we looked at the individual frequencies of each type of marker separately, we would arrive at infinitesimal numbers, concluding erroneously that children are basically unable to produce any of these types of verbal-communicative acts—greetings, thanking, action-completion markers—before their third birthday. Despite their limitations, distributional statistics reveal important facts about children's developing command of the pragmatic uses of speech in interaction. We need both competence estimates and data on use patterns for a complete picture of children's developing mastery of verbal-communicative acts, as well as of lexical, syntactic, or morphological development.

## 6.2 The Harvard longitudinal observational study

In an attempt to develop measures for assessing pragmatic development and to relate aspects of pragmatic development to other domains of language development (e.g., lexicon, syntax, and morphology), Snow and her colleagues have carried out analyses on videotaped and transcribed data from 52 children and their parents, each observed for about 20 minutes in a laboratory playroom when the children were ages 14, 20, and 32 months (see also Pan, Snow, & Willett, 1995; Pan et al., 1996). The observation sessions were structured to ensure optimal comparability across both dyads and ages. At 14 and 20 months, spontaneous language data were collected during a 5-minute warm-up and several subsequent dyadic activities. During the warm-up period, the parent and child were left alone in a small room with a set of toys, and the parent was instructed to take a few minutes to let the child become accustomed to the setting. During the remaining semistructured free-play period, the parent was asked to play with the child using the contents of four boxes. The boxes contained, in order, a ball, a cloth for peek-a-boo, paper and crayons, and a book. Parents were not told how much time to spend on each box but were asked to have only one box open at a time and to try to get to all four boxes in about 10 minutes. The sessions were terminated only when the parent had tried to engage the child in all four activities; the duration of the structured play session ranged from 10 to 25 minutes, with greater variability at 14 than at 20 months.

The protocol for parent-child interaction at the third time point also involved the four boxes. There was no warm-up period. To render the activities age-appropriate, the ball and peek-a-boo cloth were replaced by hand puppets and a toy house.

The similarities and differences in design between this study and Ninio's observational study should be noted explicitly before we go on to discuss similarities and differences in findings. First, these data were collected to describe expected developmental levels in replicable observation settings rather than to provide a detailed analysis of the process of acquisition; thus, a relatively large number of children were observed at each age, but the intervals between observations were sufficiently long that the data do not provide a good basis for drawing conclusions about age of emergence. Second, observations were carried out in a laboratory rather than in the children's homes. Although unfamiliar settings lower estimates of children's language competence and exclude many activities that might occur at home, the uniformity of interactive settings across both children and ages provides maximal comparability. The comparability and relatively large sample size make these data a basis for establishing normative expectations against which to compare the communicative behaviors of children suspected of having language problems, as well as for comparing achievements in this domain of pragmatic skills to achievements in other language subsystems.

In the Harvard project, transcription and coding also differed from the Ninio project. First, communicative intents of children and mothers were coded using the INCA-A (see Chapter 2), a system based on Ninio and Wheeler (1984b) but abridged (Ninio et al., 1994) at the Interchange level, both to reflect the more restricted interactive settings observed and to simplify coding in the hopes of providing basic data on a system that might be adopted for use by clinicians and other language practitioners. Second, since we were interested in generating data of relevance to clinical assessment, often applied to older but still preverbal children, we included in our transcripts rich information about nonverbal communicative behaviors and coded nonverbal and partially verbal or vocal communicative attempts, as well as those that consisted clearly of words or proto-words. Third, we wished to demonstrate the validity of measures derived from the INCA-A as compared to more familiar assessments of pragmatic skills. Quantitative measures we used to reflect pragmatic ability included the number of communicative attempts produced by the child per minute; the proportion of communicative attempts that were interpretable (i.e., codable) on at least the Interchange level; the extent to which interpretability was dependent on nonverbal components; and the number of Interchange types, Speech Act types, and Interchange–Speech Act combination types produced by a child at an observation. The Interchange–Speech Act–type measure is referred to here as Pragmatic Flexibility. Fourth, to assess child competence conservatively in light of the limited observational data, when comparing Interchange, Speech Act, and Interchange–Speech Act combination repertoires (i.e., type measures) across subjects, only those types produced at least twice were considered.

### 6.2.1 Pragmatic development of 14-, 20-, and 32-month-olds

As Table 6.4 (adapted from Snow et al., 1996; Pan et al., 1996) shows, children as a group increased from 14 to 32 months on all the measures of pragmatic skill used: number of communicative attempts per minute, number of Interchange and Speech Act types, and Pragmatic Flexibility. We discuss the increase in communicative attempts per minute, which include many nonverbal acts, and in interpretability in Section 6.3.1; attempts included in this count need not be transcribable or interpretable, that is, the scores reflect a real increase in children's interest in communication and not just growth in intelligibility.

At 14 months the modal child participated in just 4 different Interchange types, whereas this number grew to 7 at 20 months and to 8 at 32 months. At 14 months, most children were just beginning to engage in communicative activities in this laboratory setting. Six of the 52 14-month-olds produced no communicative acts that could be coded at the Interchange level, but by 20 months no child produced fewer than 2 interchanges. Mothers used an average of about 12 interchanges at all child ages.

Does the repertoire of Interchange types observed in this long-interval laboratory study match those reported earlier for the interview and the more intensive observational study of Ninio? There were many differences that might influence results: the coding system, the inclusion of uninterpretable utterances (those coded at the Interchange level as YYY or at the Speech Act level as yy) by Snow and colleagues, the inclusion of nonverbal communicative attempts, as well as observational setting. Although we expect differences in speech-use distribution, the basic repertoire of speech uses by mothers and children should match.

TABLE 6.4   Basic Indicators of Communicative Performance for Mothers and Children

| | Children | | | Mothers | | |
|---|---|---|---|---|---|---|
| | 14 months | 20 months | 32 months | 14 months | 20 months | 32 months |
| Communicative attempts per minute | 4.4 | 7.9 | 11.2 | 21.0 | 23.2 | 19.3 |
| Interchange types | 4.0 | 6.9 | 8.5 | 12.5 | 12.3 | 11.4 |
| Speech act types | 3.8 | 10.5 | 14.4 | 20.1 | 23.2 | 19.2 |
| Pragmatic flexibility | 5.1 | 14.2 | 22.7 | 35.6 | 40.4 | 34.2 |

Sources: Adapted from C. E. Snow, B. Pan, A. Imbens-Bailey, and J. Herman. 1996. "Learning How to Say What One Means: A Longitudinal Study of Children's Speech Act Use." Social Development 5: 56–84; B. Pan, A. Imbens-Bailey, K. Winner, and C. E. Snow. 1996. "Communicative Intents of Parents Interacting with Their Young Children." Merrill-Palmer Quarterly 42: 72–90.

At 14 months, the most commonly observed Interchanges across children were **Directing the hearer's attention, Negotiating the immediate activity,** and **Discussing a joint focus;** Ninio reported relatively fewer attention negotiations at these early ages and relatively more game-related talk (markings and moves in games together made up only about 12 percent of 14-month-olds' interpretable utterances in the Snow et al. study). The high incidence of children engaging in **Directing hearer's attention** interchanges may have to do with the novel setting and with the mothers' sense of obligation to use the contents of all four boxes. Ninio, of course, distinguished many more subtypes within the interchange coded as **Negotiating immediate activity.** Although the INCA-A lumps a wide variety of markings into a single category, nonetheless relatively few 14-month-olds (42 percent) **Marked events,** and even fewer (6 percent) produced **Performatives.** Although no interchange type was used by over 90 percent of the children at 14 months, a "core repertoire" was starting to emerge: A substantial percentage of children engaged in **Directing hearer's attention, Negotiating immediate activity,** and **Discussing a joint focus,** the most frequent interchanges (together they accounted for 34 percent of child communicative acts and over 70 percent of interpretable acts).

By age 20 months, nearly all the children engaged in **Negotiating immediate activity, Directing hearer's attention,** and **Discussing a joint focus,** which together accounted for 63 percent of child communicative acts. A second group of Interchange types (**Discussing topics related to the present, Markings, Negotiating mutual attention,** as well as **Discussing clarification of communication**) was emerging strongly at 20 months; as discussed earlier, these slightly later-emerging Interchanges are less inextricably embedded in the context of ongoing activity and reflect the children's abilities to produce more complex utterances and to conceive of communicative intentions that are distinct from nonverbal activity. For example, with scaffolding help from her mother, 20-

month-old Rachel relates the toy at hand to her memory of a televised football game in a discussion that moves from **Joint focus** to **Topic related to the present** (xxx indicates uninterpretable segment):

*Example 6.1*

| | |
|---|---|
| Child: | ball. |
| Mother: | that's a football ball? |
| Child: | yes. |
| Mother: | yeah. |
| Child: | people play. |
| Child: | xxx on the tv xxx. |
| Mother: | people play football on tv? |

Similarly, engaging in clarification of communicative attempts (one's own or those of others) requires that the child suspend focus on the here and now until the misunderstanding can be resolved (see Section 7.4). It is perhaps surprising that **Marking of an event** (*oops, uh-oh*) and **Negotiating mutual attention** (e.g., calling the mother by name) are not among the earliest-emerging Interchanges observed. **Markings**, although early-emerging, are rather infrequently occurring (see Section 6.1.3), and **Negotiating mutual attention** may simply not be necessary in a laboratory setting where mothers take it as their task to play with their children.

At 20 months, **Negotiating immediate activity** and **Discussing a joint focus** became relatively more frequent than **Direct hearer's attention**, which had been the most frequent interchange at 14 months. Whereas 10 percent of all child acts at 20 months were **Performatives**, only 17 percent of 20-month-olds produced **Performatives**, which is surprising given that all the dyads had a towel to play peek-a-boo with, a context in which performative talk should emerge. These findings mirror the patterns from the Ninio study reported earlier—an increase in **Discussions** and **Action negotiations** whereas **Attention negotiations** and **Game talk** declined. **Markings**, **Negotiating mutual attention**, and **Clarification discussions** each accounted for a small fraction of the total communicative acts produced by the children at 20 months, but by 32 months they were more general (over 80 percent of children) and more frequent.

A third set of Interchange types used by only a few children at 20 months but displayed by 54–70 percent of the 32-month-olds included **Discussing the nonpresent**, **Discussing a recent event**, and **Discussing the hearer's nonobservable thoughts and feelings**. The emergence of these more sophisticated, more decontextualized discussions echoes Ninio's findings. Consider these examples of increasingly sophisticated discussions from one child in the sample, Andrew. At 20 months Andrew gets rather generously credited with participating in **Discussions of topics related to the present** because he responds to his mother's moving from naming pictures of animals in books to eliciting information about stereotypical animal sounds. The dyad is exploiting, for purposes of discussion, well-rehearsed formats that might well have been called mimicking games had they occurred under slightly different circumstances. Only in the final example presented of Andrew at 20 months does he participate in a discussion of a past event.

*Example 6.2,* Andrew at 20 months

| | |
|---|---|
| Mother: | those are birdies. |
| Child: | birdies. |
| Mother: | and the name of these kinds of birdies they call owls. |
| Mother: | and they say hoo-hoo. |
| Child: | hoo. |

*Example 6.3,* Andrew at 20 months

| | |
|---|---|
| Mother: | there's a lamb. |
| Child: | lamb. |
| Mother: | lamb says baa. |
| Child: | baa! |
| Child: | lamb. |

*Example 6.4,* Andrew at 20 months

| | |
|---|---|
| Mother: | does that [= picture in book] look like the shark that Terry and Jamie were playing with in the pool yesterday? |
| Mother: | do you remember that? |
| Child: | shark! |
| Mother: | yeah, it does look like a shark. |

At 32 months, however, Andrew participates fully in **Discussions of topics related to the present**, even initiating them in some cases, as the following example (which occurred during book reading) demonstrates.

*Example 6.5,* Andrew at 32 months

| | |
|---|---|
| Child: | is this [= picture] a raincoat? |
| Mother: | looks like a raincoat to me. |
| Child: | can you go in the snow with this? |
| Mother: | yeah, you can go in the snow. |
| Mother: | or you can go in the rain. |

Development is reflected not only by the addition of communicative capacities but also by the recession of certain communicative activities that were frequent or even dominant at earlier ages. For example, the frequency of **Direct hearer's attention** fell from 15 percent of all communicative acts at 14 months to only 6 percent at 32 months, perhaps because older children become better able to join the adult's focus of attention and have less need to control the topic in order

TABLE 6.5    Mean Percentage of Interpretable Maternal and Child Communicative Acts in Each of the Most Frequently Occurring Interchanges

|  | 14 Months | | 20 Months | | 32 Months | |
| --- | --- | --- | --- | --- | --- | --- |
|  | Children | Mothers | Children | Mothers | Children | Mothers |
| DHA | 34 | 10 | 17 | 10 | 6 | 13 |
| NIA | 27 | 42 | 37 | 42 | 42 | 39 |
| DJF | 16 | 15 | 27 | 20 | 32 | 26 |
| MRK | 11 | 7 | 4 | 4 | 4 | 4 |
| PRP | 4 | 2 | 5 | 4 | 2 | 3 |
| PRO | 2 | 5 | 1 | 4 | 0 | 0 |
| DCC | 0 | 1 | 4 | 4 | 3 | 4 |
| NMA | 4 | 6 | 4 | 3 | 2 | 3 |
| DNP | 0 | 0 | 1 | 1 | 2 | 1 |
| DCA | 0 | 2 | 1 | 1 | 0 | 0 |
| DHS | 0 | 2 | 0 | 1 | 1 | 1 |

*Sources:* Adapted from C. E. Snow, B. Pan, A. Imbens-Bailey, and J. Herman. 1996. "Learning How to Say What One Means: A Longitudinal Study of Children's Speech Act Uses." *Social Development* 5: 56–84; B. Pan, A. Imbens-Bailey, K. Winner, and C. E. Snow. 1996. "Communicative Intents of Parents Interacting with Their Young Children." *Merrill-Palmer Quarterly* 42: 72–90.

to be able to discuss it, and also because older children have a bigger range of communicative intents to express.

As discussed previously, data on proportional use by children are more interpretable when compared to adult speech use. Since these interchanges are socially constructed, child participation in them often requires adult initiation. Both child and adult percentages of participation in the most frequent speech interchanges are given in Table 6.5 for comparison.

Adults in this study show relatively stable rates of talk **Directing hearer's attention,** initially considerably lower than the children, and of talk **Negotiating immediate activity,** initially considerably higher than the children. **Performatives,** and **Negotiating mutual attention** decline more markedly for mothers than for children, whereas **Discussing a joint focus, discussing clarification of communication,** and **Discussing the nonpresent** increase in relative frequency in maternal talk, as they do in the children's talk.

At the level of speech act, similar trends were observed: Individual children's overall repertoire expands with age, the number of children using any given speech act increases with age, different children converge on a core set of speech acts that all control, and the ability to use well-established speech acts within new interchanges grows. Some speech acts, of course, depend crucially on the interlocutor—one can only answer a wh-question, for example, after a wh-question has been asked, and one can put forth a countersuggestion only after a suggestion has been made. Thus, children's production of these speech acts must be interpreted in light of mothers' production for reasons of

complementarity rather than simply co-participation. Furthermore, some interchanges are particularly rich contexts for the diversification of the speech act
repertoire (e.g., **Discussions** of various sorts and **Negotiations**), whereas other
are limited (**Directing hearer's attention** and **Markings**; see Snow et al., 1996).

## 6.2.2 Observed speech act repertoire

Using our two-token criterion for control of a speech act category, we tallied
the number of children who displayed each speech act at each age. At 14 months,
no speech act was used by more than a third of the children. The most generally
displayed speech acts were **transfer object**, **repetition**, **statement**, **markings**,
**answering wh-questions**, **request/propose**, **prohibit/protest**, and **performative**. With the exception of **transfer object** and **prohibit/protest**, all of these are
displayed by a majority of children at 20 months. **Prohibit/protest** and **performative** are used by fewer children at 32 months than at 20 months. At 20 months,
a majority of children also displayed control of **refuse to do**, **agree to do**,
**affirmative answer to yes-no question**, and **state intent**. Most 32-month-olds
continued to engage in these speech acts, with the exception of **refuse to do**. At
32 months, **wh-** and **yes-no questions** emerged in the repertoires of a majority
of the children; the presence of answers at 14 and 20 months confirms that they
had been hearing and responding to these questions for some months before
starting to ask them. In addition, a majority of the children produced **acknowledgments**. Approximately 20 percent of the 32-month-olds displayed control
of **request reruns**, **declaration of new state of affairs**, **supply completion**, **agree
with proposition**, **disagree with proposition**, **answer in the negative to a
yes-no question**, and **request with yes-no question**.

These categories no doubt become more general during the subsequent
stage of development. Some of them reflect new abilities to operate at the
discourse level, responding to the interlocutor's propositions with **agreements**
or **disagreements** or marking episodes explicitly by **declaring a new state of
affairs**. **Requests expressed as yes-no questions** start to emerge only at 32
months, despite the fact that most children at this age are demonstrating the
ability to ask yes-no questions for other purposes and that they have been
exposed to maternal questions about their wishes or intentions frequently since
birth. Speech acts that are still extremely marginal by 32 months include some
that are characteristically parental speech acts (e.g., **approve behavior**) and
others that clearly require cognitive and discourse sophistication (e.g., **give
reason** or **criticize**).

The early-emerging speech act categories were the ones used most often
at 14 months. The proportional use of some early-emerging speech acts
declines with age, because the older children have more alternative speech act
categories at their control. Categories of speech acts used in discussion
interchanges, on the other hand, come to be both more frequent and more

widespread in the children's speech over this age range. It is worth noting, though, that categories like **transfer object**, which are used early and by a relatively high proportion of children, nonetheless never constitute more than 1 percent of the observed speech acts.

## 6.3 Refining verbal communication

Concurrent with the basic task of acquiring a verbal-communicative act repertoire, children's mastery of the speech-use system undergoes developmental changes on other dimensions during the early years. Their speech increases in interpretability, they rely increasingly on verbal rather than nonverbal means for expressing their intents, and their communicative strategies grow in sophistication. By age two children display a wide repertoire of communicative intents expressed verbally but have not yet mastered the full array of means for expressing those intents with optimal effectiveness. Control over the rules for expressing intents politely and for taking into account the other's point of view (the essence, after all, of politeness) continues to develop over several more years or decades.

### 6.3.1 Increases in interpretability

As children get older, their utterances become easier to understand, not just in terms of the words used but also in terms of the intents being expressed. Of course, 100 percent interpretability is probably never achieved—even in conversations among adults a certain low level of ambiguity about intent is maintained. However, young children's utterances are often uninterpretable at the level of signal as well as meaning.

Snow and colleagues (1996) found that 55 percent of communicative attempts produced by the 14-month-old children in their study were uninterpretable, even at the level of Interchange (see section 6.2.1 for further details). Another sizable proportion of attempts (15 percent) were interpretable at the Interchange level but not at the Speech Act level. In other words, it was often clear that the child was directing the hearer's attention to an object, but it was unclear whether the child was, for example, stating a proposition or requesting information about the object. Often, interpretation of the child's communicative attempt at the Interchange level was possible by virtue of accompanying nonverbal components (such as a point, a nod, or an operation on an object). For example, John directs his mother's attention to a football with a combination of vocalization and showing behavior.

*Example 6.6*
    Child:        vocalizes while picking up football and holding it out to his mother

speech act:   Direct hearer's attention uninterpretably except for nonverbal
              actions
Mother:       football!
speech act:   Discuss joint focus of attention with a statement

Here, it was the behavioral complex, including an act of extending the football toward his mother and a vocalization, that enabled John's communicative intent to be interpreted as **Directing hearer's attention** and that enabled his mother to proceed to a discussion of an established joint focus of attention.

### 6.3.2 Decrease in reliance on nonverbal means

During the first period of speech use, children continue to rely heavily on nonverbal communicative gestures to get their intents across, whether as the sole means of communication or accompanying verbal expressions. Some investigators even claim that during this period the communicative intent of the utterance is carried only by the nonverbal signals—gestures, actions, intonation—rather than by the accompanying expressions (cf. Barrett, 1989; Dore, 1975; see Section 3.2.2). Others holding a less extreme view (Bates, 1979; Nelson, 1985) have nevertheless pointed out that children's early speech is typically part of a behavioral complex including nonspeech action.

Children's reliance on the nonverbal channel to complement their verbal utterances gradually decreases with age; the use of the gestural mode as a free-standing channel of communication, however, follows an inverted U-shaped developmental curve. In a longitudinal study of six infants ages 8 to 15 months, Carpenter, Mastergeorge, and Coggins (1983) defined three modes of expression: **gestural**, including pointing, giving, gazing, and the like; **gestural/vocal**, a combination of gesture with "simple sounds" (e.g., *uh-uh*), apparently semiconventional key-word verbalizations; and **verbal**, words or word combinations serving a referential or descriptive function. Unfortunately, the **verbal** category included words plus gestures, so the results provide no information on the abandonment of gestures as accompaniments to verbal communication.

What we can learn from this study, however, is a rather surprising fact about gestural communication: Gestural communication alone, without an accompanying vocal component, is not an early-emerging behavior. At 8 months, children's intentional communicative moves were almost never solely gestural; more than 95 percent of communicative gestures were accompanied by a vocalization. The proportion of acts consisting of **gesture alone** increased steeply between 8 and 10 months, from less than 5 percent to about 50 percent of all communications, then declined again to about 10 percent at 15 months. Free-standing gestures had many of the characteristics of the contemporaneous verbal-communicative acts; according to Carpenter and colleagues, free gestures were used for such sharply delimited acts as protesting, requesting objects and actions, and directing attention. During this period, most of children's utterances were the nonreferential, key-word–type, presymbolic kind, similar to the earliest speech uses found in other studies (e.g., Ninio, 1993b; see Section 4.1, Table 4.2); referential and descriptive utterances (**verbal** moves as defined previously) were very infrequent, at no point surpassing 10 percent of all communications.

Communicative gestures as a free-standing means of communication are a relatively late acquisition that seems to develop in parallel with the first set of linguistic signs and in the context of very similar individual "language games." The gestural channel of communication is evidently tried and abandoned just as the linguistic system is about to undergo the major reorganization that introduces true, symbolic linguistic signals.

Carpenter, Mastergeorge, and Coggins restricted their database to child behaviors occurring in contexts of mutual or shared activity with an adult. This restriction may have excluded communicative acts designed to bring about mutual or joint action, such as **calling** to attract the adult's attention or **initiating activities**. Indeed, their coding system for types of communicative acts does not include **Calling**, nor is it mentioned among the six earliest speech acts identified. (Note, though, that **Calling** is one of the communicative acts least susceptible to purely gestural encoding.) Other types of communicative acts were also excluded, such as **verbal moves in game formats** or **greetings**. It is unclear how these restrictions affect conclusions about free-standing gestures as a distinct channel of communication.

Greenfield and Smith (1976) claimed that the nonverbal or gestural communication channel has an important role in the operation of single-word speech: Very often, children systematically combine utterances with nonverbal acts to express semantic relations between two different elements of their communicative intent. For example, children at this stage might combine the word *give* with a point at the relevant object, expressing, according to Greenfield and Smith, the semantic action-object relation; or the word *food* with a head shake, meaning "no more food," to encode negation; or—a virtuoso early production—a head shake combined with a point to another's bare feet and the words *shoes on,* glossed as something like "she doesn't have her shoes on." Even though Greenfield and Smith's claim has been criticized on theoretical grounds for a variety of sometimes contradictory reasons (cf. Brown, 1973; Dore, 1975; Griffiths, 1985; Pea, 1979), later research confirms the systematic nature of verbal-nonverbal combinations in the generation of relational meanings. For example, in a recent study, Morford and Goldin-Meadow (1992) found that children's spontaneous word-gesture combinations at the single-word stage consisted, in the majority of cases, of an expressed action word and a gestural reference to a contextual "object" argument but only rarely of a gestural "action word" combined with a verbally expressed "object element."

TABLE 6.6   Contribution of Nonverbal Information to Interpretability of Children's Communicative Attempts

| Age (in months) | 14 | 20 | 32 |
|---|---|---|---|
| Number | 52 | 48 | 37 |
| Total child communicative acts | 3,005 | 5,215 | 5,767 |
| Total acts interpretable only with help of nonverbal information | 1,408 | 1,088 | 153 |
| Number interpretable at interchange level | 750 | 1,007 | 152 |
| Number interpretable at speech act level | 310 | 522 | 142 |

Sources: Adapted from C. E. Snow, B. Pan, A. Imbens-Bailey, and J. Herman. 1996. "Learning How to Say What One Means: A Longitudinal Study of Children's Speech Act Use." Social Development 5: 56–84; B. Pan, A. Imbens-Bailey, K. Winner, and C. E. Snow. 1996. "Communicative Intents of Parents Interacting with Their Young Children." Merrill-Palmer Quarterly 42: 72–90.

Adults' reliance on children's gestures as a basis for judging their communicative intents declined as children got older (Snow et al., 1996). Communicative acts that were interpretable only with reliance on nonverbal information made up almost 50 percent of all communicative acts observed at 14 months but declined to about 20 percent and less than 3 percent at 20 and 32 months, respectively (see Table 6.6).

Of course, gestures do not disappear from the communicative system after the first three years of life. Their role in adult communication, as well as their cross-cultural variation, has been documented in work by Argyle (e.g., Argyle & Cook, 1976), von Raffler-Engel (1971), and others. However, they become less important in conveying information crucial to the interpretation of the speaker's intent at the illocutionary level; evidence that interlocutors who develop a positive mutual regard mirror each other's postures and gestures suggests that more subtle kinds of information may indeed be conveyed by gestures throughout adulthood.

### 6.3.3 Development of indirect communicative strategies

Communicative intents can be expressed in many different ways. Perhaps the most prominent example is provided by the family of directives; it is well known that apart from explicit orders or requests, typically couched in the imperative mood, there are various indirect ways in which the speaker can communicate the wish that some action be performed. Speakers may make a statement about their own wishes, as in I wish I had some paper clips; they may express a preference for some action, as in I would like you to sign this document; they may express a need, as in I need the brakes checked, or even just describe some state of affairs the listener is meant to understand needs correction, as in The car doesn't start when it's cold. If any of these is uttered in the right context, the addressee will "hear" it as a directive (see Searle, 1975, for a discussion). Other types of complex or indirect communicative strategies, such as ellipsis, have been discussed by Goffman (1976), Labov and Fanshel (1977), and MacWhinney (1984). It is clear that children need to learn to interpret and generate indirect speech acts, as well as the more explicit or direct kind.

Most of the developmental work on the acquisition of indirect communicative strategies has concentrated on indirect requests (presumably because these are thought to be more difficult to process), and our discussion will focus on them. In a seminal study of requests for action, Garvey (1975) found that children as young as 3;6–4;4 (her lower age limit) could already produce successful indirect requests for actions, although her older group (4;7–5;7) produced a larger proportion of indirect requests. These children used adultlike strategies for expressing indirect requests (cf. Gordon & Lakoff, 1971), mostly asking questions about the addressee's ability or willingness to perform an act. More infrequent strategies included questions about the addressee's reasons for *not* performing some act, reminders of the addressee's obligations, and requests not to forget to perform an act. An adult strategy not used by the children was asserting a wish for the addressee to perform the relevant act.

Ervin-Tripp and Gordon (1986) found the most prominent form of non-explicit request among 2- to 8-year-old children was the statement of speaker's need or want, a form not reported by Garvey. This difference may reflect divergent definitions of the domain investigated, with Garvey targeting requests for actions and Ervin-Tripp and Gordon directives in general. Even though Garvey's a priori restriction of her domain of inquiry is perfectly legitimate, it is surprising that she did not find any requests for action among the children's early "expression of need or want" statements. Children's early requests are severely reduced in verbal form, so it is not always obvious whether an object or an action is being requested. When a child holds out her bottle and says *Juice!* or, later on, *I want juice,* she may well intend to convey the request that the addressee perform the action of filling her bottle. Similarly, when engaged in dyadic play, children may express a request for an object but in fact be requesting help with the activity. As indirect requests of the "expression of need or want" type are among the earliest and most frequent requestive forms reported in other studies (cf. Wells, 1985), Garvey's decision evidently excluded most of children's early requests from her database.

Ervin-Tripp (1977) found that by age 2;6 children vary the form of their requests according to the addressee, using indirect forms more frequently to adults than to peers. Children are able to produce various types of indirect requests at a very early age, and they are aware of the desirability of using these indirect forms with addressees whose status is higher than theirs (Becker, 1982; Ervin-Tripp & Gordon, 1986). In dyadic interactions with peers, the proportion of indirect requests does not increase between 4 and 8 years (Levin & Rubin, 1983). These findings suggest that at a very young age children control and respond to two of the basic analytic dimensions underlying polite behavior—the social distance from, and relative power of, the interlocutor (Brown & Levinson, 1978, 1987). In Brown and Levinson's terms, face-threatening acts like requests are typically mitigated or made less direct when addressed to relatively distant and/or relatively powerful individuals. Children's abilities to conform to rules like these depend on their understanding of and ability to produce less direct forms and on their understanding of the social dimensions of power and distance. Although children evidently understand power and distance and have some idea of how to respond to them, they still do not control the full repertoire of highly mitigated forms. Hints, for example, which are the most extreme response to face threats because they are totally deniable (e.g., *I did say it was delicious, but I really didn't mean I wanted another serving*), do not emerge until about age 8.

Moreover, there is evidence that children as young as 2 (Shatz, 1978) interpret indirect requests correctly as requests for action instead of responding to their overt illocutionary force; for example, a young child hearing *Do you want to move your skates?* does not interpret this as a sincere question to which *Not really* might be an appropriate response. In fact, achieving such a misinterpretation deliberately requires considerable meta-pragmatic sophistication, as does understanding the pragmatic violations at the core of the jokes most popular with children ages 5 to 8 (e.g., *Why did the chicken cross the road?* or *What's the difference between a blueberry and an elephant?*) Children's judgments of the true intent underlying various indirect forms and of their differential politeness levels become more subtle with age (e.g., Becker, 1986; Cherry Wilkinson & Dollaghan, 1979). As Gordon and colleagues (1980) pointed out, this later development is a result less of children's increased linguistic resources than of an increase in their social understanding.

In summary, children's gradual mastery of the indirect request system exhibits the same type of developmental phenomena as their mastery of verbal-communicative acts in general. This system has its roots in early speech uses, driven by children's capacity to acquire conventional forms for expressing their own communicative intents. The system undergoes further refinement as children acquire a variety of options for expressing their requests and learn something about the rules that dictate the use of more or less mitigated forms in various social situations. Ultimately, during the school years, continued development in control over polite request forms is driven in good part by the maturation of social abilities, in particular the capacity to take the perspective of the request recipient.

### 6.3.4 Improving the effectiveness of communication

Although two-year-olds are effective in making their intentions known, they rely on the indulgence of adults rather than verbal skill to achieve their *perlocutionary goals.* They do not yet control subtle linguistic mechanisms to enhance the likelihood that the listener will be influenced. In sophisticated uses of speech, it is not enough that the listener understand that the speaker made a claim; the speaker also intends for the addressee to be convinced by the claim. Similarly, a speaker producing a directive wants it to result in the addressee actually carrying out the relevant act.

Even in the most fundamental domain of getting one's intents across, effectiveness as a communicator probably depends on the mastery of a host of cognitive principles that at present are not well understood and whose developmental history has not yet been charted. Some candidates for this list include the conversational maxims and perspective-taking.

The principle of complementarity states that the encoding of communicative intent in a verbal form involves anticipatory decoding, taking the listener's assumptions, knowledge, and point of view into consideration (Chafe, 1974; Goffman, 1983; Rommetveit, 1974). This principle underlies such pragmatically central behaviors as the choice of style and the adjustment of form and content of talk to the listener (see Chapter 8). The principles of succinctness and informativeness, as well as the other "*conversational maxims*" formulated by Grice (1975), state, roughly, that speakers speak to the point and provide necessary and sufficient information to the listener.

The control of both the conversational maxims and complementarity involves perspective-taking, that is, taking the needs, knowledge, and interpretative abilities of the addressee into account. Young children may not control these skills except in the most rudimentary way. As Greenfield (1980) suggested, very young children may even be too egocentric to understand the principle that talk is supposed to satisfy the addressee's informational requirements and instead may operate on a more primitive principle of reducing their own uncertainty in their choice of what to say. The gradual refinement of these pragmatic skills is a domain in which considerable research remains to be done.

# 7
# Children as Conversationalists

## 7.1 Overview of the problem

In the previous chapters we have described children's development toward an adultlike system for expressing communicative attempts. During the earliest period children can map utterances directly onto intentions appropriate to particular interpersonal situations (e.g., saying *bye-bye* at leave-taking, responding to maternal elicitations with imitations, providing responses in well-practiced routines, like indicating body parts or providing animal sounds). These early capacities are both communicative and highly interactive, but during this stage children are not yet really exchanging information, for example, providing statements during discussions or responding to adult requests for clarification of their utterances. Only later do they express intents related in content, as well as in form, to previous utterances from the interlocutor (e.g., providing informative answers to sincere or novel-information–seeking questions, acknowledging requests, or requesting clarification of the interlocutor's utterance).

This later-emerging ability to relate one's own utterance to the preceding utterance of the interlocutor appropriately and in a content-based way is, of course, an essential component of conversational skill. It may seem paradoxical that we identify this centrally conversational skill as late-emerging, since conversation is one of the domains in which children are widely assumed to be precocious. One goal of this chapter is to reconcile the claim of conversational precocity (which we accept) with evidence about conversational inadequacies of young children, which we will demonstrate. Their inadequacies include a tendency not to respond appropriately to many conversational-exchange starters, failures to maintain conversational topic, lack of resources for starting conversations with relative strangers, difficulties in gauging the interlocutor's state of knowledge, and other such obstacles to full participation as skilled conversationalists. Conversational skill has a number of components, some strictly linguistic and others more clearly social or interactive; young children are fairly accomplished at some yet rather poor at others.

### 7.1.1. Characteristics of a skilled conversation

Consider the following example of a highly competent conversational exchange between former spouses a couple of years after their divorce:

| Henry: | How are things with your friend? An architect, isn't he? |
| Charlotte: | I had to give him the elbow. Well, he sort of left. I called him the architect of my misfortune. |
| Henry: | What was the matter with him? |
| Charlotte: | Very possessive type. I came home from a job, I'd been away only a couple of days, and he said, why did I take my diaphragm? He'd been through my bathroom cabinet, would you believe? And then, not finding it, he went through everything else. Can't have that. |
| Henry: | What did you say? |
| Charlotte: | I said, I didn't **take** my diaphragm, it just went with me. So he said, what about the tube of Duragel? I must admit he had me there. |
| Henry: | You should have said, "Duragel!—no wonder the bristles fell out of my toothbrush." (Stoppard, 1982, p. 66) |

Characteristics of this exchange that make it highly competent (these will be remembered by those who have seen the play and can perhaps be imagined by others) include:

1. Rapid turn-taking. In fact, the effectiveness of the exchange as a piece of theater derives in part from the phenomenon called *latching,* or *immediate uptake,* in which each turn begins a microsecond before the previous one ends.
2. Avoidance of overlaps, interruptions, and dysfluencies. In addition to avoiding interturn pauses, competent conversations avoid periods of overlapping speech (although what is considered "overlapping" is highly culturally determined), interruptions of turns, intraturn pauses or dysfluencies that might elicit interruptions, and other violations of

the joint principles "only one speaker at a time" and "at least one speaker all the time."

3. Observance of obligations to respond. Certain conversational turns absolutely require a response, whereas others simply allow one. Greetings, for example, must be returned—failure to respond to a greeting is considered a social slight. Questions, unless rhetorical, must be acknowledged even if not answered, and failure to do so is a frank violation of rules for turn exchange (one children get away with a fair amount of the time).

4. Observation of obligations as a listener. In addition to responding when required, good conversationalists are expected to display attentiveness, to indicate comprehension or lack thereof, and to give the interlocutor time and opportunity to speak. Rules for listener behavior are little emphasized in the developmental literature on conversational skill; in fact, they have been attended to primarily in cross-cultural analyses, for example, analyses suggesting that Japanese conversational rules require a more active, responsible listener than do Anglo-American rules. Clearly, though, folk politeness rules in Anglo-American culture do enjoin speakers at the least to stop and give others a turn, to attend to others' speech, and so on. And in fact, such attentiveness is prerequisite to effective timing of one's own turns and to the provision of topic- appropriate responses.

5. Topic relatedness. In good conversations, like that between Charlotte and Henry, utterances relate topically to their predecessors. This principle is sufficiently strong that its inverse is institutionalized in the Gricean maxim (Grice, 1975) of relevance: No matter what answer one gets, seek an interpretation that assumes topic relevance. Children acquire this very important principle of topic development only with great difficulty and over a very long period of time. The requirement of topic relatedness leads to many additional characteristics of conversation, for example, the availability of explicit topic-change or topic-diversion strategies (e.g., *by the way, not to change the topic but . . . , that reminds me*), as well as of formulas for topic reinstatement and topic termination. The presumption of topic relevance is exploited extensively by gifted playwrights like Stoppard, who use it to force reinterpretation of utterances for humorous purposes, as in this exchange (later in the scene quoted earlier):

| Charlotte: | Do you have to go? |
| Henry: | Yes, I ought to. |
| Charlotte: | You don't fancy one for the road? |
| Henry: | No, really. |
| Charlotte: | Or a drink? |

6. Repair strategies. Whereas scripted conversations like the one quoted here typically avoid misunderstandings and failures of uptake, normal conversations are studded with various sorts of breakdowns, and thus skilled conversationalists must control polite procedures for eliciting repairs and checking on comprehension.

The difficulty of deploying skills in these several domains simultaneously generates differences in conversational skill among adults (as well as among children). That difficulty is alluded to in the Duragel exchange quoted previously and is made explicit earlier in *The Real Thing* in a speech by Charlotte to Henry (who is a playwright) and a friend who is appearing in Henry's play about a presumed adulterous wife:

Charlotte: What an ego trip! Having all the words to come back with just as you need them. That's the difference between plays and real life—thinking time, time to get your bottle back. "Must say, I take my hat off to you, coming home with Rembrandt place mats for your mother." You don't really think that if Henry caught me out with a lover, he'd sit around being witty about place mats? Like hell he would. He'd come apart like a pick-a-sticks. His sentence structure would go to pot, closely followed by his sphincter.

Charlotte is alluding here to a universal conversational rule, that witty and efficacious comebacks typically occur to one only some minutes or hours after they would have been effective—the phenomenon of *la résponse de l'escalier*.

## 7.1.2. Children's conversational skills

The paradox of children's coexistent precocity and immaturity in the realm of conversation can be explained by the need to control these various subsystems of conversational skill simultaneously. In some subsystems, for example, taking turns, children become good fairly early. In others, for example, maintaining topic relevance or observing rules of timing and obligations to respond, they are considerably less precocious. In this chapter we describe the development of children's conversational skills across these various domains.

We isolate conversational skill here as a separate topic within the domain of pragmatics somewhat artificially. Mature performance in the domain, for example, of observing rules for responses within adjacency pairs or for when and how to request clarification relates directly to developments already discussed under the rubric *communicative intents*. Similarly, developments in the domains of topic-relevance and topic-extension strategies are closely connected to those that are discussed in Chapter 8 under the rubric of *extended discourse*.

Being an effective adult conversationalist is so difficult precisely because it requires combining control over the semantic and syntactic processes of utterance planning, production, and comprehension with control over the pragmatic rules and procedures for turn-taking; for ensuring, maintaining, and recognizing topic relevance; for repairing misunderstandings or comprehension breakdowns; and for regulating proxemics and kinesics. Furthermore, conversational rules are heavily contextually dependent—they differ as a function of setting (waiting room versus doctor's office, informal discussion versus formal meeting), of role relationships, of topic under discussion, and so on. The topic *conversation* could be the opening to a multivolume discussion of complex, culturally specific, elaborated rule systems for social exchange, regulation of interpersonal relationships, and politeness—a potentially lifelong project that we will not undertake. Rather, we focus on linguistic skills that are specific to the interactive context of conversational exchange—in particular, skills associated with centrally conversational tasks, like making small talk, rather than with tasks in which information exchange or problem solving is central; Brown and Yule (1983) call the skills we focus on *interactional* and those dealing with information exchange *transactional*. Of course, conversations are meant to have content, and issues of topic relevance are directly related to content and information. Nonetheless, we take as central in this chapter (as in the entire book) the skills relevant to appropriateness and interactive effectiveness rather than to truthfulness or grammaticality.

We assume, furthermore, that it is at least theoretically possible to consider conversational rules separately from rules of social exchange more generally. A problem that recurs in every discussion of linguistic pragmatics (see Sections 1.2 and 1.3) is the fuzzy boundary between the rules for language use and the rules for social interaction; it is particularly difficult to maintain an analytic boundary between children's developing pragmatic skills and their developing sociability. This difficulty reflects, of course, the fact that the division between pragmatic systems and social systems as analytic units is imposed rather than natural; parents encouraging politeness do not distinguish among *sit up straight, don't talk with your mouth full,* and *answer when you are spoken to* as rules of politeness, and, similarly, children probably take "acting nice" as their developmental goal without distinguishing between linguistic and other sources of niceness.

## 7.2 Turn-taking as the basis of conversation

### 7.2.1 Turn-taking in adult conversations

Much of the research about adult conversation has focused on the turn-taking system; the field of conversational analysis is based on the pioneering article by

Sacks, Schegloff, and Jefferson (1974), in which detailed analyses of transcribed conversations were offered to demonstrate the degree of conformity by normal adult speakers to the conversational norms of avoiding both overlap and pauses. Sacks and colleagues also suggested that procedures for seizing turns demanded careful attention to the syntactic structure of the ongoing turn, since well-timed turn-taking required anticipating the completion of a syntactic unit by the current speaker (clause boundaries were identified as "turn-relevant" places). The conversational analysis of Sacks and his colleagues was expanded in work by Duncan and Fiske (1977), Garrod and Anderson (1987), Goodwin (1981), and many others. In addition to describing the basic system of turn alternation, these works discussed procedures for passing the turn on (e.g., asking questions), for nominating the next speaker in multiparty conversations, and so on. Although the analytic superstructure of the conversational analyst has been criticized for its tendency to dignify the trivial and glorify the obvious, these pioneering studies had the enormous impact of making clear for the first time how well structured, complex, and difficult the seemingly simple task of conversational turn-taking was.

Subsequent work within and from outside the tradition of conversational analysis proposed modifications to the notion that smooth conversational exchange is as universal and ubiquitous a phenomenon as first described (see Denny, 1985, and Murray, 1985, for reviews). At the same time, the complexity of the sorts of naturally occurring, multiparty conversations analyzed by Sacks, Schegloff, and Jefferson (1974) led many to select simpler conversational settings for analysis or to focus on circumscribed conversational problems. Thus, further work within the conversational analysis tradition has focused on specific conversational subsystems, such as the initiation (Godard, 1977; Schegloff, 1979) and conclusion of telephone conversations (Clark & French, 1981; Schegloff & Sacks, 1973). Further complexities of conversational competence emerge from analyses of specialized conversational genres, for example, ritual insults (Dundes, Leach & Özkök, 1972; Labov, 1972), service encounters (Merrit, 1976), jokes (Sacks, 1974), doctor-patient talk (Coulthard & Ashby, 1976; Mishler, 1984), and therapy sessions (Labov & Fanshel, 1977; Turner, 1972).

Competent conversationalists also display kinesic, proxemic, and gaze-control skills, on the border between linguistic pragmatics and more general social competence (e.g., Argyle & Cook, 1976; Birdwhistell, 1970; Hall, 1959; Hinde, 1972; Kendon, 1981; Key, 1975; Knapp, 1972). The points of contact between nonlinguistic and linguistic capacities emerge clearly when we see disruption of verbal turn-taking in conversations with blind adults, who cannot use gaze cues to regulate or anticipate turn exchange (Junefelt & Mills, 1990).

Cultural and linguistic differences in the regulation of conversational turn-taking and the structuring of conversation events can be enormous (e.g., Philips, 1976; White, 1989). Thus, for example, in multiparty Spanish conversations, talk by two or more speakers overlaps about 25 percent of the time but with no sense of rule violation, interruption, or confusion by participants or observers. In Swedish multiparty conversations, on the other hand, overlaps—which are interpreted as violations—are typically extremely brief, and normal turn exchange often involves an interturn silence of a couple of seconds (Fant, 1990). These differences, which can generate problems in intercultural communication, also represent socialization targets; a child raised to observe Spanish conversational rules in Swedish would presumably encounter enormous social problems, as would the Swedish-style conversationalist speaking Spanish. How do children naturally acquire their own culture's rules for timing, overlap, and turn exchange in conversation?

### 7.2.2 Children's turn-taking

The first attempts to think about children's interactions with adults from a conversational perspective were directly influenced by the work of the conversational analysts; it was reading Sacks, Schegloff, and Jefferson (1974) that led Snow to analyze interactions between two British mothers and their infants using constructs like turn, first-pair part, adjacency pair, and so on (Snow, 1977a). In applying these constructs to parent-infant interaction, contrasts with adult-adult conversation emerged; whereas adult conversationalists take turns intentionally and in fact compete for the next turn, infants are liberally given credit for turns they either did not take at all (total silence) or did not intend as communicative (e.g., burps, coughs). Mothers with infants as young as three months in Snow's study (1977a), and even younger in Kaye and Charney's work (1980, 1981), were being treated as conversational partners by their mothers during face-to-face play sessions and feeding sessions; it is thus perhaps not surprising that by eight or nine months of age such children are fairly good at the turn-taking aspect of conversation, at least in dyadic situations with adult interactants. By the time they are producing their first words, children can typically sustain long bouts of well-timed turn alternations with mothers (Kaye & Charney, 1980, 1981; Snow, 1977a). The crucial role of the sensitive adult in this accomplishment is demonstrated by the fact that with peers, the same pattern of turn alternations only appears a couple of years later; by about age three, though, children do follow rules of turn-taking with each other (Ervin-Tripp, 1979; Keenan & Klein, 1975).

Once children have learned to take their turns reliably they are faced with the problem of maintaining the turn—holding the floor. This may be a more serious problem for children than for adults, since children speak relatively slowly and dysfluently; pauses and dysfluencies represent opportunities for the interlocutor to seize a turn. Adults tend to protect children's turns, but in peer-interaction situations children must learn to hold the floor long enough to finish their own turns, a challenge that becomes greater as one's playmates become more skilled in exploiting opportunities to seize the floor. By about age four, children show some control over the use of devices like sentence-initial *and* or repetitive *et puis* (and then) as floor holders, signaling that their turn is not yet complete by initiating a new syntactic unit (Jisa, 1984–1985; Peterson & McCabe, 1987).

Much writing about conversational development has emphasized continuity—the degree to which the structure of early mother-infant interactions resembles that of adult conversational exchange. Bateson (1975), for example, referred to mother-infant interactions as *protoconversations*, and Trevarthen (1979) has argued for infant social/communicative precocity on the basis of structural similarities between infant-adult and adult-adult interaction patterns. It is also clear, though, that such periods of adult-infant conversation-like interaction alternate with periods of interaction that do not resemble conversational turn-taking, times when both parties vocalize in unison or when long silences occur (e.g., Stern et al., 1975). The tendency of Western psychologists to emphasize the continuity identifiable in some interactions (see Collis, 1985) could be taken as a reflex of precisely the same cultural tendency that leads mothers to treat infant burps or coughs as conversational turns—a cultural commitment to the principles that (1) conversation is the normal form for human interaction, and (2) babies should be accorded autonomy and interactive rights similar to those of adults.

In fact, many problems of conversational management are eased for young children (and thus the appearance of continuity is enhanced) by the availability of highly cooperative adult conversational partners. Thus, children's violations of some of the rules governing adult conversation are not considered particularly serious, and their frequent difficulties abiding by the Gricean maxims (Grice, 1975) of relevance and quantity are compensated for by adult willingness to engage in extensive repair.

How do we reconcile, though, the view that young children are rather proficient in at least the turn-taking aspects of conversation with the widely accepted view that young children are egocentric (Piaget, 1929) and engage in private speech—speech in which turn-taking does not occur? Herein lies one of the complexities of understanding conversational development; it is easy to characterize children as precocious or as hopelessly unskilled depending on what aspect of conversation one focuses on. In interaction with adults, children tend to stay involved in conversations and to look like good turn-takers. In interactions with peers, children are more likely to show disruption of turn-taking through engagement in private speech. One study of four-year-olds in dyadic interaction showed that almost half of the segments of talk (defined as talk focused on one topic) were monologic (Schober-Peterson & Johnson, 1991); however, about half of these monologic segments were unsuccessful attempts to enter into dialogue.

Children's turn-taking failures have several possible sources. Disruptions of turn-taking in infant-adult interaction, when infants are allowed to produce contentless turns, reflect the infants' lack of skill in turn-taking itself. Later disruptions can result from the undeveloped state of other conversational skills, that is, children who know they should take a turn nonetheless fail to do so because they do not understand the interlocutor or because they cannot think of anything to say on the topic. Indeed, continuation of a conversational topic in adult-child talk is often a function more of adult responsiveness (Bloom, Rocissano, & Hood, 1976) than of child-topic maintenance behaviors, although improvement in topic maintenance occurs with age (see Section 7.3). Some violations of normal conversational responsiveness by young children may also relate to deficits in their ability to comprehend implicitly nominated topics (Bacharach & Luszcz, 1979; Luszcz & Bacharach, 1983) or to other cognitive limitations on control over conversational implicature.

### 7.2.3 Violations of timing

The picture presented by Sacks, Schegloff, and Jefferson (1974) of adult conversations with minimal overlap and minimal silence is, of course, somewhat idealized even for mature conversationalists. In addition to clear violations, such as two speakers starting simultaneously and intentional or inadvertent interruptions of one speaker by another, adult conversations include periods of simultaneous speech occasioned by back channels and by chorusing. Back channels are vocal signals from the listener indicating agreement or attentiveness, frequent in Japanese conversations. Conversations among working-class North American girls are often characterized by periods of chorusing, when one or more listeners chime in with the speaker; effective chorusing requires that the speaker introduce refrains that are sufficiently predictable that unison or at least convergent chorusing is possible (Hemphill, 1989).

Although interruptions are defined as violations, it is also clear that learning to interrupt is an important aspect of acquiring conversational skill. Sometimes it is crucial to interrupt the interlocutor—when an emergency arises, for example, or when one's dinner-party conversation is being dominated by an indefatigable bore. Children do get better at interrupting ongoing adult conversations in ways that are appropriate (Sachs, Anselmi, & McCollam, 1990), but skillful interruption is one of those skills that even some adults do not fully control.

### 7.2.4 Cultural differences and listening behavior

Cultural differences in the occurrence of back channels show that acquiring conversational skill requires learning not just how and when to talk but how and when to listen as well. The role of the listener in conversation is culturally constructed in conformity with a larger set of rules about social interaction and is subject to social class and gender, as well as to cultural variation. The most familiar contrast is probably that between Japanese and Western listeners.

University faculty members teaching courses with many foreign students typically attend to the Japanese students' faces while lecturing—a response to the
Japanese listeners' active involvement in the communication. In dyadic conversations, Japanese listeners produce many back channels, nods, acknowledgments, and signals of comprehension or noncomprehension; this culturally
prescribed active listening behavior can be related to data showing that Japanese
children and adults blame the listener if communication fails, whereas North
American children and adults tend to blame the speaker under such circumstances (Flavell, 1963).

In other words, middle-class American conversation is constructed as an
interaction in which the primary responsibility for clarity of communication
rests with the speaker, who is thus required to predict or explicitly demand
information about required background knowledge and consistently to monitor
his or her own output for comprehensibility. Japanese interactions, on the other
hand, are constructed as communicative events in which speakers have considerable latitude to be elliptical, to assume shared background knowledge, and to
be unclear, because listeners are responsible to signal (non)comprehension.
Japanese children are socialized rather explicitly into their role as active,
interpretive, responsible listeners in interactions in which their mothers tell
them, for example, that visitors to the house may not really mean what they say
(Clancy, 1986). Presumably, North American children are similarly socialized
into an understanding of speaker responsibility through interactions in which
adults demand that children clarify their intentions, provide the background
information adults need to understand their narratives, make explicit unfamiliar
referents, and so on (see Blum-Kulka & Snow, 1992).

## 7.3 Topic selection and topic maintenance

### 7.3.1 Who can you talk to about what?

A paralyzing problem for the aspirant conversationalist is the issue of topic
selection. Archie Leach, an English barrister played by John Cleese in the film
*A Fish Called Wanda,* describes the problem poignantly to Wanda, an uninhib-
ited American free spirit: "Wanda, do you have any idea what it's like being
English? Being correct all the time, being so stifled by this threat of doing the
wrong thing? Saying to someone, 'Are you married?' and hearing 'My wife left
me this morning,' or asking, 'Do you have children?' and hearing 'They all burnt
to death on Wednesday.' You see, Wanda, we're all terrified of embarrassment,
that's why we're so dead." This problem, although ubiquitous, is somewhat
alleviated for adults by the availability of standard, safe, culturally prescribed
topics within speech communities—the weather in England, the playoff situation in the seasonally appropriate current sport for U.S. males, feeding and
sleeping problems for parents with young children, and so on.

Young children are greatly disadvantaged in the making of small talk by their ignorance of the standard, culturally determined list of topics that organizes casual conversation for adults (Kellermann et al., 1989), as well as by their lack of knowledge about those topics (they typically do not read the papers, watch TV news broadcasts, or follow professional sports). Instead, childhood conversations tend to develop around topics dictated by play—by available objects that constitute a shared focus of attention, by formal games, or by familiar fantasy themes stimulated perhaps by the availability of dress-up clothes or tea sets. Absent these, young children's conversations often decline into word play, mutual repetitions, or other relatively contentless talk (Garvey, 1975).

Such vocal play is one constructive low-level solution to the inability of young children to sustain social relations through simple talk, an inability that dictates the different organization of social events for different age groups. Whereas adult parties are typically unstructured in terms of activities on the assumption that conversation will constitute the major entertainment, children's parties are tightly scheduled with games, excursions, performances, and planned activities, because parents know that a group of 5- or even 10-year-olds simply will not fill up several hours with talk. In terms of Goffman's scheme for the contexts allowing talk (see Section 2.3.2 and Figure 2.1), young children can make use of the intersubjectivity created by joint attention and joint action to generate conversations and interaction in general, but they typically cannot establish sustained intersubjectivity through conversation alone; recall the late emergence of participation in **Discussions of the nonpresent** (Sections 5.5.1, 6.1.3., and 6.2.1).

Willingness to initiate topics and to use conversation as a social activity, of course, varies widely among children, as among adults. No data are available on how children are socialized either about the need to initiate topics or about the topics it is appropriate to initiate. Books providing social advice to teenagers instruct them in the sorts of things to talk about with friends or dates and how to signal to others that you are interested in friendship with them. Cultural constraints on the list of appropriate topics certainly exist; on the other hand, as Archie Leach articulated, natural affective responses proscribe or make difficult topics like family deaths, illness, and personal failures or reversals pretty much everywhere.

### 7.3.2 Procedures for topic initiation

Infants as young as 11 months of age are likely to manipulate an object that has been touched by a strange adult and to replicate the adult's actions on the object while engaging in sociable activities, like maintaining eye contact with the adult, or vocalizing (Eckerman, Whatley, & McGehee, 1979). Such events may be the entry into topic initiation for young children; these topic initiations are prelinguistic, object-mediated, and nonverbal, reflecting social abilities that under-lie and prepare for linguistic developments.

The kinds of object-mediated social initiatives described by Eckerman and colleagues are typically responded to, by middle-class Western mothers at least, with utterances that establish the topic linguistically, for example, naming the object (*yes, a ball!*) or signaling something about the appropriate response to it (e.g., *pretty* or *roll it to me!*). The form of the maternal utterance in response to child object-mediated topic nominations has considerable influence on how children later choose to initiate and extend topics themselves (Goldfield, 1987, 1990). Mothers who reliably respond with object names have children described as *referential*, who themselves rely on naming as a conversational strategy. Mothers who respond with phatic expressions (*nice!* or *pretty!*) have children who themselves are more *expressive*.

In interaction with young children, an adult's first conversational challenge is establishing a joint topic so that conversation can ensue. There are basically two possible mechanisms for doing so: a response to the child's initiation of some topic or an utterance designed to **Direct the hearer's attention** to some object or event that can serve as a new topic (see Section 8.3). In the Harvard sample (Section 6.2), every parent produced at least two, and typically more, utterances designed to **Direct the child's attention** in 20 minutes of interaction at every observation (Snow et al., 1996). **Directing hearer's attention** utterances were among the most frequent adult communicative acts (Pan et al., 1996). Evidently, even middle-class American mothers, the same type who respond to their infants' burps as conversational turns, require more content for interaction with somewhat older children.

Children in the Harvard study sample also offered their parents consider-able opportunity to follow up on a child-initiated topic. Child acts **Directing the hearer's attention** (DHA) were the most frequent type of interpretable communicative attempts children made at 14 months. The 52 children observed at 14 months produced a total of 374 communicative acts coded as DHA, but 317 of these were interpretable as DHA only from accompanying nonverbal behaviors, for example, pointing or showing. At 20 months, 48 children produced a total of 610 DHA acts, of which 221 relied crucially on nonverbal components. Only 15 of the 308 DHA acts produced by 38 32-month-olds relied on nonverbal components for comprehensibility. These data reflect consider-able development in children's capacities to nominate conversational topics and to do so verbally rather than through gesture or action. This capacity to nominate topics verbally is prerequisite to the initiation of absent, remote, or abstract topics, which both children and their parents do more successfully as the children get older.

We have in Chapters 5 and 6 (Sections 5.5.1, 6.1.3., and 6.2.1) presented information about the emergence of discussions in interactions with young children; discussions are "pure conversation," and accomplishing participation in them represents a major milestone in the development of conversational skill.

Discussions of topics that are attended to jointly by parent and child are the object- or book-mediated discussions we think of as typical in interaction with young children. All of the Harvard-sample parents engaged in such talk with children of all ages, although the percentage of children participating increased: 69 percent, 94 percent, and 100 percent at 14, 20, and 32 months, respectively (see Section 6.2.1 for a fuller presentation of these findings). Discussions of topics slightly more remote, for example, talking about one's own nonpresent toothbrush upon seeing a toothpaste ad, were coded as **Discussion related to the present**; whereas 90 percent of parents engaged in this kind of talk at all ages, only 17 percent of children did so at 14 months, although more than 50 percent did by 20 months.

Even more striking development is seen in children's ability to participate in **Discussion of the nonpresent**, for example, telling stories about past events, planning future activities, discussing theoretical issues, and so on. One child managed this at 14 months (and then only by responding to adult initiatives), but 27 percent of children observed did so by 20 months and 51 percent by 32 months. Whereas cognitive developments are clearly prerequisite to the ability to discuss nonpresent topics, new acquisitions in the domain of linguistic structures (e.g., coming to control past tense, future aspect, genericity markers, and the like) are also crucial for initiating talk about nonpresent topics. Conversely, increasing participation in the decontextualized talk coded as discussion of nonpresent topics serves as a crucial context for the continued acquisition of such linguistic structures.

### 7.3.3 Topic continuation—site of major development

Once initiated, topics need to be developed. Poor conversationalists are not necessarily unable to think of topic-initiating questions; they might think of many initiatory questions but fail to ask any follow-up questions or produce what Kaye and Charney (1981) have called *turnabouts*. When interacting with peers, children often either fail to maintain a topic (Blank & Franklin, 1980) or else use relatively primitive devices to do so. Keenan and Klein (1975), for example, analyzed conversations between twins to show that exact or partial imitation was a primary device used to maintain coherence across turns. Similarly, Garvey (1975) showed that dyads used both repetition of and ritualized variations on each others' utterances to generate conversational exchanges up through age 5. It is striking in the exchanges Garvey described that cross-turn relevance was sometimes maintained by sound-play–based cohesion rather than true topic cohesion. Reliance on imitative devices for maintaining cross-turn cohesion declines from age 2 to age 5 (Benoit, 1982). Explicit marking of cross-utterance relations with "conjuncts," like *for example, so,* and *anyway,* or with "attitudinal" expressions, like *really* or *perhaps,* is extremely rare in the speech of 6-year-olds, and 12-year-olds have not achieved adultlike frequencies

of these devices (Scott, 1984). This finding becomes fairly important in light of
the crucial role such markers are generally assumed to play in introducing
nuances of politeness, deniability, and connectedness in adult conversation
(Wardhaugh, 1985).

In adult-child conversation, adults can support topic development in
many ways—by asking appropriate questions, repairing breakdowns, or requesting elaboration. In sophisticated conversations, for example, those
where children receive a lot of adult help, each topic generates related topics,
which in turn can get developed. In the following dinner-table exchange
between 4-year-old Ethan and his parents, the first topic, gifts from Mac and
Melanie, is introduced by Father in turn 1. This topic immediately generates
a question from Ethan (who uses *at least* somewhat unconventionally to mean
something like *"but"*) about why they are getting presents in March, to which
the parents' collaborative response is rather complex, going on until turn 17
when Ethan brings up the topic of previous presents from Mac and Melanie.
This question leads to an attempt to reconstruct the contents of a videotape
that had been one of those presents, a topic that stays on the table until turn
59. This conversation demonstrates many conversational phenomena, some
of them universal and some characteristic of North American child-rearing
practices:

1. Overlap of speakers (marked in these transcripts with <and> around
   overlapped segments and used subsequently to indicate direction
   where overlapping speech should be sought)
2. Dysfluencies and self-corrections (marked with <and> around the
   dysfluent segments, then with [/] afterward)
3. The gradual transition from one topic to the next, such that two
   adjacent turns of talk are related but utterances three or four turns apart
   might be on fairly different topics
4. The embedding of narrative and explanatory segments into conversation
5. The willingness of adults to adopt child topics (Ethan introduced all
   but the first topic in this conversation), endorse the child's perspective
   (condemning the pin cushion man), and express approval of child
   accomplishments that have little importance in the adult world (e.g.,
   remembering the plot of the Pin Cushion Man)
6. The ways in which opportunities for language learning are embedded
   in conversational exchange (e.g., in line 50 Ethan finally adopts his
   parents' term *pop,* replacing his own less precise *cut*)
7. The degree to which cultural/social learning (in this case about friendship, reciprocity, gratitude, interpersonal responsibilities, ritual occasions for gift giving) can be supported by casual conversational
   exchange

**Example 7.1**

| | |
|---|---|
| 1 Father: | <and so> what did you think of the presents that Mac and Melanie gave you? [<overlap] |
| 2 Child: | they're good. |
| 3 Child: | well at least I didn't know they gave presents to people. |
| 4 Mother: | [laughs] |
| 5 Father: | well we didn't see them at Christmas time. |
| 6 Child: | why? |
| 7 Father: | because every time they were going to come down here they had snow, and every time we were going to go up there the weather was bad, so we had to wait (un)til yesterday to see them, and so <we gave> [/] we gave Michael his birthday present (be)cause we gave them their Christmas present before Christmas <xxx [/]> [overlap>] |
| 8 Child: | <and we're> their friends. [<overlap] |
| 9 Father: | yeah. |
| 10 Child: | but at least I didn't give Melanie a present. |
| 11 Father: | we, <well [/]> [overlap>] |
| 12 Mother: | <we> gave her her birthday present Honey in August when she had her birthday. [<overlap] |
| 13 Father: | and we gave her her Christmas present before, and what they gave you was your Christmas present yesterday. |
| 14 Mother: | but Michael's birthday was in January. |
| 15 Father: | yeah. |
| 16 Mother: | and we never saw him in January so that's why he got his present yesterday. Melanie remembers that we gave her present before. |
| 17 Child: | but they didn't give me a <pr(esent)>[/] present on my birthday. |
| 18 Father: | (be)cause your birthday is coming up next month. |
| 19 Mother: | last year they did. |
| 20 Father: | mmhm. |
| 21 Mother: | you know <your> [/] your videotapes with uh cartoons on them? um, which cartoons were they? [sotto voce] I don't know, Bugs Bunny and <things> like that. [overlap>] |
| 22 Mother: | those were from Michael and Melanie, and they give you <the sweatshirt that> [//] a sweatshirt that you wore yesterday, and uh they've given you other presents too. but those <are the ones I remember.>[overlap>] |
| 23 Child: | <did they Ma> give me the pin cushion um tapes? [<overlap] |
| 24 Mother: | <yes> yes. that's right, they gave you <that> [//] the tape. [overlap>] |
| 25 Father: | <mmhm.>[<overlap] |

26 Child:     but, you mean the uh the xxx [////] who's that guy who uh gets all those pins out . . . cush quash . . . [making funny noises]
27 Mother:    the pin cushion man who . . . pops the balloons?
28 Child:     yes.
29 Father:    what about him?
30 Child:     well he cuts balloons.
31 Father:    yeah.
32 Child:     and that's not very nice.
33 Father:    no it's not.
34 Child:     next time when we see the pin cushion guy tell him to not um uh cut the balloons. tell him not <to.>[overlap]
35 Father:    <you> mean tell him not to pop the balloons? [<overlap]
36 Child:     yeah.
37 Father:    okay. you can tell him too you know.
38 Child:     yeah. (be)cause he doesn't listen to people.
39 Father:    yeah.
40 Mother:    except it's a cartoon Than. <I> [/] I don't think he'll stop popping balloons because on the video he's always uh on the video . . .
41 Child:     popping.
42 Mother:    popping balloons!
43 Child:     <popping.> [overlap>]
44 Father:    <<and>> [/] and don't the balloons win in the end? [<overlap]
45 Child:     what?
46 Father:    don't the balloons win in the end? don't they find their way to get rid of the pin cushion man?
47 Child:     oh yes.
48 Mother:    do they?
49 Child:     how?
50 Mother:    I forget.
51 Father:    maybe we'll have to watch the cartoon again soon to see how.
52 Child:     I know how they put, stuff in it. <They put mmm stu(ff)> [////] they put playdough in everything, and then they swim on the pin cush guy. pin cushion guy.
53 Father:    yeah
54 Child:     and that's how the ending goes.
55 Father:    no, he can't pop their balloons any more like that.
56 Child:     n(o) yeah.
57 Father:    mmm.
58 Mother:    oh. good memory Ethan, I didn't remember that part.
59 Child:     you'll have to see it.

The cross-turn cohesion illustrated in this conversation is an issue that lies at the interface between conversation and extended discourse. Although extended discourse is treated in the field and in this book as a separate topic, we see here clearly that extended discourse is the very stuff of skilled conversation. We return to multi-party and single-party production of extended discourse in Chapter 8.

### 7.3.4 Individual differences in skill at topic continuation and topic maintenance

Any adult with a normal range of social contacts would acknowledge that conversational skill is a domain of great individual difference. The fact that normal adults can be terrible conversationalists—paradoxically, in light of infants' conversational precocity—reflects the existence of real and challenging complexities in skillful conversation.

Because adults are inclined to take on conversational responsibilities in interactions with children, and because children in peer interactions have low-level strategies (which range from tolerating silence and parallel play to simply repeating each other's utterances) for solving the problem of conversation, seeing individual differences in children's conversational skill requires giving children harder-than-usual conversational tasks. One commonly used task is some variant of referential communication—requiring, for example, that two children communicate about objects, pictures, or maps only one of them has full access to. Although these various referential communication tasks tend to be transactional (i.e., to require transfer of information and problem solving of some sort), they can be usefully analyzed for more purely interactional features as well, for example, mechanisms for establishing joint attention, shared knowledge, and mutual understanding. We discuss research along these lines in Section 7.3.5.

An alternate approach puts children in a situation where conversational exchange is the only task facing them. The task, first used by Donahue, Pearl, and Bryan (1980), involves getting children to role-play the host of a talk show—a quintessential setting for purely interactive rather than transactional conversation. The child subject is told that he or she is to interview an adult, as if for a television show like Phil Donahue's or Geraldo's. Donahue and colleagues observed child pairs, but Schley and Snow (1992) used an adult interviewee who was instructed to be politely responsive but not helpful in keeping the conversation going—that is, to answer questions but not to elaborate on responses. Precisely because no transactional task is defined, the talk-show setting is one where children's skills at initiating and maintaining topics are severely tested. In fact, some children ages 7 to 12 simply could not keep going for the four minutes we had planned; adult experimenters in these circumstances, despite extensive training and instructions to respond appropriately but avoid initiations, were unable to resist the temptation to help out by starting to ask questions themselves! Schley and Snow (1992) found that children who were rated higher as conversational partners in the talk-show task (1) used open-ended questions and questions contingent upon previous utterances more often, (2) avoided silent pauses of more than a short duration, and (3) successfully elicited elaborated responses from their adult interlocutor. Conversational skill was not related, however, to dysfluencies like self-corrections, repetitions, interruptions, or vocal hesitations, even though half the children tested were not native speakers of English.

Schley and Snow's findings concerning topic extension echo those of Dorval and Eckerman (1984), from one of the few studies of age differences in conversational skill that has looked at conversations among peers. Dorval and Eckerman found large age differences in the degree to which the talk related to topics at hand, as well as in the nature of the relations among turns. Their youngest subjects, second graders, produced the highest proportion of unrelated conversational turns. Ninth graders produced a substantial proportion of factually related turns; the twelfth graders and the adults increasingly incorporated into their conversation turns that took into account the perspective of the person being discussed. These findings extend to peer-peer conversations earlier observations by Bloom, Rocissano, and Hood, (1976) on degree of relatedness in adjacent conversational turns in adult-child interaction. Bloom and colleagues had found the incidence of children's utterances that were on the same topic as immediately preceding adult utterances and that also added new information rose from 21 percent of all utterances during stage one (MLU under 1.5, ages 19 to 23 months) to 46 percent at stage five (MLU above 3.5, ages 35 to 38 months). These findings suggest that one major component of development in conversation is learning to make responses related to the previous turn, whereas Dorval and Eckerman (1984) make clear that older children continue to improve in topic coherency and to achieve coherency in increasingly sophisticated ways. The linguistic task of achieving coherence emerges again in children's narratives and in other extended discourse productions after children have solved coherence problems in conversational exchange (see Chapter 8).

Conversational skill can play a central role in a child's access to social interaction with peers (Corsaro, 1979), in determining peer acceptance (Hemphill & Siperstein, 1990), in second-language learners' access to input in their target language (Krashen, 1985), and in making a positive impression on teachers and other powerful adults (Evans, 1987). The impression that most children develop conversational skill relatively easily and automatically may be incorrect. Shy children, for example, show deficits as conversationalists that reveal the interface between language development and personality. Reticent children speak not only less but also less complexly than their peers, using shorter utterances, single topic turns, and fewer narratives and decontextualized descriptions of nonpresent objects (Evans, 1987). Furthermore, children with language or reading disabilities (Bryan et al., 1981; Donahue, 1984; Donahue, Pearl, & Bryan, 1980, 1983) and mildly retarded children (Hemphill, 1987; Hemphill & Siperstein, 1990) show problems inter-acting with peers that may be traceable to lack of control over the subtleties of conversational skill. Bryan, Donahue and their colleagues found that in un-structured conversations poor conversationalists could "get along" by virtue of responding to the conversational initiatives of their more skilled peers, but when they were made responsible for the conversation by use of the talk-show task their deficiencies were revealed. Mentally retarded children showed more problems than language-matched, normally developing children with topic control, conversational assertiveness, topic initiation, and fluency, but they had few problems with topic transitions, requests for clarifications, and replies to initiations (Hemphill, 1987).

Precisely because the turn-taking system is more constrained for interviews than for mundane conversations (Greatbatch, 1988), one might expect this task to reduce the impact of difficulties with turn-taking per se (and thus perhaps reveal other sorts of problems) as a source of conversational ineffectiveness. As far as we know, no one has tried to relate conversational skill assessed linguis-tically to "interpersonal intelligence" (Gardner, 1983) or to other assessments of social competence. It seems likely, though, that the skills that emerge during middle childhood—responding reliably to conversational initiatives, extending the interlocutor's topic, initiating conversational topics, and taking the interlocutor's point of view—are crucial in ensuring children and adolescents of normal social contact and high regard from their potential interlocutors.

### 7.3.5 Transactional conversations: referential communication tasks

In referential communication tasks, the speaker knows something that needs to be conveyed to the listener, and the channels of communication are limited in some way (they are talking over a telephone or are seated on opposite sides of a screen so that no visual information can be communicated). Although many referential communication tasks are designed to focus on the skills of the speaker (using an experimenter, for example, in the listener role), when children are observed in both speaker and listener roles, information about their skills as listeners also becomes available. The responsibility of the listener can be increased by manipulations like giving speaker and listener somewhat different versions of a map on which a route is to be noted, thus reducing the presumption of shared knowledge. Skilled listeners in such tasks request information they need, check their own comprehension of unclear information, and in other ways contribute to skillful performance.

Children reveal remarkable inadequacies as both speakers and listeners in such dyadic communication tasks to a fairly advanced age. For example, in a study by Lloyd (1991) of route directions given over the telephone, 7-year-olds differed from 10-year-olds not just in that the speaker gave inadequate infor-mation but, more interestingly, in that the listener rarely requested additional information. In other words, children who are linguistically and cognitively capable of requesting clarification (see Section 7.4) fail to do so under conditions where it is crucial to success. Adult listeners observed by Lloyd engaged in considerable checking and requesting of additional information, even though the adult speakers in general had given adequate route descriptions. Evidently, younger children assign more responsibility for success to the speaker than do adults, who perhaps have benefited from vast experience with unsuccessful communication.

A large study of dyadic route-finding by Anderson, Clark, and Mullin (1994) compared the strategies used by 7-, 10-, and 13-year-olds. The children were warned that the maps given to listeners and speakers could be different, yet the younger children often introduced referents in statements presupposing their presence (*Go to the red church*) rather than querying their presence (*Do you have a red church?*). Anderson and colleagues described their younger listeners in the less successful dialogues as operating very much like we might characterize mediocre students: "The subjects appear to see their main goal as trying to interpret and comply with the instructions rather than as functioning as actively involved participants who must also provide information and take responsibility for establishing a common ground for the successful completion of the task" (p. 459). At the same time, individual differences within age groups in sophistication of communicative strategies were reported to be greater than age differences—a finding that is replicated for most of the conversational subsystems.

These results from referential communication tasks might suggest that young children are simply incompetent at keeping track of who knows what. Such a conclusion is, however, countered by many observations of cases in which children are fairly sophisticated in judging listeners' needs for information. For instance, when talking to a strange adult, children as young as four will explain the referents of proper nouns, both toy names (*and he came in with a Power Ranger—that's a kind of really neat toy*) and names of people (*and then Sally—she's a kid in my day care*) (Sachs, Anselmi, & McCollam, 1990). Three-year-olds adjust their descriptions of a toy to the level of knowledge of an interlocutor (Perner & Leekam, 1986). These and other results suggest that egocentric behavior on the part of children (or adults, for that matter) cannot be taken as evidence that they are incapable of taking the interlocutor's point of view but rather that coordinating perspective-taking with other communicative and linguistic demands can be very difficult.

## 7.4 Repair

Effective conversation requires the coordination of action, attention, and intention between two or more individuals; it is almost inevitable that the process of conversation will be characterized by occasional failures—failures of turn alternation, failures of uptake, failures of clear expression of intention. When such failures occur *and are obvious,* repair procedures must be in place to prevent breakdown of communication and a threat to the social relationship. Of course, many miscommunications are covert, unrecognized by one or another party to the conversation, or even if recognized, mutually unacknowledged (see Blum-Kulka & Weizman, 1988, for examples). We focus here on breakdowns serious enough that it is impossible to continue the conversation unless they are repaired.

Normally, breakdown of message transmission is repaired by the use of clarification requests—the listener asks *Huh?* or *What did you say?* or makes some more specific request for clarification (*He gave you a what?*). Clarification is a point where the development of conversation, of communicative intent (see Chapter 6), and of extended discourse overlaps; without clarification, conversation breaks down, and topics cannot be extended. How do children acquire the ability to use clarification procedures to contribute actively to repair of conversational breakdown? How do parents use clarification questions in ways that might help children learn about pragmatic and other aspects of language?

### 7.4.1 The acquisition of clarification requests

Children hear quite a lot of adult talk they cannot understand and thus might be expected to produce clarification requests early. In fact, children do not produce such requests until about age 2 (see Sections 4.2 and 5.2). Children must also learn to respond appropriately to adult requests for clarification, which they hear from an early age—fairly often in response to their own uninterpretable utterances. Child-initiated requests for clarification did not emerge reliably in the Harvard study (Pan et al., 1996; Snow et al., 1996) until 20 months, when 15 of 48 children produced them, as compared with only one of 52 children at 14 months and 31 of 37 children at 32 months (see Table 7.1).

Furthermore, children heard relatively few parental requests for clarification, although much of what they themselves produced was uninterpretable. Only 39 of the 52 children observed at 14 months heard any clarification questions during the observation, although 100 percent of the 48 20-month-olds observed and 36 of the 37 32-month-olds observed did hear clarification requests (see Table 7.1). For comparison purposes we include in Table 7.1 information about the number of child utterances that were uninterpretable; at 14 months fewer than one-seventh of uninterpretable child utterances were responded to with requests for clarification, whereas by 20 months well over half were. Clearly, parents were responding to their children's increased language sophistication by increasingly holding children accountable for their utterances and creating contexts in which children had to learn to respond to adult clarification requests.

TABLE 7.1    Repair Utterances by Children and Parents

| | Children | | | Parents | | |
|---|---|---|---|---|---|---|
| Age (in months) | 14 | 20 | 32 | 14 | 20 | 32 |
| Number | 52 | 48 | 37 | 52 | 48 | 37 |
| Total communicative acts | 3,005 | 5,215 | 5,767 | 17,070 | 15,854 | 9,904 |
| Total demanding clarification acts | 13 | 170 | 188 | 234 | 662 | 348 |
| Number producing demands for clarification | 8 | 35 | 31 | 39 | 48 | 36 |
| Child-initiated demands for clarification | 1 | 49 | 68 | — | — | — |
| Number initiating demands for clarification | 1 | 15 | 19 | — | — | — |
| Uninterpretable utterances (YYY) | 1,579 | 1,014 | 339 | — | — | — |
| Number producing YYY | 52 | 48 | 37 | — | — | — |

*Sources:* C. E. Snow, B. Pan, A. Imbens-Bailey, and J. Herman. 1996. "Learning How to Say What One Means: A Longitudinal Study of Children's Speech Act Use." *Social Development* 5: 56–84; B. Pan, A. Imbens-Bailey, K. Winner, and C. E. Snow. 1996. "Communicative Intents of Parents Interacting with Their Young Children." *Merrill-Palmer Quarterly* 42: 72–90.

Child-initiated requests for clarification during the age range 14 to 32 months were both relatively rare and fairly unsophisticated in form, consisting mostly of *Huh?* or *What?* The only child-initiated clarification request at 14 months was the following:

**Example 7.2**

Mother:    look what you made. isn't that pretty? (referring to child's drawing)
Child:     wha(t)?
Mother:    you did that. very good!

At 20 months, such examples were somewhat more frequent across the entire corpus, although a few children were particularly liberal with initiatory requests for clarification. One child at 20 months produced more initiatory clarification requests than all the other 20-month-olds together, using as well a variety of forms including *huh?* and *what?* and repeating stressed words of preceding adult utterances with a questioning intonation.

Child-initiated clarification requests were not only rare at 20 months but were also severely restricted in form. Only one example from a 20-month-old required any syntactic restructuring or analysis of the queried utterances.

**Example 7.3**

Mother:    I don't think Jane wants you to climb up on her desk, Kate.
Child:     Jane doesn't?

Every other request observed from 20-month-olds consisted of *huh, what,* or repetition of some part of the queried utterance, typically the final stressed word.

By 32 months children initiated many more clarification sequences but with formal means that were still limited mostly to *huh, what,* and repetition. Of the 188 child utterances in clarificatory sequences, 68 were child-initiated requests for clarification. Six children produced no clarificatory utterances at 32 months, whereas only one parent produced none.

### 7.4.2 Maternal clarification requests

Mothers use clarification requests in interaction with children for the standard reason—to remediate conversational breakdowns—but for additional reasons as well: as control mechanisms and as procedures for socializing children in the pragmatics of conversation. An apparent request for information can, even in adult conversation, function as a challenge to the truthfulness or acceptability of the interlocutor's utterance or as a marker of its extraordinariness on some dimension, for example:

> *The president has just resigned to join a monastery.*
> *What?*

Parents and teachers use pseudo-clarification requests in similar ways to signal to children that their statements are absurd:

> *I'm borrowing the car for the weekend.*
> *You're what?*

or that some observance of standard politeness has been omitted:

> *Gimme milk.*
> *What?*
> *Please gimme milk.*

With children under 32 months, parental requests for clarification typically focus on real communicative breakdowns but are starting to be used for derivative purposes. Anselmi, Tomasello, and Acunzo (1986) have reported that children ages 1;8 to 3;8 show no differences related to age or language stage in their response to clarification questions, which they respond to appropriately about 85 percent of the time. Frank, a child in the Harvard study, heard a particularly large number and rich assortment of clarification requests, to which he responded appropriately at 20 months, for example:

*Example 7.4*
|          |                              |
|----------|------------------------------|
| Child:   | piece.                       |
| Mother:  | oh you want a big piece here? |
| Child:   | yeah.                        |
| Mother:  | okay.                        |

He could respond appropriately as well when his mother, somewhat unusually in interaction with a child so young, used a clarification request to challenge his meaning rather than to query it:

*Example 7.5*
|         |       |
|---------|-------|
| Child:  | no!   |
| Mother: | no?   |
| Child:  | no.   |
| Mother: | yeah. |

By 32 months, Frank was more active in clarification request sequences, reflecting the substantial opportunities for practice his mother had given him. In this excerpt from a sequence of 120 consecutive utterances all on the same topic, Frank is trying to express a complex meaning his mother never fully understands (asterisks in the example indicate deleted utterances). This conversation exemplifies how central repair sequences are to the maintenance of a topic; their mastery is thus prerequisite to the production of extended discourse.

*Example 7.6*
|                |                                                               |
|----------------|---------------------------------------------------------------|
| 1 Child:       | I need a push!                                                |
| 2 Mother:      | a what?                                                       |
| 3 Child:       | push.                                                         |
| 4 Mother:      | what kind of a push?                                          |
| 5 Child:       | push the saw.                                                 |
| 6 Child:       | push saw.                                                     |
| 7 Mother:      | you mean, well you want me to give it [saw] to you and you push it [saw]? |
| 8 Child:       | no, put in the saw just like the man have.                    |
| 9 Mother:      | I don't know what you mean, just like the man has.            |
| 10 Child:      | yeah it could push.                                           |
| 11 Mother:     | make it [saw] go back and forth?                              |
| 12 Child:      | yeah.                                                         |
| 13 Mother:     | well you do that [make it go back and forth].                 |

***************************

|                |                                                               |
|----------------|---------------------------------------------------------------|
| 17 Child:      | man with saw [whining]!                                        |
| 18 Mother:     | oh, you want me to make a man with a saw?                      |
| 19 Child:      | yeah push that.                                                |
| 20 Child:      | man <has to> [?] push.                                          |
| 21 Mother:     | a bush?                                                         |

22 Child:    push.
\*\*\*\*\*\*\*\*\*\*\*\*\*\*\*\*\*\*\*\*\*\*\*\*\*
77 Child:    push saw that I have.
78 Mother:  you have?
79 Child:    yeah.
80 Child:    push saw I have.

### 7.4.3 Maternal clarification requests as feedback

The form of maternal clarification requests undergoes age-related changes, suggesting that mothers fine-tune their attempts at communication repair to children's ability to process information about reasons for the breakdown (Ninio, 1986b). Clarification demands made by 24 Hebrew-speaking mothers to their 10-, 18-, and 26-month-old children were examined. The dyads were videotaped at home in activities of their choice for 30 minutes. In the three groups of mothers, an average of 5.2 percent, 8.5 percent, and 12.0 percent of all maternal utterances, respectively, were clarification requests. The proportions of child utterances that were queried by at least one clarification demand were, on the average, 21.6 percent in the youngest age group, 22.2 percent in the middle group, and 17.1 percent in the oldest group. If noncommunicative babble-type vocalizations are also included in these statistics, the proportion of utterances queried increases to 39.4 percent in the youngest age group.

Clarification demands were found to belong to one of seven different types that vary in the information they provide about the locus of the problem with the child's utterance that caused the communication breakdown.

1.  **Rerun requests.** For example, a 10-month-old vocalized *Daddy;* her mother said *What?* **Rerun requests** provide only a general indication that a communication was not heard or understood. If problems with hearing the message can be ruled out (e.g., if there was no noise and the listener had been attentive), this indicates that some change in the utterance is necessary if it is to be understood. The clarification request itself is uninformative about the locus of the problem; it is a global negative feedback signal about the aggregate of rules that produced the utterance.
2.  **Yes-no questions that were full repetitions** of the original utterance. For example, an 18-month-old said *Key.* Mother said *Key? Go take the key.*
3.  **Yes-no questions that were partial repetitions** of the original utterance. For example, a 26-month-old said *Doll wants to see on Heidy* (a dog). Mother: *On Heidy?* **Yes-no questions that fully or partly repeat** the previous utterance without any modification are, strictly speaking, not clarification demands but demands for confirmation. As a commu-

nicative act, such clarification requests are rather ambiguous; since they stop the flow of conversation, they signal that something in the previous utterance was problematic but not why the recipient needs further confirmation of this utterance. It could be anything from needing reassurance that the previous speaker indeed had intended to say what was said, in which case there is nothing wrong with the form of the utterance, to a complete lack of understanding of what was said, because the recipient did not recognize the utterance as containing intelligible words. As a negative feedback signal this functions rather like the **Rerun request**, that is, it points to some global problem with the utterance or some part of it. Since the present speaker provides a version of what he or she had heard said, at least the previous speaker can know whether the problem was with hearing or with some other aspect of the communication. When the repetition is partial, some specific component or components of the utterance are singled out as causing the problem, but otherwise the query is as ambiguous as a full repetition.

4.  **Direct queries of the meaning of a word the child used.** For example, an 18-month-old said *Oppa.* Mother: *What is oppa?* Later, the same child said *Mana.* Mother: *Mommy doesn't understand, Roni.* These utterances provide specific information that the specified word was non-conventional.

5.  **Yes-no questions that substituted new forms** for all or part of the original utterance. For instance, a 10-month-old said *This,* looking at the strongly lit lamp we used for filming. Mother said *Light?* Or a 26-month-old complained *Oy hand, hand.* Mother comforted him, asking *Did you get hurt?* The child answered *In this,* pointing to the table corner. Mother asked, *Ah, from this?*

    **Yes-no questions with substitution of components** provide the information that the original utterance was ambiguous in some way and that the recipient had understood it in a certain way but needs confirmation of the interpretation. The substituted component or components are offered as the better alternative for saying what the previous speaker meant; they provide specific negative feedback on the appropriateness of the original component, lexical or grammatical.

6.  **Yes-no questions that were repetitions, either partial or full, of the original utterance but that also added some new material** to the original utterance. For example, an 18-month-old said *More.* Mother asked, *More flowers?* Or another 18-month-old said *To close!* Mother asked, *To close the window?* These questions provide specific information that some component of the original utterance was missing. As feedback on grammaticality, such clarification requests are fully explicit about errors consisting of the omission of obligatory components.

7. **Wh-questions that demanded product completion concerning a missing component** of the utterance. For example, an 18-month-old said *More*. Mother asked, *More what?* Or a 26-month-old, on seeing the filming setup, said *Scared*. Mother asked, *Who?* and the child answered with her own name. These questions also provide specific information about the omission by the previous speaker of an obligatory component of the sentence. Such clarification requests give fully explicit negative feedback signals about grammaticality.

The distribution of maternal clarification demands among these categories revealed that the type chosen by mothers was fine-tuned to the children's linguistic mastery. In the youngest age group (10-month-olds), where most child utterances were nonconventional vocalizations with or without communicative significance and only a few even approximated conventional words, most clarification requests were **Rerun requests** (66.4 percent), and almost all the rest were **Substitutions** (22.1 percent). Only 6.5 percent of all maternal clarification request were either **Yes-no questions** or **Wh-questions** that signaled that the child's utterance lacked a necessary component. The great majority of utterances queried by a **Rerun request** were noncommunicative babble; 91 percent of all **Rerun requests** were to this type of vocalization, compared with 44 percent of **Substitutions** and none of the other types.

In the 18-month age group, where children produced mostly one-word utterances with some two-word vertical or horizontal constructions, the average proportion of **Rerun requests** declined to 22.5 percent. The proportion of **Substitutions** stayed about the same (20.6 percent). The most dramatic increase occurred in the two categories signaling a missing component, where these two together accounted for 31.4 percent of all clarification requests.

In the 26-month age group, where all children produced multiword utterances, the proportion of **Rerun requests** declined further to 13.7 percent, along with **Substitutions** (7.3 percent). The two "expansion" categories accounted for 44.8 percent of all clarification requests.

In addition, **Partial repetitions** increased from 0 percent to 1.7 percent to 8.2 percent, whereas **Full repetitions** increased from 4.9 percent to 23.9 percent to 33.2 percent, respectively, in the three age groups. **Direct queries about unintelligible words** stayed at a low 0 percent, 1.6 percent, and 1.1 percent, respectively, in the three groups.

These results indicate that children receive negative feedback about ill-formed utterances and, moreover, that this feedback is fine-tuned to what they can be expected to process and use for modifying their rule system. For very young beginning speakers, the major informative negative feedback is the **Substitution** kind; the provision of such feedback functions to teach children to substitute more conventional forms for their own nonconventional productions. It is obvious that 10-month-olds who are just beginning to produce conventional verbal forms cannot benefit from the information that they omit obligatory components from their sentences. However, these types of feedback are increasingly appropriate as children enter the multiword stage, that is, in the 18- and 26-month age groups. For older children, such teaching is provided by **Yes-no questions that expand the children's own utterance.** In the two older age groups, children's major departure from grammaticality is errors not of commission but of omission; they simply cannot yet put all the obligatory components into a sentence. It appears that mothers, in their spontaneous conversations with their children, provide explicit information about this problem, along with some direct modeling of the more conventional, full forms the children should develop toward.

### 7.4.4 Why insist on repair?

We have devoted considerable space to the consideration of conversational repair because it constitutes a lens on several issues central to an understanding of children's development of conversational skill. First, if we see turn-taking as central to conversation, it is clear that repair is necessary for turn-taking to continue smoothly. Some repair mechanisms indeed respond directly to turn disruptions, for example, apologizing for interruptions. More common, though, are repair procedures designed to remediate breakdowns in message transmission—at the level either of the signal (*I didn't hear you*) or of the illocutionary force (*What in god's name did you mean by that?*). These repairs reveal the interlocutors' commitment to the basic presuppositions underlying conversation—that communication is possible, that information can be shared, and that different personal perspectives can be aligned. Ultimately, all of the issues we deal with under the rubric *pragmatics* have to do as well with perspective, since the simplest general formulation of all of the specific rules for speaking appropriately might be "understand and acknowledge your interlocutor's point of view."

Parents request clarification from their children for many reasons—to understand the child's message, to signal disapproval of the message, to correct the way of expressing the message. In the process, they illustrate an important central principle of effective communication: The interlocutor's perspective is often different from one's own and must be taken into account. Repair procedures lie directly on the boundary between conversation per se and extended discourse—the product of conversation in which perspective becomes a central issue.

# 8

# The Pragmatics of Connected Discourse

## 8.1 Overview

### 8.1.1 Demands on the learner

As we have seen, children start using language by connecting utterances directly to intentions embedded in interpersonal activity. Because adult interlocutors create predictable, recurrent interactive structures, children can manage effective participation and the pragmatically effective exchange of conversational turns long before they can in fact engage in the conversational exchange of novel information. Only after some months of using words to express their intentions do children start to be able to provide content-based connections between their utterances and the interlocutor's utterances, for example, to answer questions informatively, respond to greetings, agree or disagree with a statement, or in other ways respond in a topic-constrained way with new and relevant information. The emergence of this capacity for information exchange creates the possibility of extended discussions and represents a watershed for adult interlocutors, who are now no longer solely responsible for maintaining topics and providing information.

Ultimately, though, the ability to relate one's own utterances informatively to those of the interlocutor represents still incomplete control of the pragmatics of information exchange; to be successful in many forms of talk, one must take into account, in addition to what the interlocutor is saying, the interlocutor's state of mind. In other words, one must assess how much of the information to be discussed is already shared with the interlocutor, and one must consider what the interlocutor needs to know to understand new information one might wish to convey. When children are young and much connected discourse is conversational, they receive considerable help from their interlocutors in the form of both questions designed to be sure they supply relevant background information and indicators of noncomprehension when the information provided is insufficient; thus, the pragmatic requirement to take the interlocutor's knowledge into account is initially enforced conversationally. However, when children need to produce connected discourses autonomously (e.g., by taking a turn at sharing time in school or writing a letter to a distant friend), the pragmatic skills involved in assessing the interlocutor's state of mind *predictively* and not just interactively become increasingly important.

### 8.1.2 Discourse as a level of organization

We have seen in Chapter 7 various hints of how connected discourse emerges from conversation, both interactively and developmentally. Young children are capable of participating in connected discourse because of the nurturant support of adult conversational partners; tiny units of topic-centered discussions that emerge from discussions of joint foci of attention develop in length and complexity and eventually support a shift to discussions of more remote topics—topics related to the present, nonpresent topics, fantasy play, and abstract and hypothetical topics. Ultimately, these conversationally embedded stretches of discourse also free themselves from conversational support, and children develop the capacity to produce several turns in a row without prodding or feedback from the interlocutor; eventually, they are able to tell stories, give explanations, make arguments, and generate other forms of autonomous extended discourse.

   The topic of extended discourse injects into our discussion of pragmatics a new level of organization of talk. Talk is produced, of course, in utterances, which can be analyzed at the speech act level and which are further organized into stretches of talk defined by their common pragmatic business, which Goffman called interchanges. At the conversational level, talk is analyzed in turns, and sequences of turns are organized into larger units, like adjacency pairs or initiation-response contingencies. In this chapter we analyze talk organized in units like narratives, arguments, explanations, and definitions; these are socially and culturally defined units that have their own organizational principles and rules for appropriate use. Any one of these types of talk could itself be the topic of an entire book, and indeed some have been, for example, the books by Nelson and her collaborators (1986), by Peterson and McCabe (1983), by McCabe and Peterson (1991), by Berman and Slobin (1994) on narrative development, and by Donaldson (1986) on children's explanations. Given the breadth of what has been done, we cannot review the work of others in these domains. Our goals in this chapter are to locate our own and others' work on extended discourse on the map of developmental pragmatics and to present some of our own data on children's development of oral-connected discourse skills to exemplify the pragmatic analysis of these language performances.

## 8.2 Assessing the listener's state of mind

In this chapter we consider three of the most widely studied genres of connected discourse—narratives, explanations, and definitions—asking in each case how children solve the problem of taking into account in their linguistic productions the listener's state of mind. In some cases, even knowing which genre to select involves having some sense of the listener's state of mind, as well as knowledge of genre-specific rules. To understand the problems of connected discourse, we must consider how the situations of language use differ for young children and more mature language users.

First, young children talk mostly to nurturant, loving, and forgiving inti-mates, whereas adults often talk to strangers, to people with fairly different experiences and points of view, and rather frequently to people disinclined to be helpful. Second, young children receive considerable conversational support from those intimates, whereas older children and adults are expected to produce language more autonomously. In Chapter 7 we saw that older children produce longer conversational turns; a late stage in development is total absence of conversational support, for instance, the ability to give a speech or dominate the conversation at a dinner party. Finally, young children talk mostly about concrete objects and visible events in the here and now, whereas older children and adults talk as well about the past and the future, about emotions and cognitions, about abstract topics, hypotheticals, and counterfactuals. This shift in the kinds of things talked about is reflected in children's increased participa-tion in discussion of the nonpresent or of hearer's and speaker's states of mind (see Chapter 6) and in their increasing ability to make talk for its own sake a central social activity (see Chapter 7). All these changes—in interactants, in organization of talk, and in topic—increase the demands on the speaker to take into account the listener's state of mind.

"Assessing the listener's state of mind" is often referred to as "producing decontextualized language," where decontextualized language is defined as language that eschews assumptions about shared knowledge and perspective. However, the term *decontextualized language* applies only to circumstances where background knowledge is not shared, implying that the speaker's only problem is to function effectively in such situations. The pragmatic challenge is to determine precisely what kind of a situation one is faced with—whether one can count on shared background knowledge and conversational support or not. Adults often need to take into account their listeners' expertise to avoid boring them or appearing presumptuous. The linguistic problem of producing extended discourse is not that it must always be totally explicit and complete but that the speaker must decide precisely *how* explicit and complete it should be. For example, a central pragmatic problem is exemplified by the production of different lectures for introductory and advanced students—boring the advanced students is as much a pragmatic violation as is talking over the heads of the beginners.

Development of the ability to produce decontextualized language *when it is needed* is clearly one of the major accomplishments of child language users, as is establishing a basis for assessing when it is needed. The two-year-old produces communicatively effective utterances that function well as turns in a conversation, but the two-year-old's language falls short of being decontextualized on a number of points:

1. It is effective because of the conversational structure provided by adults, which embeds rather simple child utterances into a larger and more complex informational and interactive structure. Older children's language is expected to be communicatively effective even when autonomous, or isolated from conversational support, and these expectations are met only if children have the pragmatic skills to assess listener expectations and to create an implicit structure consisting of the sorts of questions the listener might ask.

2. It is effective because interlocutors already know what the two-year-old is talking about, having shared a history of experiences that provides background information about the child and about the child's activities, preferences, likes, dislikes, likely topics, and idiosyncratic linguistic forms. Only later do children start to become effective communicators with adults who share less background knowledge, by virtue of a growing recognition that shared background knowledge cannot be assumed and growing control over the language forms used to provide the required background information linguistically.

3. It is effective because the interlocutor willingly takes the two-year-old's perspective on events, displaying a willingness to find monsters scary, toppling towers amusing, and mashed carrots yucky that will decline as children get older. Thus, two-year-olds can assume a resonance with perspective that makes explicit linguistic expression of that perspective unnecessary. Older children need to acknowledge the possibility that listeners will interpret events differently from speakers and need to learn how to represent their own perspectives convincingly.

There are, then, three problems for the child acquiring the pragmatics of extended discourse: learning to operate without all of the *conversational, historical,* and *psychological* support available initially. Whereas these three types of support are typically present to some degree even in conversations between adults and certainly in those between familiars, a key aspect of developing language skill is the withdrawal of the *presumption* of these supports. Thus, for example, adults can generate connected discourse without the support of questions like *What happened after the murder?* or *How did the files get shredded?* which children would need in narrating or explaining a complex happening. Adults typically provide background information appropriate to their assessment of the status and knowledge of the interlocutor, avoiding the unwarranted assumption of shared knowledge (the fact that adults sometimes misjudge the interlocutor's knowledge does not imply they are assuming shared knowledge). Adults also provide explicit information about their "take" on events, are capable of encoding linguistically a variety of psychological stances, and often broach the task of trying to change the interlocutor's point of view; again, failure in this regard does not impugn the basic claim that adults *avoid presuming aligned perspectives,* whereas very young children do not even consider perspective as a communicative issue.

In our discussion of three genres of connected discourse, we exemplify children's problems with each of these domains of decontextualization and show how their ability to deal with each develops. Of course, other aspects of language use and cognition develop as well in the period under study and interact with those we focus on here. One major additional issue is the complexity of the information encoded in language; young children typically talk about rather simple things, topics that would require little conversational, historical, or psychological context even if discussed with a stranger. Complexity of information structure is not one of the dimensions directly relevant to pragmatics, except insofar as it exacerbates the pragmatic problems of taking the listener's state of mind into account. A second major issue is the complex of problems associated with genre. Rules for interaction in institutional settings involve some restrictions on genre that children have to learn—that good sharing time turns are narrative, whereas good answers in science lessons are explanations or definitions. Furthermore, each of these different genres has specific rules that must also be learned. Although the issues of content complexity and genre specificity cannot be ignored, we concentrate on the more centrally pragmatic problems posed by connected discourse.

## 8.3 Narratives

Narratives are defined as extended discourse forms in which at least two different events are described such that the relationship between them (temporal, causal, contrastive, or other) becomes clear. The development of narratives has been studied extensively, in part because primitive narratives can be identified very early in children's speech, and by about age four children can produce fairly complex narratives of several different sorts. In addition, it has been proposed that narratives constitute a universal, basic mode of thought—not only for the psychological matters that are the stuff of the most familiar narratives but even for thinking about how the world works. For example, scientists are described as making decisions about what experiments they need to do and how to interpret their findings by telling themselves stories rather than by engaging in deductive or expository thinking (Bruner, 1986). Whereas evidence suggests that young children understand and learn from expository genres as easily as from narrative genres (Pappas, 1993), nonetheless the narrative-primacy view has greatly influenced curricular practice for early literacy training, as well as science and social studies teaching, and in educational circles has led to a romantic attachment to "story" as the natural way of learning (see Hemphill & Snow, forthcoming, for a critique of the educational practices derived from a narrative-primacy view).

### 8.3.1 Types of narrative

*Narrative* is a superordinate term; many different kinds of narrative forms can be distinguished, although no authoritative parsing of the narrative domain is accepted in all the disciplines in which narrative is a central notion (ranging from developmental psychology to history, literary studies, and psychoanalysis). Within developmental psycholinguistics, three narrative forms have been most widely studied:

1. A *script* is a narrative about what usually happens rather than about a specific incident. Scripts are among the earliest organized narrative forms it is possible to elicit from children, and it has been proposed that they provide a basis for children's conceptual organization and event memory (Nelson, 1986). In addition, scripts can be seen as a prerequisite to the emergence of real stories, since they report deviations from the normal course of events represented in a script.

2. *Personal event narratives* include both scriptlike responses to parental queries, like *what happened in school today*, and specific anecdotes about exciting, frightening, joyful, or otherwise reportable events. A particular form of the personal event narrative that has been widely studied in both adults and children is the so-called danger-of-death or scary event story (Labov, 1981; Labov & Waletzky, 1967), used in sociolinguistic research because it typically elicits natural, unmonitored, informal speech. These danger-of-death stories have "plot" structures derived from the events—a problem and the resolution of the problem. Other personal event narratives may have less clear-cut plots, although by the age of four or five North American children typically organize their stories around a major event, referred to as the high point.

3. *Fantasy narratives* provide the structure for much of children's play, although early fantasy play often enacts scripts (playing house, playing

doctor) rather than plots. Of course, young children growing up in literate cultures are exposed to fantasy or fictional narratives through the books their parents read to them, as well as through television and films. Many children are also exposed to fantasy narratives through oral storytelling (folk tales, myths, legends); these narratives are designed for entertainment, as well as for socialization in cultural norms regarding moral and social behavior and for education about group history, heroes, religious beliefs, and so on. Children certainly borrow elements from the fantasy narratives they are exposed to for their own play narratives—in U.S. kindergarten classrooms, for example, superheroes are a recurrent theme in boys' fantasy play. In the early school years, children in many classrooms are encouraged to produce fantasy narratives, which may be dictated to an adult or written in invented or conventional spelling by the child, as a transition to reading (Graves, 1983; Paley, 1990).

### 8.3.2 Conditions of production

Children's narratives differ in the conditions of production as well as genre. Some researchers have used highly constrained elicitations of stories, for example, asking the child to tell the story represented in a wordless picture book (e.g., Berman & Slobin, 1994) to compare across languages and ages the linguistic expressions used for certain target events. To elicit less constrained fantasy stories, Wolf and her colleagues have used animal replicas to act out the first few events of a story, then asked the child to take over (Wolf, Moreton, & Camp, 1994). Others have analyzed stories emerging naturally in dinner-table conversations (Blum-Kulka & Snow, 1992; De Temple & Beals, 1991), in parent-child conversations, and in natural-seeming scripted conversations.

Peterson and McCabe (1983) developed a child version of the danger-of-death procedures, a variant in which the experimenter, chatting with the child, tells his or her own story of an injury, a visit to the doctor, or a scary event—a technique that induces most children to generate topic-related stories from their own experience. The success of this technique points up an important feature of personal event stories in natural conversations that is not always replicated in laboratory studies—that they are typically told *for a purpose*. The purpose might be as simple as maintaining interpersonal attention through discussion of shared or related topics. The stories studding naturally occurring conversations are also used to support arguments, provide explanations, answer questions, present one's point of view or a reason for one's point of view, and so on. Stories with similar topics and similar points are often, oddly enough, told in sequence by different participants in a conversation; Aston proposes they are used to establish "comity," or the public acknowledgment of a shared perspective (Aston, 1988).

Many researchers use the technique of asking parents to elicit stories from children, acknowledging how crucial to successful child narratives is the process of coconstruction with a sensitive adult who knows something about the narrated event (conversational and historical context, in our terms). Such narratives are, of course, hard to compare across children and across ages, because children have fairly different sorts of experiences to report; there is no denying that—other things being equal—car crashes, narrow escapes, and visits to the president make for better stories than playground scrapes and difficult arithmetic tests. We used the scary story elicitation technique with five-year-olds in the Home-School Study of Language and Literacy Development (Snow, 1991) and found that some children denied ever having had a really scary experience, claims typically supported by their mothers.

The technique of having children narrate events in a wordless picture book, most notably the so-called Frog Book first used by Bamberg (1987) and adopted by Berman and Slobin (1994), eliminates the differences among children in the events they have to report. Of course, children's skill in narrating the events in such a book is dependent on their understanding of the pictured events—it is obvious from the frog story narratives produced by three-year-olds that their understanding was less than complete. Furthermore, the narratives produced in response to a standard stimulus are unlikely to reflect the personal perspectives of young children (although they may from adults practiced in literary criticism) and thus fail to generate the symbolic meanings that are so central in naturally told narratives.

Each of the various narrative-elicitation methods is better for assessing some aspects of narrative skill than others, and each has some methodological shortcomings. For getting a full picture of children's narrative development, some combination would be necessary. In this chapter we use data mostly from situations in which children tell stories to an experimenter but with their mothers present to provide conversational, historical, and psychological support when needed. We used the elicitation technique, introduced by Peterson and McCabe (1983), of telling a story of a close scrape (a near collision with another car or an encounter with a large, aggressive dog), then asked the child, *Has anything like that ever happened to you?*[1] These data (and most of the extended discourse performances presented in this chapter) come from the Home-School Study of Language and Literacy Development (Snow, 1991), a longitudinal study of a group of children from low-income families observed in interaction with their mothers at home and at (pre)school from age 3 through 12 years. The goal of the study is to seek relationships between oral language skills and literacy outcomes; thus, rich data about children's performance on tasks like telling stories and giving definitions have been collected, as well as naturally occurring interactions (e.g., free play and mealtimes) during which narratives and explanations occur frequently.

### 8.3.3 Conversational support

Let us turn to a few examples of five-year-olds' scary stories to get a sense of how children approach this task and how their mothers provide conversational support. Of the 61 five-year-olds from whom we tried to elicit scary stories, 9 never managed to tell any story, and only 26 selected a topic to tell a story about and produced at least the basic story without significant help from their mothers. Of these 26, only 3 managed without at least some clarifying questions or hints from their mothers. Many children needed help in selecting an incident to tell, revealing one of the pragmatic challenges children face—that of knowing which of their own experiences is reportable. In addition, most of the children needed some help with the telling itself, producing versions their parents felt needed some elaboration or extension. Amanda's story is a good example of the kind of conversational support children often get; her mother and grandfather essentially tell the story, and Amanda simply offers a few details and reinterpretations. The experimenter asked Amanda if anything scary had happened to her.

*Example 8.1.* Amanda.

| | |
|---|---|
| Child: | nothing. |
| Grandpa: | well, no, how about not . . . getting off the bus. |
| Mother: | yeah, why don't you tell her about that? |
| Grandpa: | yeah, why don't you say, tal . . . talk about that? when Grandfather was uh . . . a little late coming around the corner with uh with the baby. |
| Mother: | she panicked, and she started getting scared and tried to . . . she wouldn't get off the bus . . . school bus. |
| Grandpa: | she wouldn't get off the bus. |
| Child: | I can't. I can't. |
| Grandpa: | why can't you? |
| Child: | because I need the um . . . |
| Mother: | she needs a note. |
| Child: | a note. |
| Grandpa: | oh, you need a note to get off the bus. |
| Child: | yeah. |

This story is typical of many we observed during dinner-table conversations as well, in that in these naturally occurring conversations it is fairly common for people to tell each other's stories and particularly for parents to tell children's stories. A similar example comes from the dinner-table conversation of an Israeli middle-class family (translated from Hebrew; from Blum-Kulka & Snow, 1992, pp. 197–198).

*Example 8.2.* Tali.

| | |
|---|---|
| Tali: | Daddy, daddy, it hurts here. |

| Mother: | D'you know that the rooster jumped on her today? |
| | They told the teacher that you cried and laughed together. |
| Tali: | Yes (laughing). |
| Mother: | She said that Tali was crying and laughing through the tears . . . rain and sun. |
| Tali: | Yes but when they brought me . . . |
| Father: | What was that? |
| Tali: | When they brought me Rom came with me, and he walked backwards. |
| Mother: | She said she was surrounded, all the kids, like flies, because the rooster had jumped on her. They brought her in. |
| Tali: | Rom too. |
| Father: | Why did he jump on you? |
| Tali: | Because I was too close to him. |
| Father: | Did you want to play with him? |
| Tali: | I was close to him and he was close to . . . |
| Father: | Did you come near to play with him? |
| Tali: | He jumped twice on my back. |
| Father: | Maybe he likes you. |
| Tali: | No, he was near me. |

Amanda's and Tali's stories exemplify an extreme of conversational support in natural storytelling, and both reveal that in natural conversation the production of extended discourse is not typically seen as a "performance," an interpretation that would enforce a single-speaker rule, but as an effort to communicate content and perspective. In the Home-School Study we actually were attempting to elicit performances from the children, using the parents' presence to ensure optimal child performance. In other families, parents accepted this goal and were less inclined to take over the storytelling completely. Nonetheless, their help or that of the experimenter was often crucial, either to keep the story going or to clarify the information being presented. In this transcript, the experimenter works hard to clarify Michelle's story, with only minimal success, after her mom suggests *tell what happened yesterday*.

*Example 8.3.* Michelle.

| Child: | I fall down the stairs. |
| Interviewer: | you did? |
| Interviewer: | how? |
| Interviewer: | on a roller skate? |
| Child: | boots. |
| Interviewer: | the boots got slippery? |
| Child: | [nods]. |
| Interviewer: | oh you tripped on boots? |

| Interviewer: | oh. |
| Mother: | where were the boots? |
| Child: | . . . on my feet. |

In the following lengthy example, Caroline needs her mother Beverly's help to tell the topic-related scary dog story, both to get started and subsequently to clarify various referents. But then in her final turn, Caroline comes out with a little story of her own, related to a topic that has emerged during the conversation but that is not directly responsive to the interviewer's elicitation. Caroline tells her own rather complicated story intelligibly and with no support, again revealing that children's extended discourse abilities are best revealed under conditions where they actually want to communicate something. In turn 8 Caroline reveals her understanding of the interviewer's limited access to necessary background knowledge, turning to her to explain away the possible confusion about Matthew's two dogs.

*Example 8.4.* Caroline.

| 1 Mother: | have you been scared? |
| 2 Child: | mmhm. |
| 3 Mother: | by whom? |
| 4 Child: | by Matthew's dog. |
| 5 Mother: | oh Matthew [laughs], yeah yeah. little dog but small dog, but she didn't really know the dog. so yeah . . . |
| 6 Child: | but I wasn't scared of the white dog. that died. |
| 7 Mother: | yeah, yeah the other one. |
| 8 Child: | Matthew had another dog and he was white. and he died. |
| 9 Interviewer: | oh. |
| 10 Mother: | yeah. but then uh . . . they . . . bought another one. that's the family wh . . . where I used to work. |
| 11 Child: | and now he's black. |
| 12 Mother: | the dog? yeah. the little dog. (be)cause they had a . . . a white one. He died, but then, she wa . . . she grew up with that dog. |
| 13 Interviewer: | oh. |
| 14 Mother: | and then uh, I mean, not grew up but . . . she was used to. but I used to work for them. |
| 15 Child: | you know. one day uh Matthew told me, "Caroline, that's so big you're six," and I said "no I'm five." then um . . . then Matthew goes "my um . . . Beverly, Beverly, she's six." she said, "no Matthew, she's still five!" |

Of course, some five-year-olds can tell topic-related stories without conversational support, like Ned in the next example.

*Example 8.5.* Ned.

| | |
|---|---|
| Child: | uh, I saw a dog. he was—my dad . . . came home. my grandpa dropped him off. and the dog tried to get in . . . the locked door downstairs. but my dad said, "hunhunh, you can't come up." |
| Interviewer: | wow, that's scary. |
| Child: | mmm. I wasn't even scared. |
| Interviewer: | oh really? |
| Mother: | it was a big dog. |
| Child: | I wasn't scared. |

This is an excellent performance for a five-year-old on a number of dimensions. First, it was topic related, following an experimenter-offered scary story about an aggressive dog. Second, Ned initiated the performance spontaneously, having himself thought of the incident he wanted to narrate and deciding how to start. Third, Ned told the whole story by himself, conveying all the necessary information about crucial characters, setting, and events—well enough that his mother did not find it necessary to elicit clarifying information. Fourth, Ned enlivens the story by using direct speech (*My dad said "hunhunh, you can't come up"*). Finally, Ned shows some attention to the principle of presenting information in the right order; the self-correction in his first line reveals his decision not to tell the "high point" of the story (he was trying to get in the door) before he had provided the necessary background information about who was involved and how the incident developed. In general, the kinds of hesitations indicated in this transcript with . . . are indicators of the skillful production of extended discourse, as they represent occasions of self-monitoring and planning. Even adults typically display dysfluencies associated with such on-line processing during the production of extended discourse, unless they are unusually fluent or well practiced.

Of course, this story could have been better. Ned undercuts its effectiveness by denying he was scared (many of the five-year-old boys we tested denied ever having been scared even while recounting events that had scared them). The story was also intrinsically fairly simple, involving essentially only dad and the dog and a single incident and response; thus, its structure did not challenge Ned's lexical and grammatical skills.

### 8.3.4 Historical support

A much less competent-sounding story from Dawn must be evaluated in light of the inherently greater complexity of the event she is reporting. In fact, it is not even clear if Dawn is telling one story or two—it is possible that she has established "snakes" as the topic and thus is telling a second story starting in the fifteenth line with *Guess what.* The difficulty of this story for Dawn is clear from her somewhat incompetent performance but also from the facts that she attempted to wriggle out of telling it (mumbling in turns 3 and 5, trying to escape physically in turn 11) and that a crucial incident (the dog's treatment of the snake) only gets told when her mother asks about it. The role of the shared historical context in contributing to Dawn's narration is clear. If her mom had not been present at the incident, it is likely we would never have gotten even a glimmer of what really happened.

**Example 8.6.** Dawn.

| | |
|---|---|
| 1 Child: | um one day, mmm mmm . . . uh my dog saw a snake uu . . . under a picnic table. |
| 2 Interviewer: | wh . . . |
| 3 Child: | th th . . . then the dog had to go to the vet. I mean . . . I mean, the puppy hospital. [looking at tape recorder] |
| 4 Interviewer: | mmhm. |
| 5 Child: | and . . . and then sh . . . |
| 6 Mother: | talk louder. |
| 7 Child: | and and . . . and, wait a minute. |
| 8 Mother: | wh . . what happened with Sandy and the snake? |
| 9 Child: | she . . she was a scared of it. |
| 10 Mother: | what did Sandy do to the snake? |
| 11 Child: | uh um . . . [tries to climb off chair] |
| 12 Mother: | no no no. [grabs Dawn] stay here and tell me. |
| 13 Child: | um. and she put her paws like this. and . . . and then she put it up again. |
| 14 Interviewer: | wow. |
| 15 Child: | guess what? I saw a long, long yellow snake that has xx yellow. um, a dead xxx and then he threw it over . . . over the red fence. |

One way to get as good as Ned at telling stories is to practice—not just to practice narration but to practice specific stories. The experience of telling stories several times represents another aspect of historical support. Brad, one of the better extended discourse producers in our study, clearly had talked with his mother about the scary incident he (after a suggestion from her) reported (in this session, the experimenter had offered his own scary story about a near-accident in a car).

**Example 8.7.** Brad.

| | |
|---|---|
| Mother: | what was scary that happened? |
| Child: | um . . . when we went in the big puddle and you thought your car . . . and you told me it would, it would die last year? |

Mother:          oh, when we drove through the giant puddles down at um the lights? down there?

Mother:          and Mama was . . . Mama was afraid that her car wasn't gonna make it through (be)cause her car died one time, and I think I got Brad a little nervous! [laughing]

Brad's mother both clarifies the specific puddle incident and explains further to the experimenter exactly why this incident was indeed scary. Brad's version is framed more as a reminiscence than a performance, a perfectly appropriate interpretation since he was addressing his mother, who had participated in the incident. His choice to make this a reminiscence, though, has certain implications for the linguistic structures he chooses—and makes clear that even if we limit ourselves to the genre of personal experience narratives, we need to incorporate into our analysis a notion like the dimension of social interchange as discussed in Chapter 2. The interpersonally agreed upon social activity for personal experience narratives might be reminiscing, instructing, informing, performing, persuading, and so on. The problems encountered by some children when they are asked to provide extended discourse in classroom settings may derive more from a misconstrual of the interpersonal activity being engaged in than from a lack of understanding of the rules of connected discourse.

### 8.3.5 Psychological support

We have emphasized in discussing the previous examples that the best stories are told for a purpose; that purpose often includes generating a temporary alignment of perspective between the storyteller and the listener. We tell some stories not so much to report facts about scary dogs or car crashes as to get the listeners to understand our fear. Unfortunately, conveying facts is easier than conveying perspectives on facts, and young children's stories often align perspectives successfully only because they can rely on empathetic listeners to anticipate the desired reaction. When they can no longer assume anticipatory alignment, they have to start working on linguistic strategies for conveying the appropriate reaction, which are referred to in work on narrative as *evaluation*.

The degree to which mothers are willing to take child perspectives on events is clear in the next transcript, again from Brad and his mother.

*Example 8.8.* Brad.

Child:           I saw something funny one da . . . yesterday when we were coming home? a truck with a board on the back? carrying a tow truck? and a tow truck carrying a car.

Mother:          a tow truck, carrying a tow truck, carrying a car—and we thought that was really funny!

| Child: | [laughs]. |
| Mother: | [laughs] huh? because you usually just see a tow truck on (with) a car. |

Here Brad's mother takes it upon herself to make the psychological perspective explicit. Evan, on the other hand, uses lots of linguistic devices to invoke his own perspective on the two events he recounts in Example 8.9, including using direct speech to represent his view in the first incident and a reenactment of his own fear in the second.

*Example 8.9.* Evan.

| Child: | yeah, Mom, and you know what? on the tv you know like I was so scared when the tv was turned off, I was like, "uhoh, there he is." |
| Mother: | oh, you felt you were seeing him places? |
| Child: | like um, like um, like um, like um I was dreaming about a Tyrannosaurus rex, and he saw me and he came after me. |
| Mother: | yeah? |
| Child: | and went and didn't pick me up. |
| Mother: | oh. |
| Child: | that like [screams]. I said, "wh- wh- wh- wh- wh- where were we? [pretending to stutter from fright] |

Even given Evan's inventive use of linguistic evaluation to express his perspective, though, his mother still provides psychological support, actively reflecting his perspective in her question *you felt you were seeing him places?* and in her reaction to the second event.

In example 8.10, Zane's mother explicitly demands he tell how he felt about going down the water slide they are discussing.

*Example 8.10.* Zane.

| Child: | hey mommy, the second one I made a very silly face, I went like this [making a silly face]. |
| Mother: | [laughing] but you don't remember . . . you can't say what it felt like? you don't remember? |
| Child: | it feel like . . . |
| Mother: | what did you think was going to happen? |
| Child: | [laughs] that I was going to xxx. |

In this excerpt from a dinner-table conversation in Brad's family, the adults essentially tell a story about Brad's *internal states,* involving him only minimally in the telling.

*Example 8.11.* Brad.

| | |
|---|---|
| Grandma: | and did you tell Dad how you ran down the hill? |
| Child: | I ran down the hill. |
| Grandma: | he was running down and xxx. couple of times he fell and rolls. |
| Mother: | way way down xxx. xxx. he loved it. Ma said we were up on top of the hill and Brad couldn't wait to run down it. Ma says "okay Brad, do you wanna go down here now?" and Brad yells out "yay." xxx and he ran down the hill just as fast as he could. |

### 8.3.6 Summary

We have presented examples of parental support for completeness and clarity of content, as well as perspective, rather than an extensive description of how children achieve those goals. This in part reflects the absence at this time of a longitudinal basis for describing children's development of the pragmatic abilities necessary for connected discourse; the cultural/psychological perspective that underlies our work, as well as considerable evidence, though, suggests that aspects of language use that parents emphasize will be adopted by children. Snow and Goldfield (1983) documented one child's spontaneous provision of information his mother had previously queried, over several sessions of reading the same book. McCabe and Peterson (1991; Peterson & McCabe, 1992) found that the sorts of questions parents ask during children's narratives predict the aspect of the narrative children elaborate a couple of years later; mothers who ask for background information have children who emphasize setting, and mothers who ask for evaluation have children who emphasize perspective. Our data, like those of McCabe and Peterson, confirm that North American mothers ask for and help with clarification of orienting information, ask for and help with clarification of the events, and, in addition, clearly model, reinforce, and demand information about the child's perspective on the story, making clear to the child that one cannot presuppose the interlocutor automatically understands the teller's point of view.

Bruner (1986) has argued that for children the difficulty of narrative lies in its juxtaposition of two landscapes, the external landscape of characters and the events they take part in and the psychological landscape of the characters' feelings, desires, reactions, and knowledge. Rather than the problem being difficulty in understanding the characters' internal states, we are arguing that the central pragmatic problem facing the producer of narrative discourse is understanding the *interlocutors'* internal states sufficiently to predict the questions they might be asking themselves, to assess their relevant background knowledge, and to be able to influence their perspective.

## 8.4 Explanations

Although connected discourse forms other than narrative have been studied sporadically, for no other form do we have a database as rich or as varied as for narrative. Explanations have been studied primarily from the perspective of the light they cast on children's thinking (Donaldson, 1986) and for their incidence in the speech children hear (Beals, 1991). It is clear from Beals's work that the explanatory genre cannot be considered distinct from narrative, as narratives are often offered to explain and explanations often contain narrative segments. Consider Example 8.12 from a dinner-table conversation in Brad's family on a stormy night (from Beals & Snow, 1994).

*Example 8.12.* Brad.

| | |
|---|---|
| Grandma: | you know what the thunder is? |
| Brad: | yeah. thunder and lightning. |
| Grandma: | yeah. and the thunder is when uh the angels are upstairs bowling. and that's one of them just got a spare. |
| Mother: | Brad should get out his Berenstain Bear almanac and let Ma read it, and that'll tell her what thunder is huh? |
| Grandma: | mmhm. |
| Mother: | tells [/] all about thunder and . . . |
| Grandpa: | that's the energy. |
| Grandma: | why should [/] why should he be brought up on a different story than you people were? |
| Brad: | because [/] that's because xxx Mommy vacuuming it. |
| Grandpa: | that's the energy huh? |
| Grandpa: | thunder is caused by energy in the clouds. |
| Brad: | yeah [/] yeah but [/] but one day I was sleeping in my bed for [/] for a long, long time, and thunder and lightning came from outside, and I was trying to (sneezes). |
| Mother: | oh bless you. |
| Brad: | and I was trying to find something that was yellow outside in the dark all by itself. and it came out. and it was thunder and lightning and I hided from it. |

Grandma's explanation for thunder is explicitly labeled a story and is contrasted with more "scientific" explanations (from the Berenstain Bears and Grandpa, respectively). Explanations about thunder flow seamlessly into more stories—in this case, Brad's story about being frightened by thunder. In the dinner-table conversations of the Home-School Study sample, about 10 percent of the utterances were classified as *both* narrative and explanatory at the same time.

### 8.4.1 Conversational support

Young children's explanatory talk is highly dependent on conversational support, in part because their understanding is limited. At the Home-School Study home visit when the children were five, we asked the mothers and children to spend a little time playing with a magnet and an assortment of metal and nonmetal objects to explore whether and how scientific explanations might be constructed (Snow & Kurland, 1995). We found that of 68 dyads observed, 62 engaged in some interactive "science process talk," or talk focused on an explanation of magnetism, although science talk constituted only 13 percent of the utterances overall. George and his mother produced a relatively high proportion of explanatory talk, of the following sort.

*Example 8.13*. George.

| Mother: | <how come> [/] how come all the silver-colored ones stick but the money doesn't stick? (putting nuts and a nickel on the magnetic base) hmm? you know why? |
| Child: | <I don't know how it does> [?]. |
| Mother: | you think money has [///] is a magnet? |
| Child: | no. |
| Mother: | (be)cause it's a different metal? |
| Child: | yeah. |
| Mother: | but it's the same color. |
| Child: | yeah. |

Clearly, if five-year-olds are to have any hope of explaining how magnets work, it will be in response to appropriate adult questions.

### 8.4.2 Historical support

Historical support is also invoked in explanatory talk, as in this conversation between Kurt and his mother (turn 7).

*Example 8.14*. Kurt.

| 1 Mother: | those keep sticking to it huh? |
| 2 Child: | mmhm. |
| 3 Mother: | you know why? |
| 4 Child: | why? |
| 5 Mother: | think. what do you think is inside that black box? |
| 6 Child: | metal? |
| 7 Mother: | what? we've talked about this before. what's inside? that makes everything stick like that [=! laughs]? like on our refrigerator? |

8 Child:          magnets.
9 Mother:         very good.

The platonic method in science teaching relies precisely on the assumption that students will eventually be able to recreate autonomously both roles in the conversations they have a history of participating in.

### 8.4.3 Psychological support

Providing explanations that take the listener's perspective into account is a great challenge, one adults fail regularly. Adults involved in scientific teaching often use metaphors in an attempt to address the students' perspective; in the discussions of magnets, the most common metaphor used by mothers was "sticking" or "stickiness" to describe the functioning of the magnet. This is, of course, a useful metaphor for the most salient property of magnets, but it is somewhat misleading in that it reminds one of glue and thus fails to account for the fact that magnets repel as well as attract.

Providing explanations is very hard for children, for reasons that have to do with the content to be explained, as well as with the pragmatic demands of providing an explanation. Nonetheless, like narratives, primitive explanations emerge very early in children's speech (Barbieri, Colavita, & Scheuer, 1990), appearing first in conversationally and historically supported contexts. Only with the emergence of sophisticated skills for assessing the interlocutor's state of mind do they become fully pragmatically effective.

## 8.5 Definitions

Definitions represent a rather special-purpose discourse form—one more highly valued in classrooms and dictionaries than at dinner tables or during play. We include definitions in our consideration of late pragmatic development because they exemplify two pragmatic problems: learning specific genres and understanding the social situation. The definitional genre is basically rather simple: It requires a superordinate and a statement of appropriate restrictions on the superordinate class named, for example:

an island is a body of land surrounded by water.
a knife is a utensil used for cutting or stabbing.
a hat is an article of clothing worn on the head.
a bicycle is a two-wheeled vehicle propelled by pedaling.

Children are typically capable of producing definitions of this general form (although perhaps somewhat less sophisticated in lexicon and syntax) by about age seven, but they still often prefer to respond to questions about words with stories or explanations rather than definitions, for example:

> What is a cat?
> My aunt had one named Boots, and it was all white and fluffy except it had black feet.

If queried further after a response like this, children as young as four will often recognize the need for a genre shift (Watson & Olson, 1987):

> Yes, but what is a cat?
> Oh, it's an animal.

By responding *it's an animal* to a normal adult in this situation, the child enters a socially constructed fiction that normal English-speaking adults might not know what cats are. The child has to understand not just what knowledge adults share but also what knowledge adults might act like they do not share for particular purposes. Obviously, it would constitute a pragmatic violation to go around explaining the meaning of all the words we used—participating in a language community means having already accepted a long list of conventions about what words mean. In a normal conversation, someone who asked *what's a cat?* would arouse surprise unless he or she could be taken for a second-language speaker or a recovering aphasic; the expected response would be to point to a cat, to provide a translation, or to elicit recognition by meowing, not to give a formal definition. Nonetheless, under certain circumstances (e.g., in classrooms and when taking IQ tests), children are expected to define simple words and to provide other answers adults could not sincerely need to know (Cazden, 1988).

Responding properly to requests for definitions requires, in effect, a metacommunicative analysis of the situation, generating an understanding that the question is not to be understood as a simple request for the information queried, like *Where's the newspaper?* or *What's this $300 phone bill?* addressed to a spouse. Requests for definitions are meant to elicit performances, and like other performances, definitions represent an intent not to communicate their content but to communicate that the speaker is capable of producing the content. Children who are very good at understanding requests for information and at expressing their own intentions directly might well have trouble with learning the rules of such performances. Initially, children may participate simply for the purpose of participating, as 10-month-olds do when playing peek-a-boo, rather than because of any understanding of the actual message they are producing. Adults typically participate in performances (e.g., marriage ceremonies, oral exams, job interviews) with a somewhat more sophisticated understanding that the questions asked are not sincere requests for the information queried but instead are attempts to enforce communication of quite a different sort.

Several different studies of children's definitions have shown that the percentage of words given a "formal" definition, that is, one that includes a superordinate and accepts the fiction of the ignorant interviewer, increases steadily with age (Snow, 1990; Velasco & Snow, 1995). In addition, though, children from families of higher social class and those attending better schools give more formal definitions than children from less educated families (Snow et al., 1996). Children who can already read or who will go on to be superior readers give formal and very complete definitions as young as 5 (Davidson & Snow, 1995), whereas poor readers may not give formal definitions even at age 10 (Velasco & Snow, 1995). Children's definitional skill is predicted by experiences at home reading books with parents (De Temple & Beals, 1991; Watson, 1989) and hearing extended discourse at the dinner table (De Temple & Beals, 1991; Snow, 1983a), as well as by exposure to academic discourse at school (Snow, 1990).

## 8.6 Summary

We have focused here on three forms of connected discourse on which the most developmental data are available. We have not included many specific types of special-purpose extended discourse whose acquisition can be of great importance in particular social settings: ritual insult exchanges, like snapping or doing the dozens; telling jokes; engaging in debates or political arguments, which are forms of discourse that one can be skilled in only after having reached a certain level of sophistication in thinking as well as talking.

The topic of extended discourse introduces new complexities in the organization of talk and in the kinds of interpersonal intentions that can be identified. Whereas it is easy to think of narratives and definitions as genres, with rules for their internal organization, explanations are somewhat less clearly a genre in that there is no clear replicable structure in explanatory speech events. What explanation has in common with narrative and definitions is that children's ability to produce autonomous explanations, like their ability to produce narratives and definitions, emerges from a long history of participating in multiparty explanations and of interactive training in the need to take into account the interlocutor's knowledge and point of view.

Indeed, all mature pragmatic functioning reflects the achievement of understanding the interlocutor's state of mind. This understanding takes the expression of communicative intents beyond its initial key-word character to the realm of pragmatic effectiveness and finesse and takes politeness beyond formulas to the establishment of social relationships through talk.

Thus we end where we started, at the problem of distinguishing linguistic pragmatics from cognitive and social competence, from psychology and linguistics, with the recognition that the boundaries cannot be sharply drawn. The central theme uniting the many different topics that fall under the rubric *pragmatics* is the theme of appropriateness. A 14-month-old is using language appropriately when he or she employs words to participate in social interactive formats, but a pragmatically effective 14-year-old must know as well how to participate appropriately in social relationships created, maintained, and transformed through language.

---

## Notes

1.  The explicit mechanism for eliciting the scary story was that the experimenter, visiting the home to observe the mother and child in a series of situations, at some point said something like: "You know, on my way over here the scariest thing happened to me. I was walking along, and this huge dog started following, and I walked faster and faster, and he kept getting closer and closer, and finally he came right up to me and grabbed my lunch bag, and I was really scared. Did anything like that ever happen to you?" If the child failed to respond, the experimenter told another story about being very frightened when almost run into by a car going too fast and again asked, Has anything like that ever happened to you? One problem with this technique is that children often took "big dog" or "car crash" as the topic rather than the intended one, "being scared."

# References

Acredolo, L., & Goodwyn, S. (1988). Symbolic gesturing in normal infants. *Child Development*, *59*, 450–466.

Ahrens, R. (1954). Beitrag zur entwicklung des physiognomie and mimikerkennens. *Z. exp. angew. Psychol.*, *2*, 412–454.

Allwood, J. (1981). On the distinction between semantics and pragmatics. In W. Klein & W. Levelt (Eds.), *Crossing the boundaries in linguistics*. Boston: D. Reidel Publishing.

Alston, W. P. (1964). *The philosophy of language*. Englewood Cliffs, N.J.: Prentice-Hall.

Anderson, A., Clark, A., & Mullin, J. (1994). Interactive communication between children: Learning how to make language work in dialogue. *Journal of Child Language*, *21*, 439–464.

Anselmi, D., Tomasello, M., & Acunzo, M. (1986). Young children's responses to neutral and specific contingent queries. *Journal of Child Language*, *13*, 135–144.

Antinucci, F., & Parisi, D. (1973). Early language acquisition: A model and some data. In C. Ferguson & D. Slobin (Eds.), *Studies in child language development*. New York: Holt, Rinehart & Winston.

Antinucci, F., & Parisi, D. (1975). Early semantic development in child language. In E. H. Lennenberg & E. Lennenberg (Eds.), *Foundations of language development: A multidisciplinary approach*, Vol. 1. New York: Academic Press.

Argyle, M., & Cook, M. (1976). *Gaze and mutual gaze*. Cambridge: Cambridge University Press.

Astington, J. W. (1988). Promises: Words or deeds? *First Language*, *8*, 259–270.

Aston, G. (1988). *Learning comity: An approach to the description and pedagogy of interactive speech*. Bologna: Ediatrice Clueb.

Austin, J. L. (1961). How to talk—some simple way. In J. L. Austin, *Philosophical papers*. Oxford: Clarendon Press.

Austin, J. L. (1962). *How to do things with words*. New York: Oxford University Press.

Bacharach, V., & Luszcz, M. (1979). Communicative competence in young children: The use of implicit linguistic information. *Child Development*, *50*, 260–263.

Baier, A. C. (1967). Nonsense. In P. Edwards (Ed.), *The encyclopedia of philosophy*. New York: Macmillan and the Free Press.

Bamberg, M. (1987). *The acquisition of narrative: Learning to use language.* The Hague: Mouton de Gruyter.

Barbieri, M. S., Colavita, F., & Scheuer, N. (1990). The beginning of the explaining capacity. In G. Conti-Ramsden & C. E. Snow (Eds.), *Children's language, Vol. 7.* Hillsdale, N.J.: Erlbaum.

Bar-Hillel, Y. (1954). Indexical expressions. *Mind, 63,* 359–379.

Barker, G. R. (1968). *Ecological psychology.* Stanford: Stanford University Press.

Barrett, M. D. (1981). The communicative functions of early child language. *Linguistics, 19,* 273–305.

Barrett, M. D. (1983). The early acquisition and development of the meanings of action-related words. In T. B. Seiler & W. Wannenmacher (Eds.), *Concept development and the development of word meaning.* Berlin: Springer.

Barrett, M. D. (1986). Early semantic representations and early word-usage. In S. A. Kuczay & M. D. Barrett (Eds.), *The development of early word meaning.* New York: Springer.

Barrett, M. D. (1989). Early language development. In A. Slater & G. Bremmer (Eds.), *Infant development.* London: Erlbaum.

Bates, E. (1976). *Language and context: Studies in the acquisition of pragmatics.* New York: Academic Press.

Bates, E. (1979). *The emergence of symbols.* New York: Academic Press.

Bates, E., Benigni, L., Bretherton, I., Camaioni, L., & Volterra, V. (1979). *The emergence of symbols: Cognition and communication in infancy.* New York: Academic Press.

Bates, E., Camaioni, L., & Volterra, V. (1975). The acquisition of performatives prior to speech. *Merrill-Palmer Quarterly, 21,* 205–226.

Bates, E., & MacWhinney, B. (1979). A functionalist approach to the acquisition of grammar. In E. Ochs & B. Schieffelin (Eds.), *Developmental pragmatics.* New York: Academic Press.

Bates, E., & MacWhinney, B. (1982). The development of grammar. In E. Wanner & L. Gleitman (Eds.), *Language acquisition: The state of art.* Cambridge: MIT Press.

Bateson, G. (1955). A theory of play and phantasy. *Psychiatric Research Reports,* 2.

Bateson, M. C. (1975). Mother-infant exchanges: The epigenesis of conversational interaction. In D. Aaronson & R. W. Rieber (Eds.), *Developmental psycholinguistics and communication disorders.* New York: New York Academy of Sciences.

Beals, D. E. (1991). *"I know who makes ice cream": Explanations in mealtime conversations of low-income families of preschoolers.* Unpublished doctoral dissertation, Harvard University Graduate School of Education.

Beals, D. E., & Snow, C. E. (1994). "Thunder is when the angels are upstairs bowling": Narratives and explanations at the dinner table. *Journal of Narrative and Life History, 4,* 331–352.

Becker, J. (1982). Children's strategic use of requests to mark and manipulate social status. In S. Kuczaj (Ed.), *Language development: Language, thought, and culture, Vol. 2.* Hillsdale, N.J.: Erlbaum.

Becker, J. (1986). Bossy and nice requests: Children's production and interpretation. *Merrill-Palmer Quarterly, 32,* 393–413.

Benedict, H. (1979). Early lexical development: Comprehension and production. *Journal of Child Language, 16,* 183–200.

Benoit, P. (1982). Formal coherence production in children's discourse. *First Language, 3,* 161–180.

Berger, P. L., & Luckman, T. (1967). *The social construction of reality.* Harmondsworth: Penguin.

Berman, R. A., & Slobin, D. I. (1994). *Relating events in narrative: A cross-linguistic developmental study.* Hillsdale, N.J.: Erlbaum.

Bertenthal, B. I., Proffitt, D. R., Spetner, N. B., & Thomas, M. A. (1985). The development of infant sensitivity to biomechanical motions. *Child Development, 56,* 531–543.

Bidell, T. R., & Fischer, K. W. (1992). Beyond the stage debate: Action, structure and variability in Piagetian theory and research. In R. Sternberg & C. Berg (Eds.), *Intellectual development.* New York: Cambridge University Press.

Birdwhistell, R. L. (1970). *Kinesics and context: Essays on body motion communication.* Philadelphia: University of Pennsylvania Press.

Blank, M., & Franklin, M. (1980). Dialogue with preschoolers: A cognitively-based system of assessment. *Applied Psycholinguistics, 1,* 127–150.

Bloom, L. (1973). *One word at a time: The use of single word utterances before syntax.* The Hague: Mouton.

Bloom, L., Rocissano, L., & Hood, L. (1976). Adult-child discourse: Developmental interaction between information processing and linguistic knowledge. *Cognitive Psychology, 8,* 521–552.

Blum-Kulka, S., & Snow, C. E. (1992). Developing autonomy for tellers, tales, and telling in family narrative events. *Journal of Narrative and Life History, 2*(3), 187–217.

Blum-Kulka, S., & Weizman, E. (1988). The inevitability of misunderstandings: Discourse ambiguities. *Text, 8,* 219–241.

Bohannon, J. N., & Marquis, L. A. (1977). Children's control of adult speech. *Child Development, 48,* 1002–1008.

Bower, T.G.R. (1966). *The visual world of infants.* San Francisco: W. H. Freeman.

Braunwald, S. R. (1978). Context, word and meaning: Towards a communicational analysis of lexical acquisition. In A. Lock (Ed.), *Action, gesture and symbol.* London: Academic Press.

Brazelton, T. B., Koslowski, B., & Main, M. (1974). The origins of reciprocity: The early mother-infant interaction. In M. Lewis & L. Rosenblum (Eds.), *The effect of the infant on the caregiver.* New York: Wiley.

Bronson, W. (1981). *Toddlers' behaviors with agemates: Issues of interaction, cognition, and affects. Monographs on Infancy, Vol. 1.* Norwood, N.J.: Ablex.

Brown, G., & Yule, G. (1983). *Discourse analysis.* Cambridge: Cambridge University Press.

Brown, P., and Levinson, S. (1978). Universals in language usage: Politeness phenomena. In E. Goody (Ed.), *Questions and politeness: Strategies in social interaction.* Cambridge: Cambridge University Press.

Brown, P., & Levinson, S. (1987). *Politeness: Some universals in language usage.* Cambridge: Cambridge University Press.

Brown, R. (1973). *A first language: The early stages.* London: Allen & Unwin.

Bruner, J. S. (1983). *Child's talk.* New York: Norton.

Bruner, J. S. (1986). *Actual minds, possible worlds.* Cambridge: Harvard University Press.

Bruner, J. S., & Sherwood, V. (1976). Early rule structure: The case of peekaboo. In J. S. Bruner, A. Jolly, & K. Sylva (Eds.), *Play: Its role in evolution and development.* London: Penguin Books.

Bryan, T., Donahue, M., Pearl, R., & Sturm, C. (1981). Learning disabled children's conversational skills: The "TV talk show." *Learning Disability Quarterly, 4,* 250–259.

Camaioni, L., & Laicardi, C. (1985). Early social games and the acquisition of language. *British Journal of Developmental Psychology, 3,* 31–39.

Carpenter, R. L., Mastergeorge, A. M., & Coggins, T. E. (1983). The acquisition of communicative intentions in infants eight to fifteen months of age. *Language and Speech, 26,* 101–116.

Carter, A. L. (1979). Prespeech meaning relations: An outline of one infant's sensorimotor morpheme development. In P. Fletcher & M. Garman (Eds.), *Language acquisition.* Cambridge: Cambridge University Press.

Cazden, C. (1970). The neglected situation in child language research and education. *Journal of Social Issues, 25,* 35–60.

Cazden, C. (1988). *Classroom discourse: The language of teaching and learning.* Portsmouth, N.H.: Heinemann.

Chafe, W. L. (1974). Language and consciousness. *Language, 59,* 112–124.

Chalkley, M. A. (1982). The emergence of language as a social skill. In S. Kuczaj (Ed.), *Language development, Vol. 2.* Hillsdale, N.J.: Erlbaum.

Chapman, R. (1981). Mother-child interaction in the second year of life: Its role in language development. In R. Schiefelbusch & D. Bricker (Eds.), *Early language: Acquisition and intervention.* Baltimore: University Park Press.

Charney, R. (1980). Speech roles and the development of personal pronouns. *Journal of Child Language, 6,* 69–80.

Cherry Wilkinson, L., & Dollaghan, C. (1979). Peer communication in first grade reading groups. *Theory into Practice, 18,* 267–274.

Cicourel, A. V. (1970). The acquisition of social structure. In H. Garfinkel & H. Sacks (Eds.), *Contributions to ethnomethodology*. Bloomington: Indiana University Press.

Clancy, P. (1986). The acquisition of communicative style in Japanese. In B. Schieffelin & E. Ochs (Eds.), *Language socialization across cultures*. Cambridge: Cambridge University Press.

Clark, E. V. (1978a). From gesture to word: On the natural history of deixis on language acquisition. In J. S. Bruner & A. Garton (Eds.), *Human growth and development: Wolfson College lectures 1976*. Oxford: Oxford University Press.

Clark, E. V. (1978b). Strategies for communicating. *Child Development, 49*, 953–959.

Clark, H. H., & French, J. W. (1981). Telephone goodbyes. *Language in Society, 10*, 1–19.

Coggins, T. E., & Carpenter, R. L. (1981). The Communicative Intention Inventory: A sytem for observing and coding children's early intentional communication. *Applied Psycholinguistics, 2*, 235–251.

Collis, G. (1985). On the origins of turn-taking: Alternation and meaning. In M. Barrett (Ed.), *Children's single word speech*. New York: Wiley.

Collis, G., & Schaffer, H. R. (1975). Synchronization of visual attention in mother-infant pairs. *Journal of Child Psychology and Psychiatry, 16*, 315–320.

Corrigan, R. (1978). Language development as related to Stage 6 object permanence development. *Journal of Child Language, 5*, 173–189.

Corsaro, W. (1979). "We're friends, right?" Children's use of access rituals in a nursery school. *Language in Society, 8*, 315–336.

Coulthard, R. M., & Ashby, M. C. (1976). A linguistic description of doctor-patient interviews. In M. Wadsworth and D. Robinson (Eds.), *Studies in everyday medical life*. London: Martin Robertson.

Cruttenden, A. (1982). How long does intonation acquisition take? *Papers and Reports on Child Language Development, 21*, 112–118.

Dale, P. S. (1980). Is early pragmatic development measurable? *Journal of Child Language, 7*, 1–12.

Dale, P. S., Bates, E., Reznick, S., & Morisset, C. (1989). The validity of a parent report instrument. *Journal of Child Language, 16*, 239–249.

Dale, P. S., & Crain-Thoreson, C. (1993). Pronoun reversals: Who, when, and why? *Journal of Child Language, 20*, 573–589.

Davidson, R. G., & Snow, C. E. (1995). The linguistic environment of early readers. *Journal of Research in Childhood Education, 10*, 5–21.

DeCasper, A. J., & Spence, M. J. (1991). Auditorily mediated behavior during the perinatal period: A cognitive view. In M. Weiss & P. Zelazo (Eds.), *Newborn attention: Biological constraints and the influence of experience*. Norwood, N.J.: Ablex.

DeHart, G., & Maratsos, M. (1984). Children's acquisition of presuppositional usages. In R. L. Schiefelbush & J. Pickar (Eds.), *The acquisition of communicative competence*. Baltimore: University Park Press.

De Temple, J. M., & Beals, D. E. (1991). Family talk: Sources of support for the development of decontextualized language skills. *Journal of Research in Childhood Education, 6*(1), 11–19.

de Villiers, J. G., & Tager-Flusberg, H. B. (1975). Some facts one simply cannot deny. *Journal of Child Language, 2,* 279–286.

Denny, R. (1985). Marking the interaction order. *Language in Society, 14,* 41–62.

Dik, S. C. (1978). *Functional grammar.* London: Academic Press.

Donahue, M. (1984). Learning disabled children's conversational competence: An attempt to activate the inactive listener. *Applied Psycholinguistics, 5*(1), 21–36.

Donahue, M., Pearl, R., & Bryan, T. (1980). Conversational competence in learning disabled children: Responses to inadequate messages. *Applied Psycholinguistics, 1,* 387–403.

Donahue, M., Pearl, R., & Bryan, T. (1983). Communicative competence in learning disabled children. In K. D. Gadow & I. Bialer (Eds.), *Advances in learning and behavior disabilities, Vol. 2.* Greenwich, Conn.: JAI Press.

Donaldson, M. L. (1986). *Children's explanations: A psycholinguistic study.* Cambridge: Cambridge University Press.

Dore, J. (1974). A pragmatic description of early language development. *Journal of Psycholinguistic Research, 3,* 343–350.

Dore, J. (1975). Holophrases, speech acts and language universals. *Journal of Child Language, 2,* 21–40.

Dore, J. (1978). Conditions for the acquisition of speech acts. In I. Markova (Ed.), *The social context of language.* Chichester: Wiley.

Dore, J. (1979). Conversation and preschool language development. In P. Fletcher and M. Garman (Eds.), *Language acquisition.* Cambridge: Cambridge University Press.

Dore, J. (1983). Feeling, form and intention in the baby's transition to language. In R. M. Golinkoff (Ed.), *The transition from prelinguistic to linguistic communication.* Hillsdale, N.J.: Erlbaum.

Dore, J. (1985). Holophrases revisited: Their "logical" development from dialog. In M. D. Barrett (Ed.), *Children's single-word speech.* New York: Wiley.

Dore, J., Franklin, M. B., Miller, R. T., & Ramer, A.L.H. (1976). Transitional phenomena in early language acquisition. *Journal of Child Language, 3,* 13–28.

Dore, J., & McDermott, R. P. (1982). Linguistic indeterminacy and social context in utterance interpretation. *Language, 58,* 374–398.

Dorval, B., & Eckerman, C. O. (1984). Developmental trends in the quality of conversation acheived by small groups of acquainted peers. *Monographs of the Society for Research in Child Development, 49,* serial no. 206.

Duncan, S., & Fiske, D. (1977). *Face-to-face interaction.* Hillsdale, N.J.: Erlbaum.

Dundes, A., Leach, J. W., & Özkök, B. (1972). The strategy of Turkish boys' verbal dueling rhymes. In J. J. Gumperz and D. Hymes (Eds.), *Directions in sociolinguistics: The ethnography of communication.* New York: Holt, Rinehart & Winston.

Dunn, J., & Kendrick, C. (1982). *Siblings: Love, envy and understanding.* Cambridge: Harvard University Press.

Eckerman, C., & Stein, M. (1982). The toddler's emerging interactive skills. In K. H. Rubin & H. S. Ross (Eds.), *Peer relations and social skills in childhood.* New York: Springer-Verlag.

Eckerman, C., Whatley, J., & Kutz, S. L. (1975). Growth of social play with peers during the second year of life. *Developmental Psychology, 11,* 42–49.

Eckerman, C., Whatley, J., & McGehee, L. (1979). Approaching and contacting the object another manipulates: A social skill of the one-year-old. *Developmental Psychology, 15,* 585–593.

Edmondson, W. (1981). *Spoken discourse: A model for analysis.* London: Longman.

Edwards, D. (1978). Social relations and early language. In A. Lock (Ed.), *Action, gesture and symbol.* London: Academic Press.

Ervin-Tripp, S. (1970). Discourse agreement: How children answer questions. In J. Hayes (Ed.), *Cognition and the development of language.* New York: Wiley.

Ervin-Tripp, S. (1977). Wait for me, roller-skate. In S. Ervin-Tripp & C. Mitchell-Kernan (Eds.), Child discourse. New York: Academic Press.

Ervin-Tripp, S. (1979). Children's verbal turn-taking. In E. Ochs & B. Schieffelin (Eds.), *Developmental pragmatics.* New York: Academic Press.

Ervin-Tripp, S. (1980). Speech acts, social meaning and social learning. In H. Giles, W. P. Robinson, & P. M. Smith (Eds.), *Language: Social psychological perspectives.* Oxford: Pergamon.

Ervin-Tripp, S., & Gordon, D. (1986). The development of requests. In R. L. Schiefelbusch (Ed.), *Language competence: Assessment and intervention.* San Diego: College Hill.

Evans, M. A. (1987). Discourse characteristics of reticent children. *Applied Psycholinguistics, 8,* 171–184.

Fant, L. (1990). Turntaking in Swedish and Spanish group discussions. Paper presented at the International Pragmatics Conference, Barcelona, Spain.

Feagans, L., Garvey, G. J., & Golinkoff, R. (Eds.) (1984). *The origins and growth of communication.* Norwood, N.J.: Ablex.

Fillmore, C. J. (1971). Verbs of judging: An exercise in semantic description. In C. J. Fillmore & D. T. Langendoen (Eds.), *Studies in linguistic semantics.* New York: Holt, Rinehart & Winston.

Fischer, K. W. (1980). A theory of cognitive development: The control and construction of hierarchies of skills. *Psychological Review, 87*, 477–531.

Flavell, J. (1963). *The developmental psychology of Jean Piaget.* New York: Van Nostrand.

Fletcher, P., & MacWhinney, B. (Eds.) (1995). *The handbook of child language.* Oxford: Blackwell.

Fogel, A., & Thelen, E. (1987). Development of early expressive and communicative action: Reinterpreting the evidence from a dynamic systems perspective. *Developmental Psychology, 23*, 747–761.

Folger, J. P., & Chapman, R. S. (1978). A pragmatic analysis of spontaneous imitation. *A Journal of Child Language, 5*, 25–28.

Forrester, M. A. (1992). *The development of young children's social-cognitive skills.* Hove, East Sussex: Erlbaum.

Gardner, H. (1983). *Frames of mind: The theory of multiple intelligences.* New York: Basic Books.

Garfinkel, H. (1967). *Studies in ethnomethodology.* Englewood Cliffs, N.J.: Prentice-Hall.

Garrod, S., & Anderson, A. (1987). Saying what you mean in dialogue: A study in semantic and conceptual organization. *Cognition, 27*, 181–218.

Garvey, C. (1975). Requests and responses in children's speech. *Journal of Child Language, 2*, 41–63.

Garvey, C. (1976). Some properties of social play. In J. Bruner, A. Jolley, & K. Sylva (Eds.), *Play—Its role in development and evolution.* Middlesex: Penguin.

Garvey, C. (1977). The contingent query: A dependent act in conversation. In M. Lewis and L. A. Rosenblum (Eds.), *Interaction, conversation and the development of language.* New York: Wiley.

Gibbs, R. W. (1984). Literal meaning and psychological reality. *Cognitive Science, 8*, 275–304.

Godard, D. (1977). Same setting, different norms: Phone call beginnings in France and the United States. *Language in Society, 6*, 209–219.

Goffman, E. (1953). *Communication conduct in an island community.* Unpublished Ph.D. dissertation, University of Chicago.

Goffman, E. (1964). The neglected situation. *American Anthropologist, 66*, 133–137.

Goffman, E. (1974). *Frame analysis: An essay on the organization of experience.* Harmondsworth: Peregrine.

Goffman, E. (1976). Replies and responses. *Language in Society, 5*, 257–313.

Goffman, E. (1983). Felicity's condition. *American Journal of Sociology, 89*, 1–53.

Goldfield, B. (1987). The contributions of child and caregiver to referential and expressive language. *Applied Psycholinguistics, 8*, 267–280.

Goldfield, B. (1990). Pointing, naming, and talk about objects: Referential behaviour in children and mothers. *First Language, 10*, 231–242.

Goldfield, B., & Reznick, J. S. (1990). Early lexical acquisition: Rate, content, and the vocabulary spurt. *Journal of Child Language, 17,* 171–184.

Goldfield, B., & Snow, C. E. (1992). Who's cousin Arthur's daddy? The acquisition of knowledge about kinship. *First Language, 12,* 187–205.

Goldman, B., & Ross, H. (1978). Social skills in action. In J. Glick & K. A. Clarke-Stewart (Eds.), *Studies in social and cognitive development, Vol. 1: Development of social understanding.* New York: Gardiner Press.

Golinkoff, R. M. (1983). The preverbal negotiation of failed messages: Insights into the transition period. In R. M. Golinkoff (Ed.), *The transition from prelinguistic to linguistic communication.* Hillsdale, N.J.: Erlbaum.

Goodenough, W. H. (1951). *Property, kin, and community on Truk.* New Haven: Yale University Press.

Goodwin, C. (1981). *Conversational organization: Interaction between speakers and hearers.* New York: Academic Press.

Gopnik, A., and Meltzoff, A. N. (1986). Words, plans, things, and locations: Interactions between semantic and cognitive development in the one-word stage. In S. A. Kuczaj and M. Barrett (Eds.), *The development of word meaning.* New York: Springer-Verlag.

Gopnik, A., and Meltzoff, A. N. (1987). The development of categorization in the second year and its relation to other cognitive and linguistic developements. *Child Development, 58*(6), 1523–1531.

Gordon, D., Budwig, N., Strage, A., & Carrell, P. (1980, October). *Children's requests to unfamiliar adults: Form, social function, age variation.* Boston: Boston University Conference on Language Development.

Gordon, D., & Lakoff, C. (1971). Conversational postulates. *Papers from the seventh regional meeting.* Chicago: Chicago Linguistic Society.

Graves, D. (1983). *Teachers and children at work.* Portsmouth, N.H.: Heinemann.

Greatbatch, D. (1988). A turn-taking system for British news interviews. *Language in Society, 15,* 401–430.

Greenfield, P. M. (1980). Going beyond information theory to explain early word choice: A reply to Roy Pea. *Journal of Child Language, 7,* 217–221.

Greenfield, P. M., & Smith, J. H. (1976). *The structure of communication in early language development.* New York: Academic Press.

Grice, H. P. (1957). Meaning. *Philosophical Review, 66,* 377–388.

Grice, H. P. (1975). Logic and conversation. In P. Cole & J. L. Morgan (Eds.), *Syntax and semantics, Vol. 3: Speech acts.* New York: Academic Press.

Griffiths, P. (1985). The communicative functions of children's single-word speech. In M. Barrett (Ed.), *Children's single-word speech.* New York: Wiley.

Gruber, J. (1973). Correlations between the syntactic construction of the child and adult. In C. Ferguson & D. Slobin (Eds.), *Studies in child language development.* New York: Holt, Rinehart & Winston.

Gumperz, J. J. (1971). *Language in social groups.* Stanford: Stanford University Press.

Gustafson, G. E., Green, L. A., & West, M. J. (1979). The infant's changing role in mother-infant games: The growth of social skills. *Infant Behavior and Development, 2,* 301–308.

Hall, E. T. (1959). *The silent language.* New York: Doubleday.

Halliday, M.A.K. (1975). *Learning to mean—Explorations in the development of language.* London: Edward Arnold.

Halliday, M.A.K. (1985). *An introduction to functional grammar.* London: Edward Arnold.

Harding, C. G. (1983). Setting the stage for language acquisition: Communication development in the first year. In R. M. Golinkoff (Ed.), *The transition from prelinguistic to linguistic communication.* Hillsdale, N.J.: Erlbaum.

Harding, C. G., & Golinkoff, R. M. (1979). The origins of intentional vocalizations in prelinguistic infants. *Child Development, 50,* 33–40.

Harré, R. (1979). *Social being.* Oxford: Basil Blackwell.

Harris, M. (1993). The relationship of maternal speech to children's first words. In D. Messer & G. Turner (Eds.), *Critical influences on language acquisition and development.* London: Macmillan.

Harris, M., Barrett, M., Jones, D., & Brookes, S. (1988). Linguistic input and early word meaning. *Journal of Child Language, 15,* 77–94.

Harrison, B. (1972). *Meaning and structure: An essay in the philosophy of language.* New York: Harper & Row.

Hay, D., Ross, H., & Davis, B. (1979). Social games in infancy. In B. Sutton-Smith (Ed.), *Play and learning.* New York: Gardiner Press.

Hemphill, L. (1987, April). Conversational abilities in mentally retarded and normally developing children. Paper presented at the Biennial Meeting of the Society for Research in Child Development, Baltimore, Maryland.

Hemphill, L. (1989). Topic development, syntax, and social class. *Discourse Processes, 12,* 267–286.

Hemphill, L., & Siperstein, G. N. (1990). Conversational competence and peer response to mildly retarded children. *Journal of Educational Psychology, 82,* 1–7.

Hemphill, L., & Snow, C. (forthcoming). Language and literacy development: Discontinuities and differences. In D. Olson & N. Torrance (Eds.), *Handbook of education and human development: New models of learning, teaching, and schooling.* Cambridge: Blackwell.

Hicks, D. (1990). Narrative skills and genre knowledge: Ways of telling in the primary school grades. *Applied Psycholinguistics, 11,* 83–104.

Hinde, R. (Ed.) (1972). *Non-verbal communication.* Cambridge: Cambridge University Press.

Hymes, D. (1972). Models of the interaction of language and social life. In J. J. Gumperz & D. H. Hymes (Eds.), *Directions in sociolinguistics.* New York: Holt, Rinehart & Winston.

Ingram, D. (1971). Transitivity in child language. *Language, 47,* 889–910.

Ingram, D. (1974). Phonological rules in young children. *Journal of Child Language, 1,* 49–64.

Ingram, D. (1989). *First language acquisition.* Cambridge: Cambridge University Press.

Jisa, H. (1984–1985.) Use of *et pis* ("and then"). *First Language, 5,* 169–184.

Johnson, M. H., & Morton, J. (1991). *Biology and cognitive development: The case of face recognition.* Oxford: Blackwell.

Junefelt K., & Mills, A. E. (1990). Turntaking in blind and sighted multiparty conversations: Swedish and Dutch compared. Paper presented at the International Pragmatics Conference, Barcelona, Spain.

Kalish, D. (1967). Semantics. In D. Edwards (Ed.), *Encyclopedia of philosophy VII.* New York: Collier-Macmillan.

Kaye, K., & Charney, R. (1980). How mothers maintain dialogue with two-year-olds. In D. R. Olson (Ed.), *The social foundations of language and thought.* New York: Norton.

Kaye, K., & Charney, R. (1981). Conversational asymmetry between mothers and children. *Journal of Child Language, 8,* 35–50.

Keenan, E. L. (1971). Two kinds of presupposition in natural language. In C. J. Fillmore & D. T. Langendoen (Eds.), *Studies in linguistic semantics.* New York: Holt.

Keenan, E. O. (1977). Making it last: Repetition in children's discourse. In S. Ervin-Tripp & C. Mitchell-Kernan (Eds.), *Child discourse.* New York: Academic Press.

Keenan, E. O., & Klein, E. (1975). Conversational competence in children. *Journal of Child Language, 1,* 163–184.

Kellermann, K., Broetzmann, S., Lim, T-S., & Kitao, K. (1989). The conversation MOP: Scenes in the stream of discourse. *Discourse Processes, 12,* 27–62.

Kempson, R. M. (1975). *Presupposition and the delimitation of semantics.* Cambridge: Cambridge University Press.

Kendon, A. (1979). Some emerging features of face-to-face interaction studies. *Sign Language Studies, 22,* 7–22.

Kendon, A. (Ed.) (1981). *Nonverbal communication, interaction, and gesture.* The Hague: Mouton.

Key, M. R. (1975). *Paralinguistics and kinesics: Nonverbal communication.* Metuchen, N.J.: Scarecrow Press.

Knapp, M. L. (1972). *Nonverbal communication in human interaction.* New York: Free Press.

Krashen, S. (1985). *The input hypothesis.* London: Longman.

Labov, W. (1972). *Sociolinguistic patterns.* Philadelphia: University of Pennsylvania Press.

Labov, W. (1981). Speech actions and reactions in personal narrative. In D. Tannen (Ed.), *Analyzing discourse: Text and talk*. Washington, D.C.: Georgetown University Press.

Labov, W., & Fanshel, D. (1977). *Therapeutic discourse: Psychotherapy as conversation*. New York: Academic Press.

Labov, W., & Waletzky, J. (1967). Narrative analysis: Oral versions of personal experience. In J. Helm (Ed.), *Essays on the verbal and visual arts*. Seattle: University of Washington Press.

Lamb, M. E., & Sherrod, L. R. (Eds.) (1981). *Infant social cognition*. Hillsdale, N.J.: Erlbaum.

Leonard, L., & Schwartz, R. (1978). Focus characteristics of single-word utterances after syntax. *Journal of Child Language, 5*, 151–158.

Levin, E. A., & Rubin, K. H. (1983). Getting others to do what you want them to do: The development of children's requestive strategies. In K. E. Nelson (Ed.), *Children's Language*, Vol. 4.

Levinson, S. C. (1983). *Pragmatics*. Cambridge: Cambridge University Press.

Lewis, M., Young, G., Brooks, J., & Michalson, L. (1975). The beginning of friendship. In M. Lewis & L. A. Rosenbloom (Eds.), *Friendship and peer relations*. New York: Wiley.

Lieven, E.V.M. (1978a). Conversations between mothers and young children: Individual differences and their possible implications for the study of language learning. In N. Waterson & C. Snow (Eds.), *The development of communication*. Chichester: Wiley.

Lieven, E.V M. (1978b). Turn-taking and pragmatics: Two issues in early child language. In R. N. Campbell & P. T. Smith (Eds.), *Recent advances in the psychology of language: Language development and mother-child interaction*. New York: Plenum.

Lloyd, P. (1991). Strategies used to communicate route directions by telephone: A comparison of the performance of 7-year-olds, 10-year-olds, and adults. *Journal of Child Language, 18*, 171–190.

Lock, A. (1980). *The guided reinvention of language*. London: Academic Press.

Locke, J. L. (1993). *The child's path to spoken language*. Cambridge: Harvard University Press.

Loveland, K. A. (1984). Learning about points of view: Spatial perspective and the acquisition of "I/you." *Journal of Child Language, 11*, 535–556.

Lucariello, J., Kyratzis, A., & Engel, S. (1986). Event representations, context, and language. In K. Nelson (Ed.), *Event knowledge: Structure and function in development*. Hillsdale, N.J.: Erlbaum.

Luszcz, M., & Bacharach, V. (1983). The emergence of communicative competence: Detection of conversational topics. *Journal of Child Language, 10*, 623–637.

Lyons, J. (1977). *Semantics*. Cambridge: Cambridge University Press.

Lyons, J. (1981). *Language, meaning and contex*. London: Fontana.

MacWhinney, B. (1984). Devices for sharing points. In R. L. Schiefelbusch & M. A. Pickar (Eds.), *The acquisition of communicative competence*. Baltimore: University Park Press.

Maratsos, M. (1973). Decrease in the understanding of the word "big" in preschool children. *Child Development, 44,* 747–752.

Markman, E. M., & Wachtel, G. F. (1988). Children's use of mutual exclusivity to constrain the meanings of words. *Cognitive Psychology, 20,* 121–157.

McCabe, A., and Peterson, C. (1991). Getting the story: A longitudinal study of parental styles in eliciting personal narratives and developing narrative skill. In A. McCabe and C. Peterson (Eds.), *Developing narrative structure*. Hillsdale, N.J.: Erlbaum.

McCune-Nicolich, L. (1981). The cognitive basis of relational words in the single word period. *Journal of Child Language, 8,* 15–34.

McShane, J. (1980). *Learning to talk*. Cambridge: Cambridge University Press.

Meltzoff, A. N., & Moore, K. N. (1977). Imitation of facial and manual gestures by human neonates. *Science, 198,* 75–78.

Mendelson, M., & Haith, M. M. (1976). The relation between audition and vision in the human newborn. *Monographs of the Society for Research in Child Development, 41,* 1–61.

Menn, L., & Haselkorn, S. (1977). Now you see it, now you don't: Tracing the development of communicative competence. In J. Kegl (Ed.), *Proceedings of the Seventh Annual Meeting of the Northeast Linguistic Society*.

Merrit, M. (1976). On questions following questions in service encounters. *Language in Society, 5,* 315–357.

Mervis, C., & Mervis, C. (1988). Role of adult input in young children's category evolution: An observational study. *Journal of Child Language, 15,* 257–272.

Miller, G. A. (1970). Four philosophical problems of psycholinguists. *Philosophy of Science,* June, 183–199.

Mischel, W. (1968). *Personality and assessment*. New York: Wiley.

Mishler, E. (1984). *The discourse of medicine: Dialectics of medical interviews*. Norwood, N.J.: Ablex.

Moerk, E. L. (1975). Verbal interaction between children and their mothers during the preschool years. *Developmental Psychology, 11,* 788–794.

Moerk, E. L. (1976). Processes of language teaching and training in the interaction of mother-child dyads. *Child Development, 47,* 1064–1078.

Montague, R. (1968). Pragmatics. In R. Klibansky (Ed.), *Contemporary philosophy*. Florence: La Nuova Italia Editrice.

Morford, M., & Goldin-Meadow, S. (1992). Comprehension and production of gesture in combination with speech in one-word speakers. *Journal of Child Language, 19,* 559–580.

Morris, C. (1938). Foundations of the theory of signs. In O. Neurath (Ed.), *International encyclopedia of unified science 1*. Chicago: University of Chicago Press.

Murray, S. O. (1985). Toward a model of members' methods for recognizing interruptions. *Language in Society, 14,* 31–40.

Nelson, K. (1973). Structure and strategy in learning to talk. *Monograph of the Society for Research in Child Development, 38,* serial no. 1–2.

Nelson, K. (1978). Early speech in its communicative context. In F. D. Minifie & L. L. Lloyd (Eds.), *Communicative and cognitive abilities—Early behavioral assessment.* Baltimore: University Park Press.

Nelson, K.(1985). *Making sense: The acquisition of shared meaning.* New York: Academic Press.

Nelson, K., and collaborators (1986). *Event knowledge: Structure and function in development.* Hillsdale, N.J.: Erlbaum.

Nelson, K., & Lucariello, J. (1985). The development of meaning in first words. In M. Barrett (Ed.), *Children's single-word speech.* New York: Wiley.

Nelson, K. E. (1977). Facilitating children's syntax acquisition. *Developmental Psychology, 13,* 101–107.

Nelson, K. E., Denninger, M. S., Bonvillian, J. D., Kaplan, B. J., & Baker, N. D. (1984). Maternal input adjustments and non-adjustments as related to children's linguistic advances and to language acquisition theories. In A. D. Pellegrini & T. Yawkey (Eds.), *The development of oral and written languages in social contexts.* Norwood, N.J.: Ablex.

Newport, E. L. (1977). Motherese: The speech of mothers to young children. In N. Castellan, D. Pisoni, & G. Potts (Eds.), *Cognitive theory, Vol. 2.* Hillsdale, N.J.: Erlbaum.

Ninio, A. (1980). The ostensive definition in vocabulary teaching. *Journal of Child Language, 7,* 565–573.

Ninio, A. (1983a). Joint bookreading as a multiple vocabulary acquisition device. *Developmental Psychology, 19,* 445–451.

Ninio, A. (1983b, May). A pragmatic approach to early language acquisition. Paper presented at the Study Group on Crosscultural and Crosslinguistic Aspects of Native Language Acquisition, Institute for Advanced Studies, Hebrew University, Jerusalem, Israel.

Ninio, A. (1984). Functions of speech in mother-infant interaction. Final Science Report to the U.S.-Israel Binational Science Foundation, Jerusalem, Israel.

Ninio, A. (1985). The meaning of children's first words: Evidence from the input. Invited article for a special issue on Pragmatic Aspects of Lexical Acquisition and Development, edited by J. Streeck. *Journal of Pragmatics, 9,* 527–546.

Ninio, A. (1986a). The illocutionary aspect of utterances. *Discourse Processes, 9,* 127–147.

Ninio, A. (1986b, March). Negative feedback on very young speakers' grammar. Paper presented at the Conference on Human Development, Nashville, Tennessee.

Ninio, A. (1988). The roots of narrative: Discussing recent events with very young children. Invited article for a special issue on Child Language Acquisition, edited by B. G. Blount. *Language Sciences, 10,* 35–52.

Ninio, A. (1989). Language development and the linguistic environment of culturally advantaged and disadvantaged children in Israel. Final Science Progress Report to the U.S.-Israel Binational Science Foundation, Jerusalem, Israel.

Ninio, A. (1990a, July). Expression of communicative intents and the vocabulary spurt. Paper presented at the Fifth International Congress for the Study of Child Language, Budapest, Hungary.

Ninio, A. (1990b). *FCA—First Communicative Acts Coding System.* Coding manual distributed by the Department of Psychology, Hebrew University, Jerusalem, Israel.

Ninio, A. (1991a, April). The expression of communicative intents in single-word utterances and the emergence of patterned speech. Paper presented at the Biennial Meeting of the Society for Research in Child Development, Seattle, Washington.

Ninio, A. (1991b, April). Is early speech situational? The relation of early utterances to the context. Paper presented at the symposium Early Communicative Development: The Centrality of Pragmatic Analysis, chaired by B. A. Pan & C. E. Snow, at the Biennial Meeting of the Society for Research in Child Development, Seattle, Washington.

Ninio, A. (1992). The relation of children's single word utterances to single word utterances in the input. *Journal of Child Language, 19,* 87–110.

Ninio, A. (1993a). Is early speech situational? An examination of some current theories about the relation of early utterances to the context. In D. Messer & G. Turner (Eds.), *Critical influences on language acquisition and development.* London: Macmillan.

Ninio, A. (1993b). On the fringes of the system: Children's acquisition of syntactically isolated forms at the onset of speech. *First Language 13,* 291–313.

Ninio, A. (1994a, June). Antecedents of syntax in the communication system. Invited lecture, Colloquium on Prelinguistic and Linguistic Communication in Children, Université René Descartes Paris-V, Centre Nationale de la Recherche Scientifique, Paris, France.

Ninio, A. (1994b). Expression of communicative intents in the single-word period and the vocabulary spurt. In K. Nelson & Z. Reger (Eds.), *Children's Language, Vol. 8.* Hillsdale, N.J.: Erlbaum.

Ninio, A., & Bruner, J. S. (1978). The achievement and antecedents of labelling. *Journal of Child Language, 5,* 1–15.

Ninio, A., & Goren, H. (1993). *PICA-100: Parental Interview on 100 Communicative Acts.* Coding manual distributed by the Department of Psychology, Hebrew University, Jerusalem, Israel.

Ninio, A., & Snow, C. (1988). Language acquisition through language use: The functional sources of children's early utterances. In Y. Levi, I. Schlesinger, & M.D.S. Braine (Eds.), *Perspectives on a theory of language acquisition*. Hillsdale, N.J.: Erlbaum.

Ninio, A., Snow, C., Pan, B. A., and Rollins, P. R. (1994). Classifying communicative acts in children's interactions. *Journal of Communication Disorders, 27,* 158–187.

Ninio, A., & Wheeler, P. (1984a). Functions of speech in mother-infant interaction: Designing a coding scheme for the description and classification of verbal-social acts. In L. Feagans, G. J. Garvey, & R. Golinkoff (Eds.), *The Origins and Growth of Communication*. Norwood, N.J.: Ablex.

Ninio, A., & Wheeler, P. (1984b). *A manual for classifying verbal communicative acts in mother-infant interaction*. Working Papers in Developmental Psychology, no. 1. Jerusalem: Martin and Vivian Levin Center, Hebrew University. Reprinted as *Transcript Analysis*, 1986, *3,* 1–82.

Ninio, A., & Wheeler, P. (1988). *A revised manual for classifying verbal communicative acts in mother-infant interaction*. Coding manual distributed by the Department of Psychology, Hebrew University, Jerusalem, Israel.

Ninio, A., Wheeler, P., Snow, C. E., Pan, B. A., and Rollins, P. R. (1991). *INCA-A: Inventory of Communicative Acts—Abridged*. Coding manual distributed by Harvard Graduate School of Education, Cambridge, Massachusetts.

Ochs, E. (1988). *Culture and language development: Language acquisition and language socialization in a Samoan village*. Cambridge: Cambridge University Press.

Ochs, E., & Schieffelin, B. (Eds.) (1979). *Developmental pragmatics*. New York: Academic Press.

Ochs, E., & Schieffelin, B. (1984). Language acquisition and socialization: Three developmental stories and their implications. In R. LeVine (Ed.), *Culture theory: Essays on mind, self, and emotion*. New York: Cambridge University Press.

Oller, D. K. (1981). Infant vocalizations: Exploration and reflexivity. In R. Stark (Ed.), *Language behavior in infancy and early childhood*. New York: Elsevier North–Holland.

Oshima-Takane, Y. (1988). Children learn from speech not addressed to them, the case of personal pronouns. *Journal of Child Language, 15,* 95–108.

Paley, V. (1990). *The boy who would be a helicopter: The uses of storytelling in the classroom*. Cambridge: Harvard University Press.

Pan, B. A., Imbens-Bailey, A., Winner, K., and Snow, C. E. (1996). Communicative intents of parents interacting with their young children. *Merrill-Palmer Quarterly, 42,* 72–90.

Pan, B. A., Snow, C. E., & Willett, J. B. (1995). *Modeling language growth: Measures of lexical, morphosyntactical, and conversational skill for early child language*. Unpublished manuscript, Harvard Graduate School of Education.

Pappas, C. C. (1993). Is narrative "primary?" Some insights from kinder- garteners' pretend readings of stories and information books. *Journal of Reading Behavior: A Journal of Literacy, 25*(1), 97–129.

Pea, R. (1979). Can information theory explain early word choice? *Journal of Child Language, 6*, 397–410.

Perner, J., & Leekam, S. (1986). Belief and quantity: Three-year-olds' adaptation to listener's knowledge. *Journal of Child Language, 13*, 305–315.

Peterson, C., & McCabe, A. (1983). *Developmental psycholinguistics: Three ways of looking at a child's narrative.* New York: Plenum.

Peterson, C., & McCabe, A. (1987). The connective and. *First Language, 8*, 19–28.

Peterson, C., and McCabe, A. (1992). Parental styles of narrative elicitation: Effect on children's narrative structure and content. *First Language, 12*, 299–322.

Philips, S. (1976). Some sources of cultural variability in the regulation of talk. *Language in Society, 5*, 81–95.

Piaget, J. (1926). *The language and thought of the child.* London: Routledge & Kegan Paul.

Piaget, J. (1929). *The child's conception of the world.* New York: Harcourt Brace.

Pinker, S. (1984). *Language learnability and language development.* Cambridge: Harvard University Press.

Ratner, N., & Bruner, J. S. (1978). Games, social exchange and the acquisition of language. *Journal of Child Language, 5*, 391–401.

Rheingold, H. L., Hay, D. F., & West, M. J. (1976). Sharing in the second year of life. *Child Development, 47*, 1148–1158.

Ricks, D. M., & Wing, L. (1975). Language, communication, and the use of symbols in normal and autistic children. *Journal of Autism and Childhood Schizophrenia, 5*, 191–221.

Rome-Flanders, T., Cossette, L., Ricard, M., & Gouin Decarie, T. (1995). Comprehension of rules and structures in mother-infant games: A longitudinal study of the first two years of life. *International Journal of Behavioral Development, 18*(1), 83–103.

Rommetveit, R. (1974). *On message structure.* London: Wiley.

Ross, H. S., & Kay, D. A. (1980). The origins of social games. In K. H. Rubin (Ed.), *Children's play: New directions for child development, Vol. 9.* San Francisco: Jossey-Bass.

Rubin, K. H., & Ross, H. S. (Eds.) (1982). *Peer relations and social skills in childhood.* New York: Springer-Verlag.

Sachs, J. (1982). Talking about there and then: The emergence of displaced reference in parent-child discourse. In I.K.E. Nelson (Ed.), *Children's language.* New York: Gardner Press.

Sachs, J., Anselmi, D., & McCollam, K. (1990, July). Young children's awareness of presuppositions based on community membership. Paper presented at the Fifth International Congress for the Study of Child Language, Budapest, Hungary.

Sachs, J., Brown, R., & Salerno, R. A. (1976). Adults' speech to children. In W. von Raffler-Engel & Y. Lebrun (Eds.), *Baby talk and infant speech*. Lisse, Netherlands: Swetz & Zeitlinger.

Sacks, H. (1974). An analysis of the course of a joke's telling in conversation. In R. Bauman and J. Sherzer (Eds.), *Explorations in the Ethnography of Speaking*. Cambridge: Cambridge University Press.

Sacks, H., Schegloff, E., & Jefferson, G. (1974). A simplest systematics for the organization of turn-taking for conversation. *Language, 50*, 596–735.

Schank, R., & Abelson, R. (1977). *Scripts, plans, goals, and understanding*. Hillsdale, N.J.: Erlbaum.

Scheflen, A. E. (1974). *How behavior means*. Garden City, N.Y.: Anchor Press.

Schegloff, E. (1979). Identification and recognition in telephone conversation openings. In G. Psathas (Ed.), *Everyday language: Studies in ethno-methodology*. New York: Irvington Publishers.

Schegloff, E., & Sacks, H. (1973). Opening up closings. *Semiotics, 8*, 289–327.

Schieffelin, B. (1990). *The give and take of everyday life: Language socialization of Kaluli children*. Cambridge: Cambridge University Press.

Schieffelin, B., & Ochs, E. (Eds.) (1986). *Language socialization across cultures*. Cambridge: Cambridge University Press.

Schley, S., & Snow, C. (1992). The conversational skills of school-aged children. *Social Development, 1*, 18–35.

Schober-Peterson, D., & Johnson, C. (1991). Non-dialogue speech during preschool interactions. *Journal of Child Language, 18*, 153–170.

Scott, C. (1984). Adverbial connectivity in conversations of children 6 to 12. *Journal of Child Language, 11*, 423–452.

Scoville, R. (1984). Development of the intention to communicate: The eye of the beholder. In L. Feagans, G. J. Garvey, & R. Golinkoff (Eds.), *The origins and growth of communication*. Norwood, N.J.: Ablex.

Searle, J. R. (1969). *Speech acts*. Cambridge: Cambridge University Press.

Searle, J. R. (1975). Indirect speech acts. In P. Cole & J. L. Morgan (Eds.), *Syntax and semantics, Vol. 3: Speech acts*. New York: Academic Press.

Searle, J. R. (1976). The classification of illocutionary acts. *Language in Society, 5*, 1–25.

Searle, J. R., & Vanderveken, D. (1985). *Foundations of illocutionary logic*. Cambridge: Cambridge University Press.

Shanon, B. (1994). *The representational and the presentational: An essay on cognition and the study of mind*. Hemel Hempsted, United Kingdom: Harvester Wheatsheaf.

Shatz, M. (1978). Children's comprehension of their mothers' question-directives. *Journal of Child Language, 5*, 39–46.

Shatz, M. (1982). On mechanisms of language acquisition: Can features of the communicative environment account for development? In E. Wanner &

L. R. Gleitman (Eds.), *Language acquisition: The state of the art*. Cambridge: Cambridge University Press.

Shvachkin, N. (1973). The development of phonemic speech perception in early childhood. In C. Ferguson & D. Slobin (Eds.), *Studies in child language development*. New York: Holt, Rinehart & Winston.

Shweder, R. A. (1990). Cultural psychology—What is it? In J. W. Stigler, R. A. Shweder, & J. Herdt (Eds.), *Cultural Psychology*. Cambridge: Cambridge University Press.

Sinclair, J., & Coulthard, R. M. (1975). *Towards an analysis of discourse: The English used by teachers and pupils*. London: Oxford University Press.

Slobin, D. (1973). Cognitive prerequisites for the development of grammar. In C. A. Ferguson and D. Slobin (Eds.), *Studies of child language development*. New York: Holt, Rinehart & Winston.

Snow, C. E. (1972). Mothers' speech to children learning language. *Child Development, 43*, 549–565.

Snow, C. E. (1977a). The development of conversation between mothers and babies. *Journal of Child Language, 4*, 1–22.

Snow, C. E. (1977b). Mothers' speech research: From input to interaction. In C. E. Snow & C. Ferguson (Eds.), *Talking to children*. Cambridge: Cambridge University Press.

Snow, C. E. (1979). The role of social interaction in language acquisition. In W. A. Collins (Ed.), *Minnesota Symposia on Child Psychology, Vol. 12*. Hillsdale, N.J.: Erlbaum.

Snow, C. E. (1983a). Literacy and language: Relationships during the preschool years. *Harvard Educational Review, 53*, 165–189.

Snow, C. E. (1983b). Parent-child interaction and the development of communicative ability. In R. Schiefelbusch (Ed.), *Communicative competence: Acquisition and retardation*. Baltimore: University Park Press.

Snow, C. E. (1990). The development of definitional skill. *Journal of Child Language, 17*, 697–710.

Snow, C. E. (1991). The theoretical basis for relationships between language and literacy development. *Journal of Research in Childhood Education, 6* Fall–Winter, 5–10.

Snow, C. E. (1995). Issues in the study of input: Fine-tuning, universality, individual and developmental differences, and necessary causes. In B. MacWhinney & P. Fletcher (Eds.), *Handbook of child language*. Oxford: Blackwell.

Snow, C. E., de Blauw, A., & van Roosmalen, G. (1978). Talking and playing with babies: The role of ideologies of child rearing. In M. Bullowa (Ed.), *Before speech*. London: Cambridge University Press.

Snow, C. E., Dubber, C., & de Blauw, A. (1982). Routines in parent-child interaction. In L. Feagans & D. Farran (Eds.), *The language of children reared in poverty: Implications for evaluation and intervention*. New York: Academic Press.

Snow, C. E., & Goldfield, B. (1983). Turn the page please: Situation-specific language learning. *Journal of Child Language*, 10, 551–570.

Snow, C. E., & Kurland, B. (1995). Sticking to the point: Talk about magnets as a preparation for literacy. In D. Hicks (Ed.), *Child discourse and social learning: An interdisciplinary perspective*. New York: Cambridge University Press.

Snow, C. E., Pan, B., Imbens-Bailey, A., & Herman, J. (1996). Learning how to say what one means: A longitudinal study of children's speech act use. *Social Development*, 5, 56–84.

Snow, C. E., Tabors, P. O., Nicholson, P., & Kurland, B. (1995). SHELL: Oral language and early literacy skills in kindergarten and first grade children. *Journal of Research in Childhood Education*, 10, 22–38.

Snow, C. E., & Winner, K. (1994, July). Where are your gloves? When did you last see them? Parents' talk about time and space. Paper presented at the Nordic Child Language Association Meeting, Reykjavik, Iceland.

Snyder, L. D. (1978). Communicative and cognitive abilities and disabilities in the sensorimotor period. *Merrill-Palmer Quarterly*, 24, 161–180.

Stalnaker, R. C. (1972). Pragmatics. In D. Davidson & G. Harman (Eds.), *Semantics of natural language*. Dordrecht: Reidel.

Stephany, U. (1986). Modality. In P. Fletcher & M. Garman (Eds.), *Language acquisition*, 2d ed. Cambridge: Cambridge University Press.

Stern, D. N. (1974). Mother and infant at play: The dyadic interaction involving facial, vocal, and gaze behaviours. In M. Lewis & L. A. Rosenblum (Eds.), *The effect of the infant on its caregiver*. New York: Wiley.

Stern, D. N., Jaffe, J., Beebe, B., & Bennett, S. L. (1975). Vocalizing in unison and in alternation: Two modes of communication within the mother-infant dyad. *Developmental Psycholinguistic and Communication Disorders*, 263, 89–100.

Stoppard, T. (1982, reprinted 1983). *The real thing*. London: Faber.

Strawson, P. F. (1970). *Meaning and truth*. Oxford: Clarendon.

Streeck, J. (1980). Speech acts in interaction: A critique of Searle. *Discourse Processes*, 3, 133–154.

Streeck, J. (1983). *Social order in child communication: A study in microethnography*. Amsterdam: John Benjamins.

Sugarman-Bell, S. (1978). Some organizational aspects of pre-verbal communication. In I. Markova (Ed.), *The social context of language*. Chichester: Wiley.

Tajfel, H. (1972). Experiment in a vacuum. In J. Israel & H. Tajfel (Eds.), *True context of social psychology*. London: Academic Press.

Tomasello, M. (1992). *First verbs: A case study of early grammatical development*. Cambridge: Cambridge University Press.

Tomasello, M., Kruger, A., & Ratner, H. (1993). Cultural learning. *Behavioral and Brain Sciences*, 16, 495–552.

Tomasello, M., & Todd, J. (1983). Joint attention and early lexical acquisition style. *First Language, 4,* 197–212.

Tough, J. (1977). *The development of meaning.* New York: Halsted Press.

Trevarthen, C. B. (1979). Instincts for human understanding and for cultural cooperation: Their development in infancy. In M. von Cranach, K. Foppa, W. Lepenies, & D. Ploog (Eds.), *Human ethology: Claims and limits of a new discipline.* Cambridge: Cambridge University Press.

Turner, R. (1972). Some formal properties of therapy talk. In D. Sudnow (Ed.), *Studies in social interaction.* New York: Free Press.

Van Valin, R. D. (1991). Functionalist linguistic theory and language acquisition. *First Language, 31,* 7–40.

Van Valin, R. D. (1993). A synopsis of Role and Reference grammar. In R. D. Van Valin (Ed.), *Advances in Role and Reference grammar.* Amsterdam: John Benjamins.

Vandell, D. L. (1977). *Boy toddlers' social interaction with mothers, fathers, and peers.* Unpublished Ph.D. dissertation, Boston University.

Velasco, P., & Snow, C. E. (1995). First and second language oral skills related to reading in bilingual children. Submitted to *Journal of the Scientific Study of Reading.*

Vendler, Z. (1972). *Res cogitans.* Ithaca: Cornell University Press.

Vihman, M. M., and McCune, L. (1994). When is a word a word? *Journal of Child Language, 21,* 517–542.

Von Raffler-Engel, W. (1971). Developmental kinesics: Cultural differences in the acquisition of nonverbal behavior. *Word, 27,* 195–204.

Vygotsky, L. (1978). *Mind in society: The development of higher psychological processes* (M. Cole, Ed.). Cambridge: Harvard University Press.

Wales, R. (1986). Deixis. In P. Fletcher & M. Garman (Eds.), *Language acquisition,* 2d ed. Cambridge: Cambridge University Press.

Wallace, A.F.C., & Atkins, J. (1960). The meaning of kinship terms. *American Anthropologist, 62,* 58–80.

Wardhaugh, R. (1985). *How conversation works.* Oxford: Basil Blackwell.

Watson, R. (1989). Literate discourse and cognitive organization: Some relations between parents' talk and 3-year-olds' thought. *Applied Psycholinguistics, 10,* 221–236.

Watson, R., & Olson, D. (1987). From meaning to definition: A literate bias on the structure of word meaning. In R. Horowitz & J. Samuels (Eds.), *Comprehending oral and written language.* Orlando: Academic Press.

Weisenberger, J. L. (1976). A choice of words: Two-year-old speech from a situational point of view. *Journal of Child Language, 3,* 275–281.

Wells, G. (1985). *Language development in the pre-school years.* Cambridge: Cambridge University Press.

White, S. (1989). Backchannels across cultures: A study of Americans and Japanese. *Language in Society, 18,* 59–76.

Wieman, L. A. (1976). Stress patterns of early language. *Journal of Child Language*, 3, 283–286.

Wittgenstein, L. (1953). *Philosophical investigations*. Oxford: Basil Blackwell.

Wolf, D., Moreton, J., & Camp, L. (1994). Children's acquisition of different kinds of narrative discourse: Genre and lines of talk. In J. Sokolov & C. Snow (Eds.), *Handbook of research in language development using CHILDES*. Hillsdale, N.J.: Erlbaum.

Zinober, B. W., & Martlew, M. (1985). The development of communicative gestures. In M. Barrett (Ed.), *Children's single-word speech*. New York: Wiley.

## About the Book and Authors

The pragmatic system consists of the rules for appropriate and communicatively effective language use. *Pragmatic Development* provides an integrated view of the acquisition of all the various pragmatic subsystems, including expression of communicative intents, participation in conversation, and production of extended discourse.

For the first time, the three components of the pragmatic system are presented in a way that makes clear how they relate to each other and why they all fall under the rubric *pragmatics*. Ninio and Snow combine their own extensive work in these three domains with an overview of the field of pragmatic development, making clear how linguistic pragmatics relates to other aspects of language development, to social development, and to becoming a member of one's culture. This book is bound to be a valuable text for advanced courses in language acquisition, as well as useful supplementary reading for an introductory course.

**Anat Ninio** is Joseph H. and Belle R. Braun Professor of Psychology at the Hebrew University in Jerusalem. **Catherine E. Snow** is Henry Lee Shattuck Professor of Education at the Harvard Graduate School of Education.

# Index

Action-negotiations. *See under* Negotiations

Anderson, A., 162

Animal sounds, 68, 89, 90. *See also* Onomatopeoia

Anselmi, D., 165

Appropriateness, 4, 9, 13, 91, 170, 192

Arguments, 172

Attempts to end activity, 123, 124, 125(fig.)

Attention, 91, 93, 96–97, 104, 112, 114, 116, 119(fig.), 121, 130, 131, 132, 133, 135–136, 154, 177

  mutual attentiveness, 67, 68, 70, 84, 96, 105, 130, 131

  *See also* Intersubjectivity

Austin,J. L., 29

Autism, 47

Back channels, 11, 151, 152

Baier, A. C., 8

Barrett, M. D., 51, 61

Bates, E., 47, 49

Bloom, L., 160

Bryan, T., 161

Bruner, J. S., 61, 89, 92, 186

Calling, 137

Carpenter, R. L., 47, 136, 137

Carter, A. L., 53

Chapman, R., 19, 20

Chorusing, 151

Clarification, 112, 114, 116, 118–119, 121, 121(fig.), 130, 131, 133, 152, 162, 163–170, 164(table), 180, 186

Coding systems, 17, 19–21, 20(table), 31–43, 37–38(table), 60, 128. *See also* Communicative acts typologies

Coggins, T. E., 47, 136, 137

Coherency, 160

Communication, 52–53

  continuity in communicative functions, 103–104

  conventions, 5, 17

  failures, 2, 28, 56, 152, 162–163

  holistic mapping style, 73, 74

  indirect strategies for, 138–140

  intents, 5, 11, 12, 15, 16, 17, 21, 43, 46–48, 49–50, 51–52, 53, 54, 56, 65(table), 72–80, 105, 112, 135, 138, 191. *See also* Meaning

  metacommunication, 28, 29–30, 35, 84, 85, 190

  nonlinguistic, 50–51, 52, 136–138. *See also* Gestures

  order of communicative acts, 104. *See also* Speech acts, order of acquisition

  prelinguistic, 11, 43, 45–48, 103, 153–154. *See also* Language, and preverbal abilities

  previous message acknowledgement, 27–28, 75–76

  referential, 159, 161–162

  refining verbal, 135–141

  transition to speech, 48–57, 84, 154

  uses of speech for, 15–43

  *See also* Communicative acts typologies

Communicative acts typologies, 18–21, 20(table), 29, 60

  Abridged Inventory of Communicative Acts (INCA-A), 39, 41–42, 41(table), 128

  First Communicative Acts (FCA) Coding System, 39–41, 64

  Ninio-Wheeler, 21–23, 31–39, 62, 91

  Parental Interview on 100 Communicative Acts (PICA-100), 39, 42–43, 69–70, 71(table), 83–84, 86–87(table), 96, 108, 127

  of prelinguistic period, 47

  *See also* Coding systems

Complementarity principle, 141

Completions, 90, 91. *See also under* Requests

Complexity, 90, 92, 93, 95, 103, 104, 175

Constructivism. *See* Meaning, constructivist conception of

Contexts, 9. *See also* Meaning,
    decontextualized; Utterances, as
    context-related
Conversations, 143–170, 172
    adult-child, 156–159
    conversational effectiveness, 140–141,
        147. *See also* Effectiveness
    conversational support, 174, 179–182,
        188. *See also* Extended discourse,
        support in
    interruptions in, 151
    multiparty, 148–149
    repair procedures, 162–170
    *See also* Discussions; Extended
        discourse; Skills,conversational
Co-presence/separation, 23–24, 26, 29,
    85, 92
Cultural issues, 5, 6, 18, 150, 156
    conversational turn-taking, 148–149
    enculturation, 12, 54, 55
    listening behavior, 151–152
    *See also* Appropriateness
Cultural Psychology, 12, 55, 56

Dale, P. S., 82
Definitions, 172, 173, 175, 189–191
Developmental psychology, 4, 12, 45
Discussions, 31, 84, 85, 88, 89, 93–95,
    104, 112, 154–155, 172
    of nonpresent topics, 42, 93, 94, 112,
        114, 116, 119–120, 121, 122(fig.),
        131, 133, 153, 155, 160, 173. *See
        also* Meaning, decontextualized
    of present topics, 114–115, 116(fig.),
        121, 130, 131, 132, 155
    *See also* Conversations; Extended
        discourse
Dore, J., 19, 20(table), 49–50, 51, 53, 55,
    59, 61
Dorval, B., 160

Early speech, 143
    developments past two years, 102–103
    repertoire size in, 83–84
    *See also* Single-word period; Speech
        acts; Utterances; *under* Pragmatics

Eckerman, C., 55, 160
Effectiveness, 4, 6–7, 140–141, 147, 174,
    191, 192
Elicitation/responses, 88–90, 92, 94, 178,
    192(n)
Empathy, 55
Empiricists, 79
*Encyclopedia of Philosophy, The*, 8
Ervin-Tripp, S., 139
Evaluation, 31, 101, 184, 185, 186
Exclamations, 60, 62, 66, 90, 91, 92, 104
Explanations, 172, 173, 175, 187–189,
    191
Expressive vocalizations, 46–47, 154. *See
    also* Exclamations
Extended discourse, 13, 14, 163, 166,
    170, 171–192
    support in, 174–175, 179–186,
        188–189

Face-to-face interactions, 23–26, 24(fig.),
    26–31, 30(fig.), 68, 107
    changes of state in, 26
    talk interchanges, 29, 30(fig.), 31–35,
        32–35(table)
    *See also* Mother-child interactions
Fantasies, 176–177
FCA. *See* Communicative acts typologies,
    First Communicative Acts Coding
    System
Feedback. *See* Negative feedback
Feelings, 93, 94, 114, 131, 186
Folger, J. P., 19
Four-letter words, 5
Frog Book, 178
Functional Grammars, 8, 60. *See also*
    Linguistics, functionalist

Games, 26, 27, 31, 47–48, 59, 60, 61–62,
    66, 68, 69, 70, 84, 89, 95, 97, 104,
    112, 114, 115(fig.), 117, 121, 131,
    137
Garvey, C., 139, 155
Genre-specific discourse, 11, 13
Gestures, 49, 138
    accompanied by vocalizations, 136–137

*See also* Communication, nonlinguistic
Gibbs, R. W., 51
Giving, 60
Goffman, E., 8, 23, 84
Goldin-Meadow, S., 137
Gordon, D., 139, 140
Grammar, 4, 49, 79, 103, 169. *See also*
    Syntax
Greenfield, P. M., 69, 70, 137, 141
Greeting, 92, 127, 137
Grice, H. P., 56, 141, 145

Halliday, M.A.K., 53, 54, 59, 60–61
Home-School Study of Language and
    Literacy Development, 178, 180,
    187, 188

Imitation, 54–57, 60, 62, 63–64, 65, 70,
    88, 89, 90, 114, 155
INCA-A. *See* Communicative acts
    typologies, Abridged Inventory of
    Communicative Acts
Infants, 45–48, 49, 55, 56
    adult interactions, 150
    *See also* Communication, prelinguistic
Initiate new activity, 123, 123(fig.)
Intents. *See under* Communication
Interactive goals, 100–102
Interjections, 66. *See also* Exclamations
Interpretability, 135–136, 138, 138(table)
Intersubjectivity, 23, 24, 25, 46, 53, 54,
    55, 56, 67, 68–69, 70–72, 84, 153

Japanese, 6, 151–152

King, Martin Luther, 6
Kinship, 5–6

Labeling, 60–61, 67, 68, 70
Language
    decontextualized, 173–174. *See also*
        Meaning, decontextualized
    deictic elements of, 10, 11, 75
    and preverbal abilities, 48–54. *See also*
        Communication, prelinguistic

skills, 4, 7, 11, 12, 13, 14, 16
    *See also* Linguistics
*La résponse de l'escalier,* 146
Leonard, L., 79
Linguistics, 191
    domains of, 4, 9
    formal analysis vs. social use of
        language, 7–8, 9–10
    functionalist, 8, 12, 13, 80
    *See also* Language
Listener's state of mind, 171–172,
    173–175, 186, 189, 191. *See also*
    Feelings; Perspective-taking
Listening behavior, 151–152, 161–162
Lloyd, P., 161

McCabe, A., 177, 178, 186
McShane, J., 19, 20(table), 59, 60
Mapping, 72, 105
    constant-to-variable, 73–77, 75(table),
        77(table), 100
    unique-to-multiple, 77–79
Markings, 27, 31, 42, 66–67, 90, 91, 92,
    104, 112, 116–118, 120(fig.), 121,
    127, 130, 131, 155–156, 165
Mastergeorge, A. M., 47, 136, 137
Meaning, 10, 53
    constructivist conception of, 12, 22, 55
    decontextualized, 51, 56, 155. *See also*
        Discussions, of nonpresent topics;
        Language, decontextualized
    and details ignored/expressed, 74
    meaningful verbal-communicative acts,
        8, 16–18, 21–23, 28–29, 60, 63
    situational, 51, 52
    social meaning, 22–23, 63
    *See also* Communication, intents;
        Semantics
Mentally retarded children, 161
Metacommunication. *See under*
    Communication
Mimicking, 68, 89. *See also* Imitation;
    Onomatopeoia
Morford, M., 137
Morris, C., 9

Mother-child interactions, 21, 80, 94, 95, 97, 98, 101, 107–141, 130(table), 133(table), 149, 150, 179, 183–185
changes in repertoire, 108, 110
convergence of mother-child speech, 114–127, 115–126(figs.)
distribution of speech uses, 112, 113(table), 114–122
maternal clarification requests, 165–170
number of interchanges, 109(table)
number of speech acts, 111(table, fig.), 112
number of types of interchanges, 109(fig.), 110
object-mediated, 154
*See also* Communicative typologies, Parental Interview on 100 Communicative Acts; Extended discourse, support in; Face-to-face interactions

Naming, 59, 78, 154. *See also* Labeling
Narratives, 172, 173, 175–186, 187
Negative feedback, 167, 168, 169
Negotiations, 27, 29, 31, 42, 84
action-negotiations, 96–103, 104, 105, 112, 114, 115–116, 117(fig.), 121, 122–127, 131, 133
Ninio-Wheeler. *See under* Communicative acts typologies
Nonverbal communication. *See* Communication, nonlinguistic
Nouns/verbs, 100, 102, 105

Observational studies, 81–83
Harvard Longitudinal Study, 127–135, 154
Ninio Longitudinal Study, 107–108, 127, 128
Onomatopoeia, 40, 61, 66, 68, 70, 88, 90, 114

Parents, 127–128, 163. *See also* Mother-child interactions
Participation, 67, 68, 69, 70, 95

Peer interactions, 47, 149, 150, 153, 159, 160
Performatives, 69, 73, 84, 95, 114, 131
Perspective-taking, 141, 170, 174, 184–185, 186, 189. *See also* Listener's state of mind
Peterson, C., 177, 178, 186
Phonology, 90
Piaget, J., 45
PICA-100. *See* Communicative acts typologies, Parental Interview on 100 Communicative Acts
Politeness, 5, 6, 11, 90, 91, 92, 117, 120(fig.), 145, 147, 191
Pragmatic development
defining domain of, 3–9, 13
of 14-, 20-, and 32-month-olds, 129–134, 130(table)
and levels of analysis, 20–21
theoretical framework, 12–13
topics studied by, 10–11
*See also* Pragmatics
Pragmatics, 12, 13, 170, 191–192
of connected discourse, 171–192
defined, 9
of early speech, 67–72, 80
rules, 4. *See also* Rules
*See also* Pragmatic development
Prelinguistic period. *See* Communication, prelinguistic; Language, and preverbal abilities
Promises, 102, 105
Propose addition of recursive act, 123, 125, 126(fig.)
Psychology, 191. *See also* Developmental psychology

Questions/answers, 40, 94–95, 102, 134, 167–170
questions repeating previous utterance, 167–168

Rationalists, 79
Reading, 191
Recent events, 93, 94

Regulating hearer's acts, 123, 124, 124(fig.)
Relevance. *See* Topic relevance
Requests, 3, 84, 134
  activity-managing, 97–100
  as asymmetrical with responses, 89
  for clarification, 163–170
  for completions, 88, 89
  for definitions, 190
  indirect, 139–140
  rerun, 167, 168, 169
  *See also* Elicitation/responses
Roles, 101, 104
  role-play, 159
Route-finding, 162
Rules, 4, 5, 6, 9, 11, 13, 80, 140, 170
  conversational, 145, 146, 147, 167
  for language use vs. social interaction, 147
  mapping, 72, 74–75, 77–78
  as presupposed, 21
  of turn-taking, 149
  *See also* Games

Sacks, H., 148, 149
Scary stories, 176, 177, 178, 179, 181–182, 183–184, 192(n)
Scheflen, A. E., 22
Schley, S., 159–160
Schwartz, R., 79
Scripts, 176
Searle, J. R., 28
  Speech Act Theory, 20, 21, 49
Self-addressed speech, 60, 61, 63, 64
Self-directed action directives, 116, 118(fig.)
Semantics, 4, 9, 12, 13. *See also* Meaning
Separation. *See* Co-presence/separation
Shyness, 160
Single-word period, 39–41, 43, 49–50, 59–67, 72–80
  communcative intents in, 79–80
  defunctionalized expressions in, 77, 78
  and gestures/vocalizations, 49
  lexicalizing addressee/speaker, 75
  and maternal models, 80

verbal-nonverbal combinations in, 137
Skills
  conversational, 143–147, 151, 159–161, 170
  metacognitive, 56
  pragmatic, 129, 148
  social-cognitive, 13, 16, 50, 105, 191
  *See also under* Language
Smith, J. H., 69, 137
Social distance/social power, 140
Social reality, 68
  current, 25–26, 26–31
  *See also* Utterances, as context-related
Sound play. *See* Vocal play
Speech acts
  changes in range of repertoire, 110, 112, 134–135, 143
  codes, categories, definitions, 37–38(table)
  emergence of, 11, 14, 48
  illocutionary, 5, 28, 49
  indirect, 138–140
  numbers of different in interaction, 111(table, fig.)
  order of acquisition, 69–70, 71(table), 84–88, 86–87(table), 93, 95, 96–105
  *See also* Early speech; Single-word period; Utterances
Statements, 93, 94–95
States of mind. *See* Feelings; Listener's state of mind; Perspective-taking
Syntax, 9, 12, 13, 78, 104, 105. *See also* Grammar
System-independence, 64

Talk interchanges. *See under* Face-to-face interactions
Text editing, 28, 35
Thanking, 91, 92, 127
Timing, 7, 145, 146, 148, 151
Toddlers, 47, 55
Tomasello, M., 54, 56, 165
Topic relevance, 145, 146, 147
Topic selection/maintenance, 152–162
Tough, J., 19, 20(table)
Trevarthen, C. B., 150

Truth, 27, 29, 63, 95, 105
Turn taking, 11, 13, 144, 145, 146, 170
  in adult conversations, 147–149
  children's, 149–151, 160
  Typologies. *See* Communicative acts
    typologies
    Utterances, 20, 22, 35–36, 172
  as context-related, 8, 10, 29, 67–68, 85,
    88, 93–94, 104, 147. *See also*
    Contexts; Social reality, current
  distribution of children's, 66(table),
    85(fig.)
  practice, 60, 61

as sensory-motor accompaniments to
  meaningful behavior, 52
  *See also* Early speech; Single-word
    period; Speech acts

Vocabulary spurt, 78, 79
Vocalizations, 49, 53–54
Vocal play, 153, 155
Vocatives, 65–66

Wells, G., 60, 61, 81, 82, 95, 103
Wittenstein, Ludwig, 7–8, 21 60, 61, 81,
  82, 95, 103